UNIVERSITIES

AND

THE LAW

CONFERENCE OF UNIVERSITY ADMINISTRATORS
& CONFERENCE OF REGISTRARS AND SECRETARIES

LEGAL GROUP

UNIVERSITIES AND THE LAW

edited by

Dennis Farrington & Frank Mattison

1990

First published in Great Britain 1990
by the Conference of University Administrators (CUA)
CUA Publications Office
Whiteknights House
University of Reading
READING RG6 2AH
United Kingdom

ISBN 0 - 947931 - 16 - 3

Printed and bound in Scotland by Betts
of Tillicoultry

Typeset at the University of Stirling

ABOUT THE AUTHORS:

RICHARD FARR was educated at the University College of Swansea where he read German and obtained his PGCE in 1968 while being Secretary of the Students' Union. Although qualified to teach, he preferred the prospect of a career in university administration, to which he thought his talents were better suited. He joined the staff of the University of Hull in 1969 as Planning Assistant in the then Buildings Office. Two rounds of reorganisation in 1982 and 1989 have seen him progress to the post of Estates Development Officer with responsibility for new work and major maintenance, as well as having an involvement in forward planning in relation to the University's academic development. He became CUA Branch Correspondent in 1985 and was Local Organiser of the 1988 Conference.

DENNIS FARRINGTON was educated at the University of Kent where he read Chemistry and the New University of Ulster where he was Secretary of the Students' Council in 1971-2. After a period in the Civil Service, taking an external London LLB in 1980, he joined the University of Hull in 1981, where he spent five years in personnel and general administration. As a staff candidate, he took the LLM degree by thesis in the field of constitutional and administrative law. He moved to the University of Stirling as Deputy Secretary and Registrar in 1986 and obtained the Open University's Advanced Diploma in Educational Management in the same year. He was Secretary to the Executive Committee of CUA from 1982 to 1988.

CHARLES HENDERSON took degrees in History and Public Administration at the University of Exeter where he was President of the Guild of Students. After two years in the Civil Service he entered university administration in the Medical Faculty of the University of Newcastle Upon Tyne. From 1971 to 1974 he was Secretary of the Medical Faculty of the University of Edinburgh. In 1974 he moved to the University of Bath as Assistant Secretary, appointed Senior Assistant Secretary in 1984 with special responsibilities for the legal aspects of technology transfer. He took an external London LLB in 1979. He is Secretary of a number of high-tech companies and acts as a consultant on university/industry issues with special reference to Intellectual Property.

FRANK MATTISON was educated at the Universities of Cambridge and Texas and took the external London LLB. He has been Registrar (now Registrar and Secretary) of the University of Hull since 1974, having previously held administrative appointments at the Universities of Leeds, Liverpool and East Anglia. He has also been a Tutor and Counsellor for the Open University and Teaching Assistant at the University of Texas. His interest in the law was stimulated by involvement with Courts Martial (not as the accused!) while doing national service, and by work as a magistrate and High Court Advocate while in the Overseas Civil Service. He is probably the only Registrar with a case cited in this work.

ROBERT SEATON was educated at the Universities of Glasgow, Oxford and Edinburgh where he took the LLB degree. He has been Secretary of the University of Dundee since 1973, having served his administrative apprenticeship in various positions in the University of Edinburgh over the preceding 11 years.

ABOUT CUA:

The Conference of University Administrators (CUA) is a registered charity. It exists for the public benefit to advance education by fostering the development of sound methods of administration of tertiary education in the university sector in the UK.

In furtherance of the above object CUA:

* arranges an Annual Conference for the exchange of ideas in the development of the administration of tertiary education with particular reference to the university sector:

* provides a forum for discussion of current problems in tertiary education:

* encourages the development of branches in individual institutions to act as a link between members and the central organisation of CUA:

* issues publications from time to time in the furtherance of the objectives of the organisation:

* facilitates the exchange of information on administrative activities:

* establishes and maintains links with administrators in tertiary education overseas in order to further the interests of tertiary education internationally:

* stimulates training activities both by provision of specific training opportunities and by the monitoring of the training programmes and policies of other organisations.

CUA welcomes to full membership all staff in the university sector in the UK who are involved in the administration and management of their institution; the bulk of its members are career administrators, but academic and senior clerical staff who wish to develop their administrative skills and to benefit from the opportunities offered by CUA are also encouraged to become members. Membership is also open to staff working in a number of specific institutions whose work relates to the administration of tertiary education in the university sector, such as the Universities Funding Council, the Research Councils, the Committee of Vice-Chancellors and Principals, the Association of Commonwealth Universities, Universities Statistical Record and the Universities Central Council on Admissions. Associate membership is open to individuals who do not qualify for full membership but who identify in some way with university administration, by working in the administration of universities or other higher educational establishments of equal status abroad or by having previously been a member of CUA.

CONTENTS

CHAPTER 2
by Frank Mattison
UNIVERSITY GOVERNMENT AND MANAGEMENT 33

CHAPTER 2 - continued

CHAPTER 3
by Dennis Farrington
THE LAW GOVERNING STUDENTS 63

CHAPTER 3 - continued

CHAPTER 4
by Robert Seaton

CHAPTER 4 - continued

CHAPTER 5
by Dennis Farrington and Robert Seaton

CHAPTER 5 - continued

CHAPTER 6 - continued

CHAPTER 6 - continued

CHAPTER 7 - continued

CHAPTER 7 - continued

CHAPTER 7 - continued

CHAPTER 7 - continued

PREFACE

The universities of the United Kingdom exist within a complex legal framework. In the first place, each of them lies within one of three distinct legal jurisdictions: those of England and Wales, of Scotland, and of Northern Ireland. Secondly, they are incorporated by one of three distinct forms of incorporation: by Statute, by Royal Charter, or (for some university institutions) under the Company Acts. Thirdly, they have the distinctive legal form known as charitable status, which takes a different aspect in each of the three jurisdictions. Finally, it should be noted that the juridical status of universities has been before the courts on only a limited number of occasions and any statement of the law must necessarily be tentative and provisional.

The team that prepared this study was jointly commissioned by the Conference of Registrars and Secretaries and the Conference of University Administrators. Our primary purpose has been to serve the practising administrator who needs a working and increasingly more precise knowledge of the manner in which the law affects his or her daily duties, and as society becomes more rule-bound, and indeed adversarial in character, so do universities. It is becoming increasingly necessary to know precisely, for example, how to transact contentious business, so as not to expose the university to procedural challenge.

But, while being concerned with the law in practice, we felt that it would be advisable to discuss the underlying legal principles. There were two principal reasons for this approach. First, it would be impossible for this study to treat the totality of the potential contact between a university and the legal process, and what an administrator needs is some idea of how the law may operate. Secondly, we regard it as important that serving administrators should have an interest in legal principle as a management tool.

For many purposes the complexities referred to above may only have practical consequences in fairly limited areas, but it is important for their existence to be recognised. Our main aim has also been to examine rather more closely areas of the law where a university qua university has, and is having, some effect upon the evolution of the law. In other areas, such as, for example, building regulations, we have largely confined ourselves to advice as to the best sources of practical information.

We were originally commissioned to undertake this study in 1986. Since then the demands placed upon university administrators have increased exponentially, and no fewer than four of the team appointed had to withdraw as a result of the pressure of work. A fifth, Ian Sanderson (Bradford) unfortunately had to withdraw on the grounds of ill-health. In addition the last three years have seen a great move into prominence and contemporary significance of legal principles as they affect universities: the jurisdiction of the

Visitor, tenure, formation of contract, variation of contract, personal legal liability of officers and members of governing bodies. Universities exist in a complex setting, and they are themselves highly complex organisations. Whilst we have made every effort to state the law as we understand it, the expert reader may find many issues of interpretation and explanation with which he will disagree, or omissions of which he will rightly be critical: a penalty paid by any pioneering work produced by administrative practitioners. Accordingly neither the CRS, the CUA, the authors nor their universities can accept any liability for any loss or damage whatsoever or howsoever arising from the use or adoption of any guidance or advice given in this work.

We have taken much advice in the preparation of this study, and grateful acknowledgements are due to all those who, by way of information or advice, have contributed to this work. Of these we wish to mention Tom Owen, former Registrar of the University College of Wales, Aberystwyth for his researches into the legal nature of universities, and Patrick Birkinshaw, Senior Lecturer in Law at the University of Hull for advice on recent developments in Administrative Law. Particular acknowledgements are due to Marion McClintock (Lancaster) for the preparation of the index.

We are nevertheless very conscious of the many shortcomings of this work, for which we are solely responsible. The law is generally as stated on 1st April 1989, but the opportunity has been taken to discuss items of current interest up to 31st July 1989.

Authorship is as stated in the contents. An indication has been given of the major variations from English Law: Bob Seaton was responsible for drawing attention to the principal differences as far as Scotland is concerned and Dennis Farrington for Northern Ireland. Of the two editors Dennis Farrington assumed full responsibility for all the manifold aspects of book production including the preparation of statute and case lists, and liaison with the publisher. In this connection he wishes to record his personal thanks to those staff of the University of Stirling who have given practical help, in particular Monica Cessford and Tony Osborne.

Richard Farr (Hull)
Charles Henderson (Bath)
Robert Seaton (Dundee)

Dennis Farrington (Stirling) Co-editors
Frank Mattison (Hull)

This book is not a legal textbook nor is it a set of handy hints for harassed administrators. It is a general guide to those aspects of our legal system which impact significantly on the university world which is, in many respects, unique. The medieval and Victorian ghosts are still clanking their chains here, not only in the form of the Visitatorial jurisdiction in England and Wales but also in much of the important case law affecting the special position of corporate bodies, the procedure for the proper conduct of meetings and the rights which universities enjoy over land and other property. Equally the growth of legislation having an impact on our work has accelerated exponentially over the past fifteen years.

Although this is not a legal textbook the layout adopted by the authors is similar to a legal work in a number of respects. Readers unfamiliar with such texts will find that they are confronted almost immediately by apparently incomprehensible lists of cases and statutes. These are for reference only but a brief word of explanation may be useful. Our legal system is based on both common law, derived from custom and from case law made by the courts, and on statute law, which is itself interpreted by the courts. Decided cases are therefore of great significance and are cited by reference to one of the sets of Law Reports, the majority of which should be accessible readily in any university library with a law reference section. The most common sets of Reports cited here are the All England Reports (abbreviated to All ER) and those undertaken by the Council of Law Reporting and identifiable by the courts in which the cases cited have been heard, e.g. QB for Queen's Bench Division of the High Court, Ch for the Chancery Division, etc. English cases before 1865 appear in private reports, commonly cited by the initials of the reporters' names. Scots law cases may appear in, for example, the Session Cases (SC) or the Scots Law Times (SLT) series.

The reasons for decisions which are normally binding on lower courts are contained in the ratio decidendi of judgments. Statements made by judges in the course of their judgments which are not strictly binding but have significant persuasive force are referred to as obiter dicta and both these expressions are used in this work. Statutes are listed chronologically by year group and alphabetically within a year group. Until 1962 a statute was assigned a chapter number in the Parliamentary session corresponding to the regnal year of the current monarch. Thus the Public Order Act 1936 is cited as 1 Edw 8 and 1 Geo 6 c.6 being the sixth Act to receive Royal Assent in the first (and only) regnal year of King Edward VIII and the first regnal year of King George VI. Since 1963 this has been replaced by a chapter number within the calendar year. So the Education Reform Act 1988 is cited as 1988 c.40, simply the fortieth statute to receive Royal Assent in 1988. The statute list also shows where reference has been made to a particular part, section or schedule of an Act. Acts of the Parliament of Northern Ireland (1921 to 1972) are included for convenience.

There are some terms from which non-lawyer readers, especially those with no knowledge of Latin, will recoil in horror. Scots law is perhaps slightly more obscure than English in this respect, using words such as feu, delict, poinding, interdict, caveat and sist quite liberally. English law can produce tort, chose in action, certiorari and such useful definitions as "'Dower' includes 'freebench'"[Settled Land Act 1925 s.117(1(vi))]. Do not be put off by this apparent gobbledegook: much of the early development of our law was influenced by Norman and Roman practice and the legal profession in its widest sense has not had much incentive to modernise its terminology. In fact the incomprehensibility of so much law to laymen was one driving force behind the concept of "Universities and the Law". Hopefully we have succeeded. The method adopted is to attempt to explain each piece of legal jargon on first appearance in the text.

There are a few basic concepts, such as the meaning of "contract", used frequently in the book. In English law a contract at its most simple is an agreement which the courts are willing to enforce. This of course rules out many agreements of a non-contractual nature, for example that the Registrar will give the Finance Officer a free lift home after the Senate meeting, or one rendered void by statute, for example a wager on the outcome of the deliberations of the Car Parking Committee. Some contracts have to be made in writing and a few under seal, a small red disc in the case of individuals not possessing their own coat of arms or an impression of an heraldic symbol in the case of universities. Except in the case of contracts under seal, there must be "consideration" i.e. at its most basic there must be money or money's worth changing hands. In Scotland a binding contract exists once there is agreement by the parties on the essentials - demonstrated most clearly by the system of buying a house by the exchange of "missives" - and in some cases there is no requirement for consideration. The Scots do not share the English attachment to seals, although documents executed by universities and university companies are normally sealed.

You will also come across the concept, and some of the detailed practice, of judicial review of administrative action. Although it is generally accepted that "administrative law" is just another branch of the legal system in all parts of the United Kingdom, it is an important one for university administrators. It deals with the supervision by the Courts of actions of the Executive and institutions governed by statute (such as the UFC and the ancient Scottish Universities), whether they have acted outside their authority (ultra vires) or otherwise. The English orders of certiorari (removing a decision of an inferior tribunal into the High Court for review) and mandamus (a directive by the Court), the injunction (which may be mandatory or which more usually will prohibit an activity) and declaration (a statement of the legal position by the Court) and their Scots and Northern Irish equivalents are all means by which this supervision is exercised. Their meaning in each case should be clear from the context. The concept and principles of natural justice are introduced where they occur in the text.

Although we cannot be held responsible for the use of "sexist" language in judgments and the work of other authors, we have tried to eliminate its use so far as possible in our original work. For the avoidance of doubt, unless there is any specific contrary implication, the masculine includes the feminine and vice versa.

An area not covered by this work to any significant degree is practice and procedure, very different in the three jurisdictions and in different causes of action. It is experience and expertise in these areas which distinguishes the practising from the academic lawyer and a fortiori from those of us who have learned the law but are far from being learned in it.

DJF

TABLE OF CASES

CHRONOLOGICAL LIST OF STATUTES

CHAPTER 1

UNIVERSITIES AND THE LAW

1. LEGAL DEFINITION OF A UNIVERSITY

1.1 Introduction

The first question is whether it is important to have a legal definition and the second is, does one exist? The orthodox views given in such publications as Halsbury's 'Laws of England' (Volume 15, paras 280-295, 4th edition), the Robbins Committee Report (Appendix 4) and in such ministerial pronouncements as that of Norman St John Stevas in the House of Commons on 1 December 1972 (Hansard), lead one to believe that it is important to have a legal definition and that that definition contains certain essential elements.

1.2 Absence of Statutory Definition

There is, as yet, no adequate statutory definition of a university. The College Charter Act 1871 defines college or university as including "any institution in the nature of a college or university".[1] The Universities (Scotland) Act 1889 defines universities as "Scottish Universities".[2] The Race Relations Act 1976 defines a university as including "a university college and the college, school or hall of a university".[3] The Education Act 1944 refers to university education only in passing and without definition: it was not part of the statutory system of education, the codification of which is the principal purpose of that Act. The Education Reform Act 1988 in section 235 (1) states that a university includes a "university college and any college, or institution in the nature of a college, in a university". It does not define a university as such. Section 214 (2) dealing with unrecognised degrees does, however, for the purposes of that section refer to "a university, college or other body which is authorised by Royal Charter or Act of Parliament to award degrees". This is discussed later.[4] It will be noted that, since a non-university body may be authorised to grant degrees, the power to award degrees cannot, under this Act, be the exclusive right of a university. Thus the section does not contribute to the definition of a university.

The only case to consider the question in any depth concerned St David's College, Lampeter, in 1951.[5] In that case, Vaisey J held that the word "university" is not a term of art and accepted without criticism the list of essential attributes of a university advanced by Counsel for the defendants, the Ministry of Education, in arguing that St David's College was not a university. The essential attributes referred to were as follows:

a) The institution should admit students from all parts of the world:

b) There should be a plurality of masters amongst the academic staff:

c) Teaching should be carried out in at least one of the higher faculties, that is, divinity, law, or medicine:

d) There should be provision for residence of students:

e) The institution should have the right to confer degrees:

f) Most important and essential of all, the institution should be incorporated as a university by the sovereign power of the State.

Vaisey J continued

> "I have left until last what is stated to be the most obvious and most essential quality of a university, that is, that it must have power to grant its own degrees. Here we find the very curious situation that the royal prerogative of granting degrees in the various faculties and branches of knowledge has been granted to this particular institution subject to a very strict limitation. It is only entitled to grant the degrees of Bachelor of Arts and Bachelor of Divinity. It has not of its own essential power any right to grant degrees, but to that limited extent the royal privilege has been acceded to it by royal concession .... but, if the word "university" is not one of art, I have to try to see what it means, regard being had to those particular qualities which I have enumerated ... I cannot help feeling that this extraordinarily limited power of granting degrees, which has throughout been regarded as being the test for the solution of this problem, is an indication that this institution falls short of a university properly so called ... Judging the matter both on broad principles and on the narrow principles of its limited powers and the absence of any express intention of making it a university by the sovereign power, I think that the plaintiffs have not discharged the onus of satisfying me that the college ought to be called and to be considered, in accordance with the proper meaning of the English language, a university".[6]

1.3 <u>The consequences of the absence of a statutory definition</u>

One consequence of the absence of a common law or statutory definition of a university is that any individual can "create" a university, and provided that there is no intent to deceive or defraud, can operate as such. It was reported in 1954 that a newsagent in Birmingham was selling degrees of the University of Birmingham, and the Department of Education and Science indicated at that time that there was no basis for intervention. The degree certificates on sale bore no resemblance to those of the University proper. Bogus degrees have now been the subject of legislative intervention. (See $ 3.4 infra.)

In the absence of a statutory definition one must, by the normal rules of statutory interpretation, look to the "ordinary" everyday meaning for a definition of a university. The Oxford English Dictionary defines a university as

> "the whole body of teachers and students pursuing, at a particular place, the higher branches of learning; such persons associated together as a society or corporate body having the power of conferring degrees and other privileges, and forming an institution for the promotion of education in the higher branches of learning, the colleges, buildings etc, belonging to such a body".

Chambers Dictionary defines a university in similar terms as

> "an institution of higher learning with the power to grant degrees, its body of teachers, students, graduates, its college/s, or its buildings"

and this definition is cited in the legal reference work Words and Phrases Legally Defined.[7]

Reflection on developments in higher education since the Lampeter case in 1951 will indicate that a number of the allegedly essential attributes of a university are clearly lacking in a number of modern universities. For example, a considerable number of institutions do not teach in one of the higher faculties. A number of degree-awarding bodies make no provision for residence, e.g. the Open University. Further, a number of institutions widely recognised to be of university status have the right to confer degrees in a number of limited fields, such as Cranfield and the Royal College of Art.

There is an important unorthodox view of this question. It maintains that there is no legal need for a legal definition of a university and that, if there is such a need, it is not necessary for universities to be incorporated by the sovereign power. A modern example lies in the development of the University of Buckingham which began as the University College of Buckingham.

This institution did at its inception not call itself a 'University' but it was recognised by a number of universities and professional bodies as providing university level education. It had no Charter but, instead, was incorporated by registration as a company limited by guarantee. Unlike the case of St David's

College in 1951, the present Government recognised the University College of Buckingham for the purposes of the award of mandatory student grants and later granted a Charter.

Academic writers have occasionally considered the question of the need for incorporation of a university. H S Fearns, in an article entitled 'Towards an Independent University' in 1969, when the setting up of UCB was being discussed, stated that

> "sponsors of universities must secure a Charter from the Privy Council. Nothing in the laws of the United Kingdom requires it, but the nature and structure of British society do. Many employers, particularly those organised as professions, will recognise the degrees of a Chartered Institution. Although the true Charter of any university is the quality of its staff and students, any independent university must have the official endorsement which the Charter implies."[8]

Fearns, therefore, makes the important distinction between what the law requires as an essential step in the formation of a university, and what practical politics require.

In their book 'Power and Authority in British Universities', Moodie and Eustace refer to the subordination of the universities to the State in that the legal form, statutes and powers of all British universities are defined by the State. This is both in the sense that the university as a corporation is subject to the general rules of society, and specifically that a university, nowadays at least, obtains its Charter from the Privy Council and cannot change it without the latter's consent.[9]

The most detailed analysis of this unorthodox view of the question of incorporation of universities is contained in an article by D J Christie in Public Law, Winter 1976 entitled 'The Power to Award Degrees'.[10] Christie traces the history of the mediaeval scholastic guilds and the steady growth towards corporate status made necessary by the need to have the various privileges associated with such status.

2.THE LEGAL PERSONALITY OF CORPORATIONS

2.1 The Creation of Corporations

Corporate bodies are brought into being in three main ways:

(a) By statute, for example British Telecom and a small group of universities (usually on re-organisation, such as Newcastle and Durham in 1963).

(b) By registration under the Companies Acts 1948 to 1976 (e.g. The University of Sussex until 1962).

(c) By the grant of a Charter in the exercise of the Royal Prerogative.

There are significant differences between these types of corporation in relation to their powers and to the liabilities of their members.

2.2 The powers of Corporations

Statutory corporations and those incorporated by registration under the Companies Acts have only those powers conferred directly or indirectly by their instruments of creation. An illegal use of powers is open to attack under the doctrine of ultra vires, only partly modified for companies by s.9, European Communities Act 1972.

Chartered corporations in England and Wales on the other hand have all the powers of an ordinary natural person of sound mind and of full legal capacity. Their powers cannot be modified even by the creating Charter, but there is the risk that the Crown may annul the Charter if the institution ignores the expressed or implied limits placed on its powers. In Sutton's Hospital case in 1612 it was held that a restriction in a charter was "simply an ordinance testifying the King's desire, but it is but a precept, and it does not bind in law."[11] In the more recent case of British South Africa Co. v De Beers Consolidated Mines Ltd in 1910 in the English Chancery Division, Swinfen Eady J. confirmed

> "...not only can the chartered company bind itself by acts as to which no power is affirmatively given by the charter, but even if the charter by express negative words forbids any particular act, the corporation can nevertheless at common law do the act, and if it does, it is bound thereby, and the result is only that ground is given for a proceeding by scire facias in the name of the Crown, repealing the charter."[12]

In the case of Jenkin v Pharmaceutical Society of Great Britain in 1921 it was held, however, that a member may obtain an injunction to restrain any act which might put the charter of the corporation at risk.[13] In universities subject to the jurisdiction of the Visitor,[14] the Visitor rather than the Court would have to decide and this would then raise the problem of the powers available to him to give effect to his judgment.

In Scotland a chartered corporation may enter into any contract not expressly forbidden by its charter.[15] However, the principle governing restrictions on its activities is related to the expenditure of money: whether or not a given application of its funds is a breach of trust. In Kemp v Corporation of Glasgow,[16] the contention that a chartered body may do anything which an individual might lawfully do was not accepted.

In relation to the debts and liabilities of corporations, which particularly at times of insolvency or liquidation are the ultimate responsibility of all members of statutory corporations, members' liabilities limited by shares or by guarantee extend only to the amounts not previously paid up. The shareholders of a company limited by shares, or subscribers of a company limited by guarantee, can be asked to find some cash out of their own pockets to meet the debts of the corporation. However, chartered corporations, although their liability is not limited, have the privilege at common law that their members are not liable for their debts. The Charter, however, may impose a liability which would provide a remedy for the creditors of the chartered body to pursue their claims into the pockets of the members.

2.3 Grant of Charter as exercise of Prerogative Power

It is important to realise that no group of individuals has the legal right to a Charter. It is granted by

> "virtue of the Prerogative Royal and of the special grace, certain knowledge and mere motion"

of the sovereign body represented by the Queen in Council.[17] The Privy Council has made available a Memorandum of General Principles for the granting of Charters in the hope, presumably, of discouraging frivolous applications. The College Charter Act 1871 provides that a copy of any application for a Charter for the foundation of any college or university which is referred by the Queen in Council for the report of a Committee of the Privy Council must be laid before Parliament, together with a copy of the Draft Charter, not less than 30 days before the Committee reports on it.[18]

3. THE POWER TO GRANT DEGREES

3.1 Introduction

It is this topic, rather than the question of legal creation and personality and powers of Universities, which has attracted most attention in recent years. The orthodox view is set out in Halsbury's 'Laws of England' and is also referred to in Appendix 4 of the Robbins Committee Report which referred to the problem of 'degree mills'.[19]

The orthodox view is that the power to grant degrees derives from the Royal Prerogative. In the St.David's case in 1951, this assertion was made by reference to sections of Blackstone's 'Commentaries on the Laws of England' 1765 dealing with the Sovereign as the "fountain of honour and office and privilege".[20] Mr St John Stevas (as he then was) in the House of Commons on 1 December 1972, as a junior Education Minister, repeated this view.[21] The Crown may delegate the exercise of a prerogative power to a subject: this is called a franchise. The orthodox view, therefore, argues that the only legal award of a degree is made by a university or other body possessing the power delegated to it by the Sovereign Power of the State. The acid test of this assertion lies in the question of what remedies are available, and at whose suit, to attack the purported unauthorised and illegal exercise of the power to award degrees.

3.2 Is the power inherent or conferred?

Christie's article deals with this question at length and concludes that no remedies are available to prevent the abuse, if abuse it be, of degree mills. Christie, therefore, attacks the assumption that universities must have the power to award degrees conferred upon them. Certainly, current legal practice in the award of Charters to modern universities is to insert a clause in the Charter granting the power to award degrees. This is supposed to be evidence of the grant of the franchise by the Crown. Christie argues from historical analysis that a university degree is not an honour emanating from the Crown in the sense of a peerage or an Order of Chivalry, but instead a degree has a "private and domestic character".

He argues, further, that the power to award degrees is original to universities, that is, it is innate and inherent in the character of universities and need not be conferred upon them. Christie rejects on historical analysis the view that the authority of the Roman Catholic Church in mediaeval times to award degrees and licences to teach the dogmas of the Church passed to the

English State at the time of the Reformation and became part of the Royal Prerogative. Mediaeval universities awarded degrees before the Reformation and without the authority of the Holy See.

Certainly, in post-Reformation times the Crown in this country has only been peripherally involved in granting degrees. For example, the issue of a Royal Mandate to a university to grant a degree to a specified individual has been unknown since 1689. Further, there is the power available to the Archbishop of Canterbury to award "Lambeth degrees".

Christie goes on to argue that, since the power to award degrees is original to universities, the focus of discussion shifts from the basis of the power to the legal attributes of the university itself. If there is an authoritative legal definition of a university, there will be found a legal definition of the power to award degrees. If there is no legal definition of a university, it follows that the law is unable to distinguish between universities and "degree mills". Therefore the power of the latter to award degrees must be regarded as being on exactly the same legal basis as that of bodies which would normally be regarded as universities according to non-legal criteria.

An important argument in Christie's article relates to the distinction to be drawn between the legal basis of the power to award degrees and what he describes as the recognition system. Originally these systems were informal agreements between universities to recognise the gradus or degree of another university for the purpose of appointment of teachers who may have obtained a further academic qualification in the nature of a licence. In modern Britain, the State and its various organs and bodies created or recognised by the State, such as the General Medical Council, operate a recognition system. Christie urges that one should avoid the conclusion that, because the State has the power to recognise the degrees of particular institutions, it also has the power to award or sanction the award or delegate the power to award university degrees.

On the basis of Christie's analysis it would therefore appear perfectly legal for the University College of Buckingham to have described its qualifications, not as licences, which was its practice, but as degrees, even though the College had not been awarded a Royal Charter. It is interesting to note that the University College secured recognition of its licence on a piecemeal basis from a number of Universities and professional bodies such as the Law Society and the General Council of the Bar.

3.3 The conferment of degrees by other means

T A Owen pointed out an example of degrees being awarded quite legally in the United Kingdom without the benefit of a franchise from the Crown.[22] He challenged the common assumption that, though a degree granting power did not make an institution into a University, that power, to be legal, must derive exclusively from the Crown. He pointed out that degrees were being granted "quite legally in Britain" in the case of Heythrop College in Oxfordshire which was empowered in 1965 by the Holy See to confer degrees of Bachelor, Licentiate and Doctor in Philosophy and Theology. (The College is now part of the Faculty of Theology of the University of London and prepares students for London degrees.)

3.4 Bogus Degrees

Sections 214-216 of the Education Reform Act 1988, which came into force on 30 November 1988, relate to the new offence, to be enforced by local authority trading standards officers, of granting awards which may be taken to be degrees of UK institutions where the award is not a recognised award for the purposes of those provisions. "Recognised bodies" for the purposes of the Act include all UK Universities, the Archbishop of Canterbury, the CNAA, Cranfield Institute of Technology, London Business School and the Royal Colleges of Art and Music.[23] There is also a separate list of bodies which provide courses in preparation for the degree of a recognised body, or which are constituent colleges, schools etc of universities (for example the Schools and Senate Institutes of the University of London). A third list sets out recognised awards which would otherwise be unrecognised (e.g. Degree of the Utter Bar of the Inns of Court, Master of Horticulture of the Royal Horticultural Society).

Thus the conclusion is that a university with the power to award a UK degree is one defined by the Secretary of State for Education and Science. The problem of defining a university is not addressed.

4. GENERAL EXTERNAL CONTROLS

4.1 Statutory

Until the passing of the Education Reform Act 1988, legislation specifically controlling the universities was comparatively rare. The Universities of Oxford and Cambridge, the ancient Scottish Universities (St Andrews, Glasgow, Aberdeen and Edinburgh), and the Universities of Durham and Newcastle-upon-Tyne were incorporated by statute, and the College Charter Act 1871 prescribed the methods by which petitions for Charters from, inter alia, would-be universities are to be considered. There was also quite extensive control exercised by statute over the landowning aspects of College management (primarily Oxford and Cambridge Colleges, but also including the University of Durham).[24] There were two passing references to universities in the Education Act 1944, relating to the provision of further education and inspection.[25] Complete control can, of course, be exercised over any chartered body by Act of Parliament. Under the Chartered and Other Bodies (Temporary Provisions) Act 1939 the Universities and Colleges (Temporary Provisions) Order 1939 was made, enabling universities and colleges to make emergency statutes without complying with the full terms of their charters.

Powers outside those contained in charters can be granted by private Act of Parliament. The University of Sheffield (Lands) Act 1948 empowered that University to acquire certain lands.

By virtue of s.338 of the Public Health Act 1936 a collegiate body is defined as a sewage authority with the statutory powers of entry on land for the purposes of directing or constructing sewers.

The Atomic Energy Authority Act 1954 gives the authority to make grants or loans to universities for the conduct of research (subject to the approval of the Lord President of the Council and the Treasury). The Building Control Act 1966 exempted university building from the controls contained in the Act as being "Public Works". Section 8 of the Chronically Sick and Disabled Persons Act 1970 provides, inter alia, that university buildings constructed after that date should have means of access to and within the building and parking facilities and sanitary conveniences for the needs of persons using the building who are disabled. The Control of Pollution Act 1974 classifies university refuse as household waste.[26]

The Sex Discrimination Act 1975 prohibits discrimination in the terms of admission, the refusal or deliberate omission to accept an application for admission, or, after admission, access to any benefits, facilities or services.[27] The Race Relations Act 1976 makes it unlawful for the governing body of a university to discriminate against a person in the conditions of an offer for admission, or in the way of affording him as a student access to any facilities of the University.[28] S.36 however permits a university to do anything for the benefit of persons not ordinarily resident in Great Britain in affording access to facilities for education and training or any ancillary benefits, where it appears to the University that the persons in question do not intend to remain in Great Britain after their period of education or training there.

The Universities and College Estates Acts 1925 and 1964 should also be noted. The 1964 Act freed land transactions in colleges in any university from the restrictions imposed by the Ecclesiastical Leases Acts 1571, 1572, 1575 and 1836. The powers of the Minister of Agriculture over dealings in real property by the Universities of Oxford, Cambridge and Durham were thereby largely removed.[29]

The Leasehold Reform Act 1967 safeguarded the position of land required for public purposes, and specifically extended to any university body.[30] Local authority and university bodies were empowered to oblige tenants acquiring the freehold to accept covenants restricting the carrying out of development or clearing of land as are necessary to reserve the land for possible development by the "authority" i.e. the university. Specific power is given to the Secretary of State to exercise compulsory purchase powers on behalf of universities.[31] By s.28 a university landlord can obtain from a Minister of the Crown a certificate that within the following ten years the property will be required for relevant redevelopment (development for purposes other than investment purposes). These include the purposes of any related university body, i.e. a college of the same university, the tenant's claim to have the freehold or an extended lease to be of no effect, although compensation is to be paid.

There is also a reference to universities in the Extra-Parochial Clergy Measure 1967, which empowers a diocesan bishop to license a clergyman for any university, with chapel or not, to provide all services but the solemnisation of marriage, without the consent of the Minister of the Parish in which the university premises are situated.

It is principally in terms of grants to attend universities that Parliament has been at all active. For example, the Education Act 1975 empowers the Secretary of State to exclude postgraduate courses from grants, and Awards Regulations are made under s.1 of the Education Act 1962 as amended by s.1 of the Education Act 1975.

Under the Road Traffic Regulation Act 1967 s.1(1)(b) the appropriate Minister, on application in that behalf being made by the governing body of a university in receipt of a grant of public moneys, and after holding, if he thinks fit, a public enquiry shall have the power to make a traffic regulation order as respects a road not being a trunk road. This has the effect of giving roads in the vicinity of a university campus the status, for legal purposes, of trunk roads.

By virtue of the Companies Business Names (Amendment) Regulations 1982, made under ss.31-32 of the Companies Act 1981 (now consolidated in the Companies Act 1985), the approval of the Secretary of State for Trade and Industry is required for the use of the word 'University' in or as part of a company or business name, and the Department of Education and Science is specified as the relevant public body which is to be requested to give an indication of any objection to the use of those words. In 1986 the Education (No.2) Act placed certain obligations on, inter alia, universities in England and Wales, with regard to freedom of speech.[32]

The relative absence of legislation regarding universities is noteworthy. Taylor and Saunders[33] argue that the reason for this was because "the general powers and duties conferred by the principal Act (the Education Act 1944) were so far reaching". This enabled such profound changes as the assumption of responsibility for the universities by the Secretary of State for Education and Science to take place without specific enactment. It is also possibly worthy of note that a charter may be wholly or partially revoked by a subsequent Act of Parliament.[34]

4.2 Ministers and Law Officers

As with statutory regulation there are few instances of legal controls being exercised by Ministers of the Crown. Certain courses leading to the right to practise a profession, eg teaching, require the specific approval of the Secretary of State for Education and Science. The National Health Service Act 1977 imposes certain duties upon the Secretary of State (for Health) to make available such facilities as he considers are reasonably required by any university which has a medical or dental school in connection with clinical teaching and with research connected with clinical medicine or clinical dentistry. Certain ministerial powers over universities exist by virtue of their status as charities, in circumstances where their special status as exempt or excepted charities do not apply. For example, it is a general rule of law that a charity cannot make ex gratia payments, but only payments for the purposes of the charity. In certain circumstances the Attorney-General can give authority to charity trustees to make such payments out of funds held on charitable trusts.[35] The Attorney-General also has the power to institute proceedings to dissolve corporations on a proceeding known as scire facias on the Crown side of the Queen's Bench Division, and the basis under which such proceedings may be taken include a corporation doing something which is prohibited or not authorised by the Charter notwithstanding the validity of that act as done: the legal doctrine of ultra vires does not apply to a chartered corporation such as a university.[36] The power to amend university statutes to conform with changes in local government introduced by the Local Government Act 1972 was vested in the Secretary of State for the Environment. Except as provided in specific legislation, change in a Charter or Statutes can only be initiated by the University itself. The Secretary of State for Scotland had certain powers in relation to the office of Principal and Regius chairs at certain of the ancient Scottish Universities.

Generally, however, the Government did not until 1988 use legislation as a means of exerting control over the universities.

> "Legally speaking, universities are today completely their own masters. None of the clauses, usual in Charters and Acts of Parliament creating new semi Governmental agencies, giving Ministers power to issue directions or giving the Treasury power to control numbers and remuneration of staff, are to be found in even the newest university charters...."[37]

Until 1988 control was exercised through the power of the purse and in the giving of advice to the University Grants Committee. The Education Reform Act 1988, however, has the effect of placing much of the relationship between universities and the source of the instrument of government of most of them, the Crown, on a statutory basis. The essence of the Act, so far as universities are concerned is

(a) to replace the University Grants Committee by a Universities Funding Council whose relationship with universities is prescribed by Statute;

(b) to appoint University Commissioners with powers to amend university statutes so as to eliminate from 20 November 1987 on appointment or promotion, contracts where only the employed person may lawfully give notice of termination and provide for

(i) dismissal by virtue of redundancy by an appropriate body

(ii) dismissal by virtue of good cause by an appropriate officer

(iii) disciplinary procedures against members of staff

(iv) appeal and grievance procedure for members of staff;

(c) to exclude the visitatorial jurisdiction in respect of any dispute relating to a member of academic staff concerning his appointment or termination except in the hearing of appeals or grievances;

(d) to "nationalise" the polytechnics and certain colleges and to provide for the grant of funds to them and general supervision by a Polytechnics and Colleges Funding Council.

In relation to the Scottish Universities the Under-Secretary for Scotland stated in 1965:

"The Secretary of State will find himself when the Bill (Universities (Scotland) Bill) is passed, in an anomalous position. His relationship with one group of universities, Strathclyde, Dundee, Heriot-Watt and Stirling will be in one form, while his relationship with the second group, Aberdeen, St. Andrews, Edinburgh and Glasgow will be in another form... This is not a logical or defensible position and my Right Hon. Friend would like to free himself as soon as possible from the anomaly... It is equally desirable, from the universities' point of view that the powers of each component of a university should be set out explicitly. None of the enactments sets out the powers of a senate in full, for example."[38]

4.3 The University Grants Committee

The University Grants Committee, which ceased to exist on 14th July 1989, was itself a non-statutory body existing by virtue of the prerogative powers of the Crown: its existence was the consequence of a Treasury Minute. Its terms of reference were:

1919 To enquire into the financial needs of university education in the United Kingdom and to advise the Government as to the applications of any grants that may be made by Parliament towards meeting them.

1946 To enquire into the financial needs of university education in Great Britain; to advise the Government as to the application of any grants made by Parliament towards meeting them; to collect, examine and make available information on matters relating to university education, at home and abroad, and to assist, in consultation with the universities and other bodies concerned, the preparation and execution of such plans for the development of the universities as may from time to time be required in order to ensure that they are fully adequate to national needs.

1962 "at home and abroad" was replaced by "throughout the United Kingdom".

As a non-statutory body it did not exercise its control over the universities by legal process, but rather through financial control, and the conditions attached to grant. Whilst the Committee no longer exists, its legal position is of some interest as a precursor to examining the legal position of the Universities Funding Council and its powers and liabilities. Whilst the relationship between the UGC and individual universities was not regulated by law it is considered that an application for judicial review could have succeeded against the UGC. The principle of judicial review has been held to extend to a self-regulating unincorporated association which had no statutory, prerogative or common law powers.[39] The UGC was much more than this in that it had certain prerogative powers. The judicial rule applies not by virtue of the source of a body's powers and duties but rather to their nature, and exercising public law functions means that the court had jurisdiction.[40] In another case a board was characterised as

> "a servant of the Crown charged by the Crown, by executive instruction, with the duty of distributing the bounty of the Crown...I do not think that this court should shrink from entertaining the application merely because the board have no statutory authority: they act with lawful authority, albeit such authority is derived from the executive and not from Act of Parliament".[41]

Equally it appears that the process of administrative regulation did not apply to the UGC as it did not fall within the scope of the Parliamentary Commissioner for Administration.

4.4 The Universities Funding Council

Many sections of the Education Reform Act 1988, however, have the effect of greatly extending the legal controls exercised by the Secretary of State or his agents. Hitherto, as pointed out above, control has been exercised only in relation to the university system as a whole and not to individual institutions through conditions attached to grant rather than through statutory powers. It can be argued that through the exercise of powers in this way a future Secretary of State could be more exposed to legal challenge than in the past.

For example, s.131(6) provides that the Universities Funding Council shall have power to make payments subject to such terms and conditions as they think fit. There is, however, a corpus of administrative law which indicates that the courts have the power to enquire into the fitness of those terms and conditions, even without the insertion of the word "reasonable" between "such" and "terms". In addition, sub-section (9) of the same section requires the governing body to give the Council such information as the Council may require for the purpose of the exercise of any of their functions under this section.

The full plenitude of legal power is, however, contained in s.134 which empowers the Secretary of State to impose such additional functions on the UFC as he thinks fit. The question will arise as to whether this will empower him to instruct it as to a course of action in relation to an individual university. By virtue of sub-section (7) the condition attached to grant shall not relate to the making of grants or other payments to any specified institution but sub-section (8) compels the UFC to comply with any directions given to them by the Secretary of State. Neither of the Funding Councils shall be regarded as the servant or agent of the Crown, or as enjoying any status, immunity or privilege of the Crown.[42] There appear to be two consequences of this provision. First, the operations of the UFC (but not the Department of Education and Science or the Research Councils) will not be subject to the Parliamentary Commissioner for Administration. Secondly, it will not be a defence to claim for non-performance of a contract that the UFC has frustrated its performance. The defence of force majeure, ie a contract the performance of which has been frustrated by Crown action, will not apply to acts of the UFC.

On the other hand impossibility of performance arising from the actions of the UFC could discharge a contract under the doctrine of the implied term i.e. where the performance of the contract depended upon the continued existence of a certain state of affairs which fails to continue.[43] Thus contracts of service or for services could be discharged if their performance depended upon the continued existence of a certain subject at the university in question, and the UFC subsequently specifically withdraws all funds for the pursuit of that subject at that university.

What seems clear is that the actions of the UFC are susceptible to judicial review. The UFC is a statutory body performing "public" functions and proceedings could therefore be instituted under Order 53 of the Rules of the Supreme Court (RSC). To be granted leave to institute proceedings an individual or body is required to have a "sufficient interest" in the outcome. A sufficient interest does not entail a direct financial or legal interest. It appears to be a mixed question of fact and law: a question of fact and degree and the relationship between the applicant and the matter to which the application relates, having regard to all the circumstances of the case.[44] There is little doubt that a university would have a sufficient interest: there is a direct link between the UFC and individual universities, and the UFC has certain legal duties in relation to them. Whether an individual academic whose career is at risk of being ruined or damaged by the action of the UFC has an interest is a more difficult issue. There is no direct relationship and it is doubtful if he could succeed unless the court accepted the principle of a chain of relationships as in the Finnegan case.[45] Legal issues appear to be in conflict: on the one hand if there is a wrong there must be a remedy, on the other if there is no legal duty there can be no interest which the court can protect.[46] The court might take the view that it was for the university to institute proceedings and not the individual. Certainly the replacement of the UGC by a statutory UFC will inevitably require much more attention to be paid to legal matters in considering the relationship between universities and the State.

4.5 The University Commissioners

Substantial powers to change the nature of tenure are contained in ss. 202 to 208, but the University Commissioners provided for in these clauses are more restricted in the terms of the exercise of their functions than either the Secretary of State or the Universities Funding Council. They will, by virtue of s.202, have to have regard to enabling qualifying institutions to provide education, promote education, and engage in research efficiently and economically and to apply the principles of justice and fairness. It is interesting that the latter prescription was felt to be necessary, given the legal presumption that anyone performing a statutory duty will, in so doing, be bound by the rules of natural justice.

The powers of the Commissioners are to amend the Statutes of universities as necessary so as to enable any appropriate body or section thereof to dismiss any member of the academic or equivalent staff for redundancy. The Act defines redundancy as the fact that the institution has ceased, or intends to cease, to carry on the activity for the purpose of which he was appointed or employed or to cease to carry it out, or intend to, in the place in which he carried out his work, or that the requirements for that activity have ceased or diminished or are expected to cease or diminish. It also provides the Commissioners power to ensure that there are provisions to remove for "good cause" which includes reasons within s.57(2) of the Employment Protection (Consolidation) Act 1978.

The Statutes as amended by the action of the Commissioners apply to all appointments made or contracts of employment entered into after 20th November 1987. The powers are restricted in such a way in order to safeguard the position of staff already in post, and the DES press notice originally issued stated "the Bill provides (Clause 132) that staff currently in post who have tenure should retain it as long as they continue in their present appointments, but that those newly appointed, or promoted to permanent posts after 20th November 1987 should no longer have this special measure of protection."

4.6 The Visitor

All universities in England and Wales, except Oxford and Cambridge, are eleemosynary corporations, that is to say, their purposes include the perpetual distribution of the bounty of the founder.[47] The Universities of Oxford and Cambridge are civil corporations. As eleemosynary corporations other universities have an office known as Visitor and the Charters of those universities in England and Wales incorporated by Charter provide for a Visitor.[48] In the absence of express identification the Lord Chancellor is Visitor.[49] The general nature of a visitatorial jurisdiction is to settle dispute between members of a corporation, and to inspect and regulate the corporation. A typical article in a charter providing for the office of Visitor is that from the University of Nottingham:

"We Our Heirs and Successors Kings and Queens of the Kingdom and Dominions aforesaid shall be and remain the Visitor and Visitors of the University of Nottingham through the Lord President of Our Council for the time being and in exercise of the Visitatorial Authority We Our Heirs and Successors shall have the right from time to time and in such manner as We or They shall think fit to direct an inspection of the University its buildings laboratories and general equipment and also an enquiry into the teaching research examinations and other work done by the University."[50]

When Lord Upjohn was appointed Visitor to the University of Essex in 1964 his terms of reference were:

"to hear and determine all questions concerning (1) the construction of the Charter, Statutes, Ordinances and Regulations of the said University and (2) the due and lawful exercise by any of the Statutory bodies named in the statutes of the powers and duties conferred upon them by the Charter, Statutes, Ordinances or Regulations of the said University".[51]

A Visitor can exercise his jurisdiction either on his own initiative or on the receipt of a petition, but it has been held that a Visitor should not interfere in matters relating to membership, unless the circumstances involve illegality or corruption.[52]

> "In many situations, for example, it might be an abuse of power, and a justifiable source of grievance on the part of the foundation, if the Visitor entered on matters which, by the Statutes of the Foundation, were expressly left in the discretion of specially designated officers or members...If the Visitor declines to interfere with their decisions on matters which depend on academic or scientific or other technical judgment then it seems to me quite impossible to say that he has committed any error of law, unless the decisions in question are so plainly irrational or fraught with bias, or some other obvious irregularity that they clearly cannot stand."[53]

A Visitor is therefore a standing authority at all times for the domestic affairs of the corporation, and he derives his authority from the founder's right to determine matters concerning his own creation. As Lord Hardwicke, L.C. said in <u>Attorney General v Talbot</u>

> "The Chancellor (of the University of Cambridge) is visitor (to Clare Hall College). The powers are absolute and final; and cannot be taken away by the courts of law in this kingdom. Such also is the intent; and notwithstanding what has been said, it is the most convenient jurisdiction; for though perhaps it may be sometimes absurd, yet it is less expensive than a suit in law or equity; and in general has been exercised in a reasonable manner."[54]

Some years ago the authority of the Visitor was overshadowed by the Courts. In 1981 Dr Peter M Smith argued

> "Once a relationship has been established which is governed by the general laws of the realm over which the Visitor can have no jurisdiction, the Visitor is wholly excluded from considering any question concerning that relationship."[55]

and this view was upheld in <u>Casson v University of Aston in Birmingham</u> where Lord Hailsham LC said

> "No visitor can have jurisdiction in any matter governed by the Common Law."[56]

More recently however the courts have been more ready to uphold the jurisdiction of the Visitor and the "absolute and final" nature of the Visitor's jurisdiction has been confirmed in a line of cases extending to the present day: the most recent examples being Hines v Birkbeck College in which, after quoting a long series of cases, Hoffmann J commented

> "The existence of so much judicial and academic guidance is usually a sign that the law is in an unsatisfactory state."

and ruled

> "It follows that the matters in dispute between Professor Hines and the college are within the exclusive jurisdiction of the college visitor and his claim against the college in this court must be struck out"[57];

and Thomas v University of Bradford,[58] which has led to legislative intervention. By virtue of s.206 of the Education Reform Act 1988 the exclusive jurisdiction of the Visitor in relation to wrongful dismissal has been removed so that university staff may bring actions in the Courts for such dismissal in the same way as the great majority of other employees. This will take effect for each university in situations where there has been no reference to the Visitor, and when its statutes have been amended by the Commissioners.

In the Thomas case a lecturer's contract of employment had been terminated, and this had the effect of terminating her membership of the University. Thomas's complaint was that, in dismissing her, the University had failed to follow the procedures set out in its Statutes. The University pleaded that the matters pleaded in Thomas's Statement of Claim were within the exclusive jurisdiction of the Visitor. The House of Lords held that, if a dispute arose between a university and a member of the University over his contract of employment with the University which involved questions relating to the internal laws of the University, or the rights and duties derived from those laws, the Visitor had exclusive jurisdiction and could reinstate and order the payment of arrears of salary or damages in lieu of reinstatement. The important point to note in the judgment is that the Visitor had jurisdiction, in other words constitutes a Court, or domestic tribunal, a Court admittedly outside the normal structure but a Court nevertheless, like a Court Martial (which has jurisdiction in matters of military law), a Consistory Court (which deals with issues of ecclesiastical law of the Church of England), or the Court of Chivalry (which deals with claims to coats of arms).

As a Court the Visitor is subject to the supervisory jurisdiction of the Supreme Court in terms of errors as to jurisdiction, or defects in procedure, or points of law, just as is any other court, but not by way of an appeal.

The visitatorial jurisdiction is appellate or by way of review according to the circumstances.[59]

> "It has no exact analogy with that of the ordinary courts. It cannot be usefully defined, beyond saying that the Visitor has untrammeled power to investigate and right wrongs arising from the application of the domestic laws of the charitable foundation."[60]

If Thomas had sued the University of Bradford for breach of contract, rather than for failure to observe its own Statutes there is a possibility that the High Court would have accepted jurisdiction. By virtue of complaining on the procedural rather than the substantive issue, the claim before the Courts fell. In Page v The University of Hull however Auld J held that it was impossible to interpret a university contract of employment without reference to Charter and Statutes and there was consequently no basis on which the courts could intervene.[61]

The jurisdiction of the Visitor extends over all bodies within and members of the corporation, and if he acts outside his jurisdiction the court order known as mandamus can be obtained, and the powers of the court to intervene even where the visitatorial jurisdiction is exercised by the Crown or the Queen in Council.[62] However, disappointed candidates for admission to a university will have no prospect of success if they petition the Visitor because a Visitor is not entitled to interfere with the discretionary powers of the members of the corporation, unless they exercise that discretion wrongly.[63] A Visitor may, however, wish to satisfy himself that the discretion has been correctly and fairly exercised.

Any exercise of the visitatorial power is a judicial act, and a Visitor cannot therefore determine a case without giving both parties a hearing.[64] The procedure does not, however, have to be according to the rules of common law: it has been held sufficient for the parties to be able to state their case in writing.[65] A Visitor, in determining a dispute, has power to make an award for costs.[66] Thus

> "The mode of exercise of the visitatorial powers is infinitely flexible, provided that he acts judicially."[67]

None of the Scottish universities, whether established by Statute or by Royal Charter, has an office of University Visitor. It may be that the University Court - that is, the governing body of the University, more equivalent to the Council than to the Court of an English University - has a slightly more pronounced role in the determination of domestic disputes and grievances, since typically there is provision for the Court to be asked to review any decision of the Senatus. There is also, in five of the eight Scottish universities, an office of Rector who traditionally represents the interests of students, collectively or individually, but the Rector has no legal jurisdiction in the resolution of disputes and grievances other than as a member of the University Court. In general, therefore, if a matter is not resolved internally by the constitutional bodies of the university, the only remaining recourse available to a member of the university is to take the issue to the courts.

4.7 The Courts

A university, which is an eleemosynary or charitable corporation, is subject to control by the courts insofar as exclusive jurisdiction is not vested in the Visitor. As a corporation a university has a legal personality distinct from that of its members and notice served on a member who has no authority to receive notices is not equivalent to notice to the corporation.[68]

Notwithstanding the fact that most universities in England and Wales are Crown creations, that is, they are incorporated by royal charter, they are not subject to Crown control except to the extent provided by their charters, and by virtue of not being subject to control by the Crown are not entitled to Crown immunity on the ground that they are performing a public duty or providing a public service.[69]

The courts will intervene to protect a person against being a member of the corporation against his will.[70] Notwithstanding this general rule of law, many universities had to amend their statutes in the late 1960s and early 1970s to provide for the non-membership of the Exclusive Brethren as staff or students. On the other hand the courts will also protect a corporation against its members. The books of a corporation are only open to inspection by members of the corporation for the purposes of the corporation. Neither individually nor collectively are members entitled to demand inspection except in cases where there is a dispute between members themselves, or between the corporation and an individual member thereof.[71]

If it is proposed to expel members of a corporation, the offence for which expulsion is proposed must be clearly specified, but the extent to which a corporation such as a university can exclude the principles of natural justice in relation to the expulsion of members is not settled.[72]

The courts will permit corporations to lessen the extent of their authority by internal rule, but powers cannot be increased by Ordinance or Regulation.[73] The terms in which a corporation such as a university must make its decisions are, in the absence of any special provision to the contrary in its constitution, as at common law, that is, by a show of hands followed, if necessary, by a poll, i.e. count of the votes.[74] The Courts will also permit a non-statutory corporation to do anything that an ordinary individual can do unless restricted directly or indirectly by statute.[75] This includes the power to deal with its property and to incur liabilities in the same way as an ordinary individual.[76] For example, corporations have been permitted to use their funds to resist any attack upon their property, rights, or to indemnify their servants.[77]

In terms of torts or wrongs committed a university is liable to be sued for any tort provided that it is a tort in respect of which an action would lie against a private individual,[78] the person by whom the tort is committed is acting within the scope of his authority,[79] and the act complained of is not one which the university would not, in any circumstances, be authorised by its charter and statutes to commit.[80] The courts have held corporations liable for a very wide variety of torts and it is considered that universities would likewise be held liable. These include trespass,[81] wrongful distress of goods,[82] assault,[83] negligence,[84] nuisance,[85] false imprisonment,[86] infringement of patent rights,[87] keeping a dangerous animal,[88] breach of trust,[89] fraud,[90] malicious prosecution,[91] and libel.[92] A chartered corporation, such as a university, can perform any act, even those expressly prohibited or not authorised by its charter, that can be undertaken by an individual, except certain criminal offences,[93] but if it does so it may forfeit its charter.[94]

To establish the liability of a university the relation of agent or servant would need to be established in relation to the person actually committing the tort in question.[95] This is defined as vicarious liability.

Whilst universities would be held liable for many such torts, the courts would also protect them from torts committed against them. A university could probably sue in respect of a libel affecting its property[96] or its reputation, unless the imputation is made solely against individual members of staff.[97] A university would be held to have an academic reputation to protect in the same way as a trading corporation is entitled to defend its trading reputation.[98]

A university has certain special rights and obligations under its charter i.e. those different to all those that it has in common with all corporations. These include, for example, the duty to examine students, and the right to award and confer degrees and to confer titles. The extent to which the courts will protect these rights is at least doubtful, even if pecuniary loss can be demonstrated, where such a right is infringed. The principal cases involving interference with rights granted under charter relate to ferries and markets. The owner of a market granted by charter is entitled to protection against unjustifiable interference with the market, as is the owner of a ferry, but the courts have been very restrictive in their grant of relief and this restriction has been confirmed in a recent application for an injunction.[99] The possibility of damage to the working of the institution is not enough: "an allegation of damage alone will not do. You must have in our law injury as well as damage".[100] An injunction will not be granted to restrain a threat of act or acts likely to cause damage but which is not otherwise unlawful.[101]

As with civil liability so with criminal liability. A university can commit any offence other than those for which the sole penalty is death or imprisonment or which cannot be committed vicariously, and where intent is required for the conviction on a criminal offence it has to be obtained from those who represent the "directing mind" of the university and control what it does.[102]

The universities' status as charities renders them liable to a further set of controls by the courts. As charities founded by royal charter they cannot be re-founded or re-established by the court, but they can be regulated and controlled by the courts in financial matters and in doing so the court is entitled to have regard to altered circumstances, and apply a <u>cy pres</u> scheme to alter the basis of the charity, but is not, by so doing, able to upset the constitution of the governing body.[103] <u>Cy pres</u> is a special term meaning as near as possible to the mode specified by the donor.

A charity is any institution which is established for charitable purposes and is subject to the control of the High Court in the exercise of its jurisdiction with respect to charities.[104] The advancement and propagation of education and learning generally are charitable purposes, even in the absence of any poverty in the class of beneficiaries.

Universities, as eleemosynary, or charitable corporations are trustees for their corporate property, and as such are subject to the jurisdiction of the courts except in circumstances where the Visitor has jurisdiction.[105] Special powers are therefore needed, and these are normally given in statutes, to permit university property to be invested more widely than permitted for trust funds. A university, as trustee, does not have to give reasons for its actions in relation to trust funds for which it is responsible, but if it does, it will be subject to the jurisdiction of the courts, though the court is generally reluctant to interfere with a discretionary authority, and the charters of most universities have an article, prescribing that wherever possible a beneficial construction be placed upon the acts of the university.[106]

4.8 The Charity Commissioners

The Charities Act 1960, which does not, in general terms, apply to Scotland or Northern Ireland, provides for the continuance of a body of Charity Commissioners for England and Wales and provides them with certain powers and duties. For the purposes of the Act charities fall into three classes: those fully within the jurisdiction of the Charity Commissioners or the Secretary of State for Education and Science in respect of his responsibilities for educational charities, excepted charities, and exempt charities. All universities are either excepted charities or exempt charities, but even so there are certain matters in relation to which the Charity Commissioners can act. Exempt and excepted charities do not have to register with the Charity Commissioners, or the Secretary of State.[107] The Commission has a general power to institute enquiries with regard to charities: the power extends to excepted charities; but not to exempt charities.[108] The form of the enquiry can include the furnishing of accounts and statements in writing and includes the power to call for documents and search records.[109] Neither excepted nor exempt charities are required to furnish the commissioners with audited accounts.[110] A local authority may, with the consent of the Charity Commissioners, carry out a review of the working of any group of local charities with the same or similar purposes in the Council's area.[111] Exempt and excepted charities are not excluded.

The original purposes of a charitable gift may be altered to allow an application cy pres.[112] There have been several cases in which gifts to universities or associated institutions have been modified under the cy pres principle.[113] Charities established by Royal Charter, such as most universities in England and Wales, are subject to the court's jurisdiction in relation to the application of a scheme cy pres to any property, but where the scheme would require the amendment of the Charter, it cannot take effect until the Charter is amended.[114] Any charity property, including that held by an exempt or excepted charity, may be by order of the court vested in the Official Custodian for Charities. Where the Charity Commissioners are of the view that a charity, other than an exempt charity, ought to apply for a scheme for the administration of a charity but unreasonably refuse or neglect to do so the Commissioners may proceed to do so.[115] The Charity Commissioners can also bring any excepted charity under their general supervision removing officers of the charity, vesting the property of the charity in the official custodian, freezing the assets of the charity.[116] The Commissioners may also authorise any dealings with the property of any charity, which is expedient in the interests of the charity, notwithstanding the powers possessed by the charity.[117]

The Charity Commissioners have the power to give advice to any trustee, general, excepted or exempt, on the application of those charged with the management of the charity and unless the advice is improperly obtained, trustees are protected if they act in accordance with that advice.[118]

They also have the power to control the taking of legal proceedings by excepted charities (not exempt charities) in charity proceedings; a restricted class of legal action relating to the administration of the charity.[119] An important case relating to the definition of a person who may take charity proceedings is Bradshaw & Another v University College of North Wales and Another.[120] In that case certain farm lands were conveyed to the defendant college (University College of Wales, Aberystwyth) on charitable trusts for certain educational purposes and the general purposes of the College. A dispute arose between the donor and the College, which was taken up after her death by her executors. In 1982 the disputes were resolved by a deed of compromise, the executors covenanting not to instigate or assist thereafter in any action or proceeding to enforce or challenge the performance of the trusts created by the 1976 conveyance. In 1986, however, the executors commenced proceedings for an order that the College should furnish reports of its administration of the charitable trust and that in the event of any breach of duty the College should pay an appropriate sum to the trust and be replaced by 5 named new trustees. The College, supported by the Attorney-General, applied to have the summons struck out on the ground that the plaintiffs as executors had no interest in the Charity within the meaning of S28(1) of the Charities Act 1960 as being "persons interested" in the Charity entitled to bring proceedings under S28(8) as neither they, nor the estate of the original donor had any locus standi as beneficiaries under any of the charitable purposes of the trust nor could the land conveyed in 1976 revert in any circumstances to the estate of the donor. Their interest was no more than that of any member of the public whose guardian in the enforcement of charities was the Crown. In Scotland, however, the situation is somewhat different in that an heir of law or executor of the founder of the charity has an interest which entitles him to see that the trust is properly administered.[121]

Where any charity has the power to alter its instrument, as do universities in respect of the making of amendments to their charters or statutes (subject to their allowance by the Privy Council) or by Ordinance, no exercise of that power can validly have the effect of ceasing to be a charity in relation to property acquired as a benefaction, or the income from such property.[122]

The Scots law of charities is relatively simple, with charitable purposes being regarded as trusts for

(i) the relief of poverty:

(ii) the advancement of education:

(iii) the advancement of religion:

(iv) other purposes beneficial to the community.[123]

In practice a group or organisation wishing to obtain charitable status submits to the Inland Revenue details of its constitution, in particular its charitable objectives, and a copy of its accounts, and the positive decision of the Inland Revenue is then final. No further registration of the charity is needed in Scotland and there is no such body as the Charity Commissioners. The Scottish Universities are of course recognised charities in this way and, for example, can apply to the courts for a cy pres scheme for an educational endowment.

4.9 The National Audit Office

The Comptroller and Auditor-General was granted access to universities' books in 1968, and the arrangements for public audit are now contained in s.135 of the Education Reform Act 1988 and the National Audit Act 1983. Except as provided by statute the Comptroller and Auditor-General has complete discretion as to the manner in which he carries out his functions. The powers of the Comptroller and Auditor-General include carrying out examinations into the economy, efficiency and effectiveness with which a body has used its resources in discharging its functions. This does not extend to questioning the merits of the policy objectives. The legal route by which the Comptroller and Auditor-General had access to a University's books was, between 1983 and 1988, not altogether clear. During that period the basis for access was a "decision" by Government in 1967,[124] but s.6 of the 1983 Act prescribes that, for bodies such as universities, the right derives from an "agreement" made before the passing of the Act, between that body and a Minister of the Crown.[125] A prospective complication could have arisen with the change in tuition fees which will result in many universities deriving less than 50% of their income from public funds as defined in the Act (which excludes moneys from Local Education Authorities) and 50% is the normal threshhold for the rights granted to the Comptroller and Auditor-General.[126] However s.135 of the Education Reform Act 1988 makes the books open irrespective of whether or not the 50% threshhold is exceeded, but only in respect of grants from the Universities Funding Council.

Footnotes - Chapter 1

See generally, Halsbury's Laws of England on Charities and Corporations

1. s.3
2. s.3
3. s.78
4. See $ 3.4 infra
5. St David's College, Lampeter v Minister of Education [1951] 1 All ER 556-562
6. Ibid, at p 561
7. London, Butterworth 1970) Vol 5 p 249
8. In Towards an Independent University, 1969 Institute of Economic Affairs Occasional paper 25 pp 23-4)
9. R Eustace and G C Moodie, Power & Authority in British Universities London: Allen & Unwin 1974 pp 20-21
10. pp 358-396
11. 10 Co Rep 1a, 23a
12. British South Africa Co v De Beers Consolidated Mines Limited [1910] 1 Ch 374 at 375
13. Jenkin v Pharmaceutical Society of Great Britain [1921] 1 Ch 392
14. For a discussion of the role of the Visitor see $ 4.6 infra
15. Conn v Corporation of Renfrew [1906] 8 F 905
16. [1920] SC (HL) 73
17. See, for example, the Charter of the University of Bath, 1966
18. s.2
19. Committee on Higher Education (Chairman Lord Robbins) Higher Education Cmnd 2154, Appendix 4, paras 1-17
20. loc.cit. n.5 supra at p.560
21. Hansard 1 December 1972 at pp 875-878
22. Universities Quarterly (1972) 26 pp 271-282: the author is indebted to Mr Owen for a note on this point
23. See The Education (Recognised Bodies) Order 1988, The Education (Listed Bodies) Order 1988 and The Education (Recognised Awards) Order 1988 [SIs 1988 Nos. 2036,2034,2035 respectively]
24. See for example the Universities and Colleges Estates Acts 1925 and 1963 and the Universities and Colleges (Trusts) Act 1943
25. s.42(4) Schemes for further education, now repealed by Schedule 13, Education Reform Act 1988. s.82 of the 1944 Act specifically empowers any local education authority to provide financial assistance to any university or university college.
26. s.30(3)(a) This does not, without further regulation, exempt waste from university halls of residence from collection charges: see Mattison v Beverley Borough Council "The Times" 6 February 1987

27. 1975 c.65 s.22
28. 1976 c.74 s.17
29. 1964 c.51 s.2
30. 1967 c.88 s.28
31. Ibid s.29(6)(b)
32. 1986 c.61 s.43
33. Taylor G & Saunders J B, The Law of Education London, Butterworths, 1976, p.3
34. See Halsbury, Laws of England, London Butterworths 1974 Vol 9 para 1393 and R v Massory [1738] Andr 295
35. Re Snowden [1970] Ch 700
36. Jenkins v Pharmaceutical Society of Great Britain [1921] 1 Ch 392
37. Richard Griffiths,"Are the Universities their own Masters?" Page Fund Lecture, University College Cardiff, 1968
38. Mrs Judith Hart, Under-Secretary of State for Scotland, speaking at the Scottish Standing Committee (H,C.) 7 December 1965
39. R v Panel of Take-overs and Mergers ex.p. Datafin [1987] 1 All ER 564
40. Ibid.
41. R v Criminal Injuries Compensation Board ex.p. Lain [1967] 2 All ER 770 at 778 per Lord Parker CJ
42. Education Reform Act 1988 s.134(10)
43. Krell v Henry [1903] 2 KB 740
44. R v Inland Revenue Commissioners ex.p. National Federation of Self-Employed and Small Businesses Ltd [1982] AC 617
45. See Chapter 3, $ 5.7, infra
46. National Federation case n.44 supra at p.647
47. R v Dean and Chapter of Chester [1850] 15 Q B 513
48. Shelford, The Law of Mortmain [1836] p 23
49. A-G v Dedham School [1857] 23 Beav 350 at 356; affirmed Patel v University of Bradford [1978] 3 All ER 841 at 845
50. University of Nottingham Calendar 1988-89
51. Bridge, Keeping Peace in the Universities - The Role of the Visitor, 86 LQR 531 (1970)
52. R v Hertford College [1878] 3 QBD 693 at 701, CA
53. R v University of London ex parte Vijayatunga [1987] 3 All ER 204 at 213
54. Att-Gen v Talbot [1747] 3 Atk at 674
55. The Exclusive Jurisdiction of the University Visitor LQR (1981) pp 610-647 at p 642
56. Casson v University of Aston [1983] 1 All ER 88 at 91 per Lord Hailsham LC
57. Hines v Birkbeck College [1985] 3 All ER 156
58. [1987] 1 All ER 834

59. Bishop of Chester v Harward and Webber [1787] 1 Term Rep
60. R v University of London ex.p. Vijayatunga [1988] QB 322 at 344-345 per Simon Brown J; approved in R v Her Majesty The Queen in Council ex.p Vijayatunga [1989] 3 WLR 13 per Bingham LJ at p.21
61. Unreported
62. R v Bishop of Ely [1788] 2 Term Rep 290. A prohibition can also be granted by the court if a Visitor exceeds his jurisdiction: R v Bishop of Chichester [1787] 1 Term Rep 650
63. Ibid at p. 701: this is not contrary to natural justice by analogy with such cases as Stuart v Haughley Parochial Church Council [1935] Ch 452 and R (Hennessy) v Department of the Environment [1980] NI 1
64. R v Cambridge University [1723] 8 Mod Rep 148; R v Bishop of Ely [1788] 2 TR 290 per Buller J at 336
65. Shelford, Law of Mortmain (1836), 379;
66. Case of Queen's College [1821] Jac 1 47 affirmed in Thomas v University of Bradford [1987] 1 All ER 834
67. R v University of London ex parte Vijayatunga loc.cit. n.60 supra
68. Steward v Dunn [1844] 1 Dow & L 642 at 649
69. BBC v Johns [1964] 1 All ER 923.Also in Scotland, Greig v Edinburgh University [1868] LR 1
70. R v Askew [1768] 4 Barr 2186 at 2200
71. R v Merchant Tailors Co [1831] 2 B & Ad 115. See also the right of a University Court to receive the minute of any proceeding in the Council, Chapter 2, $ 2.8, infra
72. Gaiman v National Association for Mental Health [1971] 2 All ER 362 at 380, 381
73. R v Weymouth Corporation [1741] 7 Mod Rep 373
74. Re Horbury Bridge Coal Iron and Waggon Co [1879] 11 Ch.D. 109 at 115 CA
75. See n.36 supra
76. Baroness Wenlock v River Dee Co [1883] 36 Ch.D. 675 at 685 n
77. Peel v LNWR Co [1907] 1 Ch. 5 at 21, CA, per Buckley, LJ
78. Greer v London General Omnibus [1859] 7 CBNS 290 at 303
79. Barwick v English Joint Stock Bank [1867] LR2 Exch 259
80. For the general principle see Mill v Hawker [1875] LR 10 Exch 92
81. Ibid.
82. Smith v Birmingham and Staffs Gas Light Co [1834] 1 Ad and El 526
83. Whittaker v LCC [1915] 2 KB 676
84. Hardaker v Idle District Council [1896] 1 QB 335
85. Campbell v Paddington Corpn [1911] 1 KB 869
86. Moore v Metropolitan Rly Co [1872] L R 8 QB 36
87. De Vitre v Betts [1873] LR 6 HL 319
88. Tilburn v People's Palace & Aquarium [1890] 25 QBD 258 CA
89. A-G v Leicester Corporation [1844] 7 Beav 176

90. Lloyd v Grace Smith & Co [1912] AC 716
91. Cornford v Carlton Bank [1900] 1 QB 22
92. Pratt v British Medical Association [1919] 1 KB 244
93. R v Birmingham & Gloucester Railway Co [1842] 3 Q B 223 at 232
94. Eastern Archipelago Co v R [1853] 2 E & B 856 at 870
95. Fisher v Oldham Corporation [1930] 2 KB 364
96. Linotype Co Ltd v British Empire Type Setting Machine Co Ltd [1899] 81 LT 331, HL
97. National Union of General and Municipal Workers v Gillian [1946] KB 81
98. On the analogy of a local authority Bognor Regis UDC v Campion [1972] All ER 61
99. Associated Newspapers Group plc v Insert Media Ltd [1988] 1 WLR 509
100. Day v Brownrigg [1875] 10 Ch.D. 294 at 304,per Sir George Sersel MR
101. Associated Newspapers case n.99 supra at p.513,per Hoffman J.
102. See supra. Also Tesco Supermarkets Ltd v Nattrass [1972] AC 153
103. Re Whitworth Art Gallery Trusts, Manchester Whitworth Institute v Victoria University of Manchester [1958] 1 All ER 176
104. Charities Act 1960 s45(1)
105. A-G v St. Catherine Hall, Cambridge [1820] Jac 381 at 392
106. Re Beloved Wilkes' Charity [1851] 20 L J Ch 588 The general rule of construction is that a grant made by the Crown at the suit of a subject is to be taken most beneficially for the Crown: Eastern Archipelago Co v R [1853] 2 E & B 856. But see The University of Hull Calendar 1987-8 P A40 Charter, Article 24

    > "Our Royal Will and pleasure is that these Presents shall ever be construed benevolently and in every case most favourable to the University and the promotion of the objects of this Our Charter."

107. Charities Act, 1960 s.4(4)
108. Ibid. s.6(1)
109. Ibid. s.6(3)
110. Ibid. ss.8(1) & (7)
111. Ibid. s.11
112. Ibid. ss.13-15
113. e.g.Re Lysaght, Hill v Royal College of Surgeons [1965] 2 All ER 888
114. Charities Act, 1960 s.15
115. Ibid. s.19
116. Ibid. s.20
117. Ibid. s.23
118. Ibid. s.24
119. Ibid. s.28
120. [1988] 1 WLR 190

121. Encyclopaedia of the Laws of Scotland Vol 3 (1937) p 228 para 500
122. Charities Act 1960 s.30(2)
123. Commissioners for Special Purposes of Income Tax v Pemsel [1891] AC 531
124. University Development 1962-7 Cmnd 3820 Para 597
125. National Audit Act 1983 S.6(3)(d)

CHAPTER 2

UNIVERSITY GOVERNMENT AND MANAGEMENT

1. COMMON LAW AND CORPORATIONS

1.1 Introduction

In England and Wales the Common Law has developed a substantial body of rules and principles determining the manner in which all corporations must be governed and managed, and it is considered that this body of rules and principles applies to eleemosynary corporations such as universities to the extent that their own instruments of government do not make other provision. Many of the provisions in university charters and statutes are in fact designed to qualify or modify common law rules, as are many of the rules enunciated in Ordinances and Regulations, such as standing orders for the conduct of business. Parliament has also enacted a vast body of rules for the conduct of business of companies and local authorities: except in cases in which university institutions are incorporated under companies legislation these rules do not, directly, apply, but they may well be used as guides (by the Visitor or the Courts in cases where such issues come before the Courts) to determine the propriety of any particular procedure of government or management. For universities incorporated by statute, rules governing the behaviour of statutory corporations may apply. Parliament had, until 1988, enacted comparatively little legislation directly controlling government or management.[1]

1.2 Legal Personality

In Common Law a corporation has full legal personality when it is complete, that is, when every office and place in the corporation (where numbers are precisely defined) is filled.[2] Thus, if the head of a corporation, e.g. the Chancellor, bequeaths land to such corporation, i.e. the university, that bequest is void, because the bequest must take effect, as a testamentary disposition, at the moment of death, and at that moment the corporation is incomplete.[3] Hence most university charters and statutes provide for the legal capacity of the university in the event of offices being vacant.[4]

It is also a rule of Common Law that the concurrence of a majority of the governing body present and voting is sufficient to bind the corporation, regardless as to what proportion that majority might be to the whole governing body.[5] This again explains the more elaborate quorum and voting rules in charters and standing orders to amend statutes or amend or suspend standing orders.[6] There are likewise restrictions on the right to appoint deputies. A deputy cannot be appointed to act for an officer of the corporation unless there is clear authority to do so in the constitution of the corporation.[7]

1.3 Natural Justice

In some circumstances the rules of Common Law appear to cut across the rules of natural justice: the prohibition against being judge in one's own cause, and the right to a hearing. An office was defined in GWR v Bater as:

> "a subsisting permanent substantive position which had an existence independent of the person who filled it, and which went on and was filled in succession by successive holders".[8]

The power to remove from office, where it exists by virtue of a vote by the governing body, is subject to very strict interpretation by the courts, and if a majority is required that majority must be of the whole body, including the persons to be removed.[9] Here again university rules for the conduct of business normally exclude from voting rights those with a personal interest in the outcome.[10] The rules regulating the right to a hearing are not settled. A nineteenth century case is evidence for the view that an officer of a corporation cannot be removed from office until he has had a hearing, or at least the opportunity of a hearing.[11] But in a twentieth century case the view was expressed, obiter, that the extent to which the constitution of a corporation can exclude the principles of natural justice in relation to the expulsion of members is not settled.[12] In that case Megarry J thought that an article giving an unrestricted power of expulsion ought to be taken into account with all other factors in determining whether the principles of natural justice had any application.

1.4 The "whole body" of the corporation

A corporation's powers are vested in the "whole body" of the corporation.[13] In the case of a university the whole body is conventionally the congregation: the total membership of the University presided over by the Chancellor, supported by the other University officers, with the Court, Council, Senate, Faculties, Convocation and students present. Thus it is that charters and statutes define the powers and duties of the various authorities of the universities in considerable detail so as to avoid the common law principle.

2. THE TRANSACTION OF BUSINESS

2.1 Introduction

Common Law principles also enter the techniques by which business is transacted. As most decisions in universities are made by collective bodies - Councils, Senates, boards, committees - the Common Law principles governing the conduct of private meetings apply, except to the extent that they are qualified by the instrument of government, or intra vires rules made thereunder. A regulation must not be opposed to the constitution,[14] and if a regulation purports to abridge a discretionary power it can be held void as being an attempt to amend the constitution.[15] It is also a basic tenet of Common Law that regulations must be reasonable. Even in the absence of precise rules defining the power to make regulations that power extends to all the purposes for which the corporation was created.[16]

2.2 Notice

The means by which the various authorities of a corporation meet are regulated by Common Law. A meeting must be convened by proper authority,[17] and it must be held upon notice that would give every member of a board etc an opportunity of attending.[18] Notice of meeting can be given in various ways: an entry in the Almanac of meetings, the giving of specific notice, or the circulation of an agenda list. If, on the other hand, a member of, for example, a university Council whom it is reasonably possible to summon to a meeting is not summoned, that meeting of Council will not have been validly convened, even though the omission was accidental and as a result, for example, of clerical error.[19] In the case of a company there are usually in the articles very elaborate provision for the service of notice. For example

> "Properly addressing it, prepaying and posting a letter containing the notice and to have been effected in the case of a notice of a meeting at the expiration of 24 hours after the letter containing the same is posted, and in any other case at the time at which the letter would be delivered in the ordinary course of post".[20]

Likewise there are provisions in the articles of companies for the failure to give notice by reason of accidental omission, and in the event of any dispute over notice the Court or Visitor would be concerned at the extent of the omission in determining the validity of the proceedings.[21] It is of some comfort to know that an irregular procedure cannot be upset if the majority of members approve of the action,[22] but the failure to give notice is construed, not as the denial of the right of the member but rather as being the cause of a material defect in the meeting itself.[23] Charters and statutes sometimes prescribe the form of notice to be given, e.g. for business at annual and special general meetings of a university Court in England (Scottish universities have no body equivalent to the Court of an English university), but in general terms the rules governing the giving of notice, if made at all, are contained in standing orders. If standing orders are silent the general principles of Common Law apply in their entirety.

It is not sufficient just to give notice. The form and content of the notice of business has been subject to fairly extensive legal interpretation. A body within a corporation, e.g. the Senate, which can act in certain matters on behalf of the university cannot act except upon a special summons for the particular business to be transacted.[24] The notice convening the meeting should state definitely that it will be held and must contain sufficient information about the business to be transacted to enable members to decide whether or not to attend.[25] If the notice is misleading the Court will restrain the holding of the meeting, or restrain the corporation from acting upon decisions made at meetings where the business to be transacted was imperfectly communicated in the notice.[26]

> "A notice must be stated fairly: it must not be stated so as to mislead. It must give a fair and candid and reasonable explanation of the purpose or purposes of the meeting."[27]

In Baillie v Oriental Telephone and Electric Co. Ltd, Lord Cozens-Hardy MR said

> "The notice ... seems to me to be not frank, not open, not clear, and not in any way satisfactory - it was tricky."[28]

There must also be a reasonable relationship between the notice given and the business actually transacted.[29] The validity of business transacted under "any other business" upon an agenda could be called in question. Whether business transacted is validly transacted turns upon the particular facts of each case.[30] Judicial interpretation, which would be followed by a Visitor, is that notice is not to be construed with excessive strictness,[31] but it is unsound to transact business other than that of an informal character without giving proper notice.[32]

The period of notice is subject to definition at Common Law. Twenty one days' notice means 21 clear days between the day on which the member, allowing for the ordinary time for the post in England, would receive the notice and the day on which the meeting is to be held. In other words, neither the day of posting the notice nor the day of the meeting itself can be counted as within the period of notice.[33] Lord Mansfield in Pugh v Duke of Leeds stated the general rule of law in the computation of time is that fractions of a day are not reckoned.[34]

> "Date does not mean the hour or the minute, but the day of delivery, and in law there is no fraction of a day."

In applying that rule Chitty J. went on to remark

> "It is no wonder to my mind that persons who do not read statutes with care and have not legal knowledge at their finger's end should make a mistake in a matter such as this."[35]

2.3 Quorum

As stated above, the Common Law quorum rule is that the major part of the persons entitled to attend must be at the meeting, and any decisions are validly made by a majority of those present.[36] However, as far as third parties or strangers to the corporation are concerned, an act apparently valid on the face of it will be good in favour of such a third party acting in good faith and without notice of any irregularity.[37] The active participation of a non-member in the proceedings of a meeting, but not his presence,[38] will, unless the contrary is specifically prescribed in the domestic rules of the corporation, invalidate the proceedings.[39]

A person who is entitled or invited to attend a meeting cannot be counted as a contribution to the quorum, unless he is entitled to vote upon the matter under consideration.[40] The essence of membership of a university board or committee is the right to vote, notwithstanding quite frequent confusion in universities about the concept of non-voting "membership". Restrictions on the right to vote will also have an effect on the calculation of the quorum. Student members are commonly excluded from participating in the transaction of "reserved business",[41] members of staff cannot vote on matters relating to their own salaries or conditions of service, and lay members who may be suppliers or contractors to the University will commonly have restrictions placed upon them by standing orders. Unless otherwise prescribed it is sufficient for there to be a quorum at the commencement of business.[42] The calculation of a quorum must also be by reference to the total size of the body, including any casual vacancies.[43]

2.4 Voting

The form of voting in corporations, including universities, has, as might well be imagined, been the subject of extensive review. At Common Law votes at all meetings are to be taken by a show of hands, that is, the visual impression, as at a trade union branch meeting, which will determine where the majority lies on the issue before the meeting. If a show of hands does not clearly reveal the majority, or on the demand of any member present, a poll may be taken, that is, the votes are counted. In the absence of any special regulations to the contrary in the instrument of government, or regulations validly made thereunder, it is this, the Common Law rule, that must prevail.[44] Voting by a show of hands means the counting of the persons present, who are entitled to vote, and who choose to do so by raising one hand.[45]

Within a corporation incorporated by Charter, such as a university, there is no second or casting vote allowed to the chairman except by the express provision in the constitution, or by long usage.[46] In chartered bodies therefore, a regulation empowering a casting vote may be void.[47] In the case therefore of the voting being equal, the motion is lost.[48]

In certain circumstances, notably under the companies' legislation, provision exists for the exercise of a vote by proxy, but there is no right at Common Law to vote by proxy.[49] It is understood that, except in cases where a university institution is incorporated under the Companies Acts, there is no provision within the university system for a proxy vote to be exercised as such. On the other hand there is commonly a power to delegate powers to transact business, and this may include delegating the right to exercise a vote at a meeting. In addition to the general power of delegation, university statutes quite commonly provide that a Pro-Vice-Chancellor may act for the Vice-Chancellor. It is considered that this would include the right to exercise the Vice-Chancellor's vote on a university body. In terms of calculating a quorum there is argument that a Pro-Vice-Chancellor sitting on a committee in his own right, and as acting for the Vice-Chancellor, cannot be treated as two persons for the purposes of calculating the quorum.[50]

Universities quite commonly require special majorities for the transaction of special business, for example, the making of statutes, the enactment of ordinances by a special procedure on the grounds of urgency, or the rescission of a motion passed at an earlier meeting in the session. If such a special majority is required, for example two thirds or three quarters of those present and voting, a declaration by the Chairman that it was carried could be challenged.[51] In the case of a university incorporated by charter this would be by appeal to the Visitor (to the Courts in Scotland).

2.5 The Chairman

2.5.1 Introduction

The essence of a meeting has two particular ingredients: there must be two persons present and there must be someone in control.[52] In universities the presiding officer is sometimes prescribed in statutes: the Chancellor commonly presides at meetings of university Courts, a Pro-Chancellor at meetings of the

Council, and the Vice-Chancellor at meetings of the Senate. For committees, the appointing body customarily appoints the chairman. Where, however, the Chairman is not appointed by a duly constituted authority, it is the task of the committee to elect a chairman. Any person who is candidate for the chair cannot himself conduct the election. This is a natural extension of the rule of natural justice that no one can be judge in his own cause.[53] Any irregularity in the appointment of a chairman must be the subject of an immediate challenge: tacit consent validates the appointment.[54]

The power to remove a chairman is regarded as essential to the good order and management of a corporation.[55] In a university, however, a chairman normally holds the appointment ex officio or is appointed by a superior body: it is only rarely that he will be appointed by the body over which he presides. It is only in the latter case that the meeting itself has power to remove the chairman, unless a procedure for the suspension of the chair is prescribed in standing orders. In the former the only remedy is to petition for the removal from the office by virtue of which the chair is held, or to petition the appointing authority.

2.5.2 The Task of the Chairman

The task of the chairman has been subject to extensive legal interpretation and is summarised in Shaw and Smith's Law of Meetings.[56] It includes

(i) determining that the meeting is properly constituted and that a quorum is present;

(ii) informing himself as to the business and objects of the meeting;

(iii) preserving order in the conduct of those present;

(iv) confining discussion within the scope of the meeting and reasonable limits of time;

(v) deciding whether proposed motions and amendments are in order;

(vi) formulating for discussion and decision questions which have been moved for the consideration of the meeting;

(vii) deciding points of order and other incidental matters which require decision at the time;

(viii) ascertaining the sense of the meeting by

(a) putting relevant questions to the meeting and taking a vote thereon;

(b) declaring the result;

(c) causing a count to be taken if duly demanded;

(ix) dealing with the minutes of proceedings;

(x) adjourning the meeting where prevailing circumstances justify that course;

(xi) declaring the meeting closed when its business has been completed.

2.5.3 The Maintenance of Order

The constitution of a meeting and quorum has already been discussed.[57] In terms of the maintenance of order at a meeting of a university committee the question of how to maintain order as against those who have a specific right to attend is a difficult one. In normal circumstances the disciplining of those who have a right to attend is a matter for the statutory body or committee by virtue of the fact that such power is reasonably necessary for the exercise of the functions of the body.[58] Standing orders will sometimes vest the power to expel a refractory member, or to adjourn the meeting. The general experience of the disruption of meetings in universities points to adjournment or suspension of the proceedings as being the best weapons in the hands of the chairman.

2.5.4 Order of Business

The proper conduct of business at a meeting involves an order for the business to be transacted. The order is normally defined by an agenda paper or list which will set out items in the intended chronological order. Unless, however, there are precise regulations in standing orders controlling the order of business or vesting discretion in the chairman, the meeting as a whole has discretion as to the order in which items are taken.[59]

2.5.5 Irregularity of Procedure

If the chairman's handling of the procedure at a meeting is irregular it does not necessarily mean that the business transacted will be upset by the Courts (if a stranger to the corporation is involved) or the Visitor (if members of the corporation only are affected by the decisions made). Where a corporation is competent to rectify an irregularity in the management of its internal affairs, the Court will not as a rule interfere to compel rectification.[60] The majority of any authority or committee can regularise any irregularity in the proceedings by approving of them,[61] unless the irregularity is such as to amount to a fraud.[62]

In regulating the conduct of business the chairman has a duty to exclude irrelevancies. His purpose is to keep within the defined scope, to ascertain the true sense of the meeting having regard to the time available for the purposes of the meeting, and he has an inherent duty to conduct the proceedings with impartiality.[63] He is, however, exempt from personal liability in respect of the conduct of the meeting provided that he acts bona fide and honestly.[64]

2.6 Limits on Freedom of Discussion - Defamation[65]

As the holding of a meeting of a university Court, Council, Senate, board or committee is not a statutory obligation the proceedings are not absolutely privileged in terms of the law of defamation. However, fair comment can be a defence provided that it is a comment and not an assertion of fact, that the comment is a matter of public interest, and the comment must be fair and not actuated by malice.[66] However, the proceedings of corporations are protected by qualified privilege[67] and fair and accurate reports of the findings of university Councils will likewise be protected.[68] If one member of a university made a statement which was prima facie (at first sight) defamatory of another in the course of university business it is a matter which would be within the jurisdiction of the Courts, notwithstanding its "domestic" nature, because the dispute did not relate to the internal laws of the foundation.

2.7 Motions

The chairman of a body can put motions to a meeting without the necessity of a seconder.[69] At Common Law a seconder of a motion is not required though it is normal practice for standing orders to require a seconder of each motion from the floor. The chairman is obliged to accept every motion proposed provided that it is relevant[70] and that it is a material question brought before the meeting.[71] A motion the purpose of which is not clear can be rejected by the chairman. Under the accepted conventions of procedure in England only one amendment can be under consideration at any one time: under Scottish procedure more than one amendment can be considered simultaneously.[72]

An amendment can propose

(a) to omit certain words; or

(b) to insert certain words; or

(c) to omit certain words from and replace them by others in any part of the original motion; or

(d) to add words to the original motion.

What an amendment should not do is have the effect of negating the original motion, that can be achieved by a negative vote on the substantive motion.[73] The Chairman is likewise under an obligation to accept every amendment within the prescribed form provided that it is intelligible and preserves the intelligibility of the original motion, and provided also that it does not purport to negative a motion that has been accepted by the committee meeting within any period that might be prescribed by standing orders (e.g. the current academic session).

The prescribed form of an amendment, therefore, is that

(l) It is not <u>ultra vires</u> the meeting;

(2) It is not irrelevant;

(3) It is not redundant;

(4) It is not inconsistent;

(5) It is not vexatious;

(6) It is a proper exercise of any discretion granted to the chairman.[74]

Once the debate on a motion has commenced it is not required of a chairman that he should carry the debate through to a decision on that motion with such amendments as might be proposed. There are a number of procedural motions that can be employed to terminate discussions. These are:

(l) The previous question, that the motion "be not now put";

(2) The clause, that the motion "be now put";

(3) That the meeting "proceed to next business";

(4) That the discussion on the motion be adjourned;

(5) That the meeting be adjourned;

(6) That the motion "lie on the table";

(7) That the motion "be referred back (to committee)";

(8) That the chairman leave the chair.[75]

Procedural motions take precedence over substantive motions and discussion on them is either limited or excluded.[76] Where discussion is limited a motion to adjourn will take precedence over other procedural motions.

The power to adjourn a meeting is, at Common Law, vested in the meeting itself, and not in the hands of the chairman.[77] The chairman has, however, a general discretion to adjourn a meeting in the face of disorder,[78] or if prescribed in the rules of procedure. If the rules of procedure remit the power to the chairman "with the consent of the members" a motion to adjourn is void.[79]

2.8 Minutes

Finally, there is a responsibility vested in the chairman for the keeping of minutes. There is no obligation at Common Law for minutes of meetings of corporations or the authorities thereof to be kept, and the charters and statutes of universities do not prescribe the keeping of minutes. However, the supervisory role of one authority in a university over another will necessarily involve some keeping of records at least so that that supervisory function can be exercised. For example, it is sometimes prescribed that at the Annual General Meeting

> "Any member of the court may require that any Resolution or Minute of the proceedings of the Council in relation to any particular matter shall be read in full".[80]

In precise terms a minute is concerned only with recording the fact that a meeting was held and that certain decisions were arrived at.[81] A minute will record:

(1) the nature of the meeting;

(2) the time and place at which it was held;

(3) how constituted, i.e. who was in the chair and what other members were present;

(4) what persons were in attendance, but not as members;

(5) the full terms of resolutions adopted;

(6) the subject matter of financial transactions considered by the meeting;

(7) all specific business upon which decisions were taken.[82]

A report of a meeting is an account of what transpired, and narrates, in greater or less detail, the course of proceedings including the arguments advanced for or against any particular course of action, and the options considered.[83]

Minutes can be written up from rough notes made at the time of the meeting.[84] The confirmation of minutes at the next meeting does not confirm the substantive decisions made at the meeting the minutes of which are being confirmed, and refusal to confirm the minutes does not render the decision made void.[85] Discussion on the motion relating to the minutes must be confined to the record, and not to the decisions. The chairman's signature of authentication need not be written at the meeting to which the minutes relate.[86]

At Common Law confirmed minutes are not conclusive evidence as to the making or otherwise of decisions at the meetings to which the minutes relate. A resolution may be proved by other evidence, even if not minuted.[87] If standing orders prescribe the conclusive nature of confirmed minutes that will be binding on members of the corporation.[88] Confirmed minutes do not prevent a challenge to the validity of the minute whether by quorum, or adequacy as to the form of notice.[89] If minutes are to have some evidential value they need to be prepared within a reasonable time after the meeting to which they relate.

2.9 The Supervision of Committees

As mentioned above, the Court of an English university may exercise a certain supervisory function in relation to the Council, but the allocation of powers as between Court and Council are so defined in charters and statutes as to prevent any possibility of the Court exercising detailed control over the Council which is normally defined as the governing body and executive. There is some analogy between Court as being approximately equivalent to the general meeting of a company, and Council as being the board of directors. Although the resolution of a dispute beteen Court and Council is within the exclusive jurisdiction of the Visitor it is considered that the rule enunciated in Automatic Self-cleansing Fitter Syndicate Co. v Cunninghame[90] would apply, and that not even a resolution of the Court would invalidate an act of Council acting within its statutory powers. The only course of action open to Court would be to alter the composition of Council, insofar as it is open to Court to do so, or to make statutes for consideration by the Privy Council re-defining the relationship.[91]

The convening of meetings of Court, other than the annual general meeting, is normally undertaken by the Council of the University, or there can be provision for the requisition of a meeting by a certain number of the members of Court.[92] A meeting convened on any other instructions is void[93] unless subsequently validated by the Council.[94] If a group is authorised to convene a university body, for example, a meeting of the Court convened by Council, it is not enough for each member of the group to agree individually but the group must agree collectively.[95] Any delay, however, in challenging the validity of the basis on which the meeting is summoned will amount to condonation.[96] At Common Law, once a meeting has been convened there is no power to postpone it, but power to postpone may, by standing orders, be vested in a chairman.[97]

3. THE LEGAL POSITION OF UNIVERSITY OFFICERS AND MEMBERS OF UNIVERSITY AUTHORITIES

3.1 General

As has been pointed out, a corporation is recognised by the law as having a personality distinct from its members, in other words the corporators as members of the corporation are something wholly different from the corporation itself. One important consequence of this distinct legal personality is that a plaintiff's rights against individual members of the corporation are limited, in general terms, to the extent that individual liability is prescribed in the charter or statutes of the corporation. Members of the corporation are thus not, unless the contrary is expressly prescribed, liable to be charged with the debts of the corporation. Given that the presumption of law lies against personal liability, it would require express words to set that liability aside. In Re. Sheffield & South Yorkshire Permanent Building Society it was contended that the ex-members of a building society were liable to contribute to the debts of the society as far as the debts or liabilities were incurred while they were members, but Charles J. stated

> "that contention assumes that the individual members of a corporation are liable for the debts of the corporation: an assumption which I have no doubt is a wrong one, unless the charter creating the society or some Act of Parliament has created that liability".[98]

On the other hand it has been held that where the officers or directors of a corporation or company actively participate in an act which is beyond the power of the corporation to perform, they are each, to the extent of participation, personally liable for the consequences.[99] In a university setting the powers of the Council can be expressly delegated to a group of officers or an individual officer if the statutes of the university empower such delegation. In such circumstances it could be argued that there is a personal liability for actions taken under delegated powers, unless the act of delegation expressly excluded personal liability. There is no distinction in respect of whether the members of the university acting under delegated powers are employees or lay members of Council. For this purpose they are agents, and there is a convergence of the position of servant and agent from the point of view of practical consequences.[100] In addition statute provides for the personal responsibility of managers and licence-holders in a variety of ways.[101]

The situation becomes more complex still when one considers the position of a charity. Where charity trustees use the trust money for their own purposes, for purposes not in accordance with the trust, occasioning the destruction of trust property, or improperly alienate it, they are strictly liable to make good any deficiency or loss. It is however the duty of charity trustees to protect the trust property, but they are not bound to look with more prudence to the affairs of the charity than to their own. On the other hand a corporation can be a trustee for charitable purposes,[102] and as charitable corporations exist solely for the accomplishment of charitable purposes, their whole raison d'etre is to be trustee for the charity.[103] As the charter and statutes of an English university commonly prescribe that it is the Council, and not the members of Council, that is trustee for university property, liability for the actions of the university lies with the Council and not the members thereof.[104] A university, as a corporation, is liable for the protection of its property but the courts will tend to greater leniency in the case of corporations in judging the management than in cases where individuals are trustees.[105]

Lord Langdale MR said

> "I should be sorry to say anything from which it could be inferred that corporations and colleges are not bound strictly to perform the trusts they undertake, but it is evident that, in changing corporations consisting of fluctuating members, they cannot be dealt with as individual persons, for, by so doing, we should visit the present members with the consequences of errors committed by their predecessors, whom they do not in any case represent".[106]

Thus it can be said that there is a general presumption against the individual and personal liability of members of the Council of a university for acts or omissions of the Council, but there may be circumstances in which that immunity can be set aside.

3.2 Individual Officers

3.2.1 The Chancellor

The Chancellor of a university is normally, ex officio, the presiding officer at meetings of the Court of the university. As presiding officer or chairman of the Court he has the legal responsibilities and powers of a meeting chairman, but his exercise and performance of those powers and duties will be subject to the jurisdiction of the Visitor in respect of any complaints by members of the university, and to the courts where any plaintiff can establish locus standi sufficient to commence proceedings.

A Chancellor may resign by writing addressed to the Court and can only be removed from office for "good cause" as defined by the Court.

3.2.2 Pro-Chancellors

Pro-Chancellors, in the absence of the Chancellor, exercise all the powers of the Chancellor except that of conferring degrees. In addition, a Pro-Chancellor may be Chairman of the university Council and hence his powers and duties are those associated with the Chairman of a meeting. Like the Chancellor, a Pro-Chancellor may resign by writing addressed to the Court, and can only be removed from office for "good cause" as defined by the Court. Some Pro-Chancellors, however, hold office for a limited term and their appointment can therefore lapse by virtue of not being re-elected by the Court.

3.2.3 The Vice-Chancellor

The Vice-Chancellor is commonly described as the principal academic and administrative officer of the university. The official powers and duties ascribed to a Vice-Chancellor tend, however, to be rather limited. In the absence of the Chancellor he presides at congregations of the university and confers degrees. He is almost invariably ex officio Chairman of the Senate or equivalent body and has a general responsibility for maintaining and promoting the efficiency and good order of the university. The specific powers accorded to Vice-Chancellors in relation to students vary: in some cases the power to refuse to admit as a student is unconditional, and does not have to be reported. In such cases the only remedy is by way of petition to the Visitor, but it is considered that only in exceptional cases would the Visitor intervene, by virtue of the general principle that the Visitor does not interfere in the general management of the corporation to which he is Visitor. In other cases there is a statutory obligation to report the refusal to the university authority which has the power to regulate admission to courses: normally the Senate. The consequence of the obligation to report is not well defined.

Vice-Chancellors also have the power to suspend or exclude students from any part of the university or its precincts. As the "precinct" is normally expressly mentioned as a second area it is assumed that it means the environs, rather than the space defined by the boundaries of the property, i.e. the immediate neighbourhood of the university. In exercising these powers a Vice-Chancellor should normally apply the rules of natural justice, i.e. the nature of the charge which is the basis of the potential exclusion should be known to the student, and the student should be given an opportunity to answer the charge.[107] In addition the Vice-Chancellor would not exercise his powers if he were personally involved in the charge e.g. an assault upon him or his room.

3.2.4 Pro-Vice-Chancellors

Pro-Vice-Chancellors normally have two sets of powers: reserve and original. The reserve power is to act as Vice-Chancellor during a vacancy in the office or during the absence or inability of the Vice-Chancellor, e.g. in a disciplinary case involving the Vice-Chancellor personally. The original powers are those which may be vested in him by Statute or Ordinance.

3.2.5 Other Officers

Universities have a variety of other officers: Treasurers, Deans, Registrars, Secretaries, Bursars, Librarians. The duties and powers of such officers are variously defined in statutes, ordinances, and regulations. Where such officers perform quasi-judicial functions, as in the application of regulations or codes of discipline, they are bound to observe the rules of natural justice, but in performing administrative tasks no such limitation applies. A test of whether a person is acting judicially or administratively is set out in Durayappah v Fernando:

> (1) What is the nature of the property held, the status enjoyed or services to be performed by the complainant of injustice;
>
> (2) In what circumstances or upon what occasions is the person claiming to be entitled to exercise the measure of control entitled to intervene;
>
> (3) When a right to intervene is proved what sanctions in fact is the latter entitled to impose upon the other.[108]

3.3 Judge in One's Own Cause

The structure of university government is such as to make officers with regulatory authority members of one or more of the university authorities, such as Senate or Council. That being so, university procedures are fraught with the risk of a person being judge in one's own cause. Some illustrations will suffice. If a Senate is trapped in its chamber by a student demonstration, the members of the Senate charged with responsibility for student discipline might have been present. Even if they were not there is quite commonly a right of appeal to the Senate in discipline cases. In either case there is a distinct possibility of members of a disciplinary tribunal qua members of Senate being judges in their own cause.

It is impossible to summarise exactly the varied legal advice that universities have received in such cases, but the general gist is that members of the inferior body should play no active part in the transaction of that business at the superior body. Mere membership of the superior body will not necessarily invalidate the proceedings, but active participation could do so. A case which might influence the Visitor considering a petition against expulsion from the university or a staff removal from office under "good cause" procedure is Cooper v Wilson.[109] In that case a Watch Committee, in considering an appeal from a Chief Constable's dismissal of a police officer, allowed the Chief Constable to sit with them during their deliberations, and the Court of Appeal held that the proceedings should be quashed as a breach of natural justice. Similarly in R v Sussex Justices ex parte McCarthy,[110] an acting Clerk to the Justices, with an interest as solicitor in civil proceedings in a traffic accident case, retired with the Justices in a criminal case over the same accident. He did not take part in the decision to convict, as his opinion or advice was not sought by the bench, but the conviction was quashed. In neither case could justice be seen to be done. In neither case was the person whose presence offended against the rule of no man being judge in his own cause a member of the relevant authority, Watch Committee or Magistrate's Bench, but in R v Hendon R.D.C. ex parte Chorley,[111] the presence of a member of the authority vitiated the proceedings. In that case, an application for planning permission, a member of the Council with an interest in the use of the land had voted on the resolution. It might be that a Visitor would not take such a strict view of the need to ensure that justice must be seen to be done as the Courts, but the principle stands.

In more recent cases the courts have taken a pragmatic view of how a person performing a judicial function comes to a case with "clean hands". In R v Frankland Prison Board of Visitors ex.p. Lewis[112] it was held that, as the Board was required to perform dual administrative and judicial functions and having regard to the nature of prison disciplinary hearings, the fact that an individual member of the board had gained background knowledge of a prisoner by virtue of his administrative functions did not necessarily disqualify him from dealing with that prisoner in a disciplinary hearing. The test was "would a reasonable and fair minded person sitting in court and hearing all the relevant facts have a reasonable suspicion that a fair trial for the applicant was not possible".[113] It is all a question of degree.

In R v Kent Police Authority ex.p. Godden it was held that a medical practitioner giving a decision as to whether a person was permanently disabled was performing a quasi-judicial function and under a duty to act fairly. He was not acting as a doctor. His decision would affect not merely pension rights but standing in the community, his ability to get other work and the like, and as the doctor in question had previously been involved he did not come to the case with clean hands.[114]

3.4 Deputies

In general terms a corporation cannot appoint deputies to act for it unless clear authority to do so exists in the charter or statutes.[115] A Pro-Vice-Chancellor is an example of such a deputy; he can substitute for the Vice-Chancellor.

Where there is power by charter for an authority to appoint a deputy, the latter has all the powers of his principal, unless he is appointed as a special deputy.[116]

3.5 Delegation

The concept of delegated powers has come to prominence consequent upon the Jarratt Report on University Efficiency Studies[117] and the Education Reform Act 1988, where it is enacted that the University Commissioners have to secure that the statutes of each qualifying institution include

(a) Provision enabling an appropriate body, or any delegate of such a body, to dismiss any member of the academic staff by reason of redundancy; and

(b) Provision enabling an appropriate officer, or any delegate of such an officer, acting in accordance with procedures determined by the Commissioners, to dismiss any member of the academic staff for good cause.[118]

In addition many universities have express powers in their statutes to delegate the powers of university authorities to individuals or committees. What, then, in the legal sense, is delegation, and what consequences flow from delegation?

Delegation is defined as the devolution from an agent upon another person of a power or duty entrusted to the agent by his principal. Delegatus non potest delegare is the maxim which lays down the general rule that an agent cannot delegate his powers or duties to another, in whole or in part, without the express authority of the principal, or authority derived from that principal.[119] Wills J. pointed out in Huth v Clarke

> "Delegation, as the word is generally used, does not imply a parting with powers by the person who grants the delegation, but points rather to a conferring of an authority to do things which otherwise the person would have to do himself. The best illustration of the use of the word is afforded by the maxim, Delegatus non potest delegare, as to the meaning of which it is significant that it is dealt with in Broom's Legal Maxims under the law of contracts: it is never used by legal writers, so far as I am aware, as implying that the delegating person parts with his power in such a manner as to denude himself of his rights. If it is correct the word 'delegate' means little more than an agent".[120]

A delegate therefore is an agent with a high-flown title. There is also a connection with the law of master and servant. Birkett L.J. in Mainwaring v Billington said

> "My own view is that for there to be a delegation of a statutory authority it must be made clear that it is a statutory duty that is being delegated, and that what is being said is not mere instruction as to how the workman should carry on his work".[121]

3.6 Agency

A university officer or committee, therefore, who exercises the powers of a university authority by virtue of a formal act of delegation is an agent of the university authority. The rules which define the relationship between the authority (Council or Senate), the delegate (committee or officer), and third parties either within the university (where jurisdiction lies with the Visitor) or externally (where jurisdiction lies with the courts) are those of the law of agency.

As between principal and agent, respective rights and duties rest upon an express or implied contract,[122] but a term will not be implied merely because it is reasonable to imply it: it must necessarily be implied in the nature of the contract.[123] The relationship is also of a fiduciary nature and imports into it elements of the law of trusts.[124]

If an agent or delegate is given instructions as to the manner in which he must perform his duties, he must carry them out in that manner.[125] In exercising his discretion an agent can use his own judgment but must always have the interests of his principal in mind.[126] In the absence of express authority an agent must not purport to bind his principal by contract.[127] On the other hand the implied authority of university Senates acting in the course of their employment must be considered, as university statutes commonly validate contracts made under the implied authority of the Council.[128]

An agent must employ proper care, skill and diligence in the performance of his delegated powers and duties, and can be held liable to his principal for any loss occasioned by his want of proper care, skill or diligence.[129] There is, however, no absolute standard, and each particular case must be judged by its own circumstances.[130] The standard of care required will vary according to the officer. A permanent officer, such as a Vice-Chancellor or Registrar, could well have a higher standard expected of him in the performance of delegated tasks than a member of the academic staff holding university office for a limited term, such as Pro-Vice-Chancellor or Dean.

Lay members of Council are frequently vested with delegated powers. As they perform their tasks on a gratuitous basis they are only bound to use such skill as they have,[131] except where they have represented themselves as possessing particular skills, in which case the amount of skill requisite is that appropriate to the representation and reasonably to be expected in the circumstances.[132] Thus the chairman of a finance committee who is a chartered accountant exercising delegated powers could be expected to bring to the task a higher degree of skill and financial acumen than, say, a head teacher. In general terms, however, the degree of care and diligence expected of a lay person exercising delegated powers is such as persons ordinarily use in the conduct of their own affairs.[133] A lay person acting as agent is not liable for failing to act unless he has undertaken to do so. If he undertakes to act and performs his duties negligently he is liable under the normal rules of negligence.[134]

3.7 The Liabilities of a Delegate or Agent

If a principal is convicted of a criminal offence as a result of the negligence of the agent, in cases where the liability is absolute, and the principal has not himself been guilty of any fault, he can recover the whole penalty.[135] In other cases the normal rule is that, subject to the form of delegation, a principal has a right to bring an action for damages against the agent. A university authority commonly delegates to a committee or group. In such circumstances one member of such a group is not liable for the acts or defaults of the other members of the group,[136] unless he has expressly or tacitly authorised such acts or defaults.[137]

3.8 The Rights of an Agent or Delegate

An agent or delegate is entitled to be indemnified for such liabilities as he might incur and such losses suffered as were in contemplation when the agency was undertaken. By implication a contract exists between the principal and the agent to reimburse him and to indemnify.[138] The extent of that indemnity is not only any losses actually sustained but also, in accordance with the principles of equity, the full amount of the liability incurred.[139]

However, the right to indemnity or reimbursement is not unlimited. An agent cannot recover in respect of expenses or liabilities incurred in consequence of his own default[140] or breach of duty, or transactions which were outside the scope of his authority and are not subsequently ratified by the principal.[141] There is no right of indemnity in the case of a transaction contrary to public policy,[142] but there is a right of indemnity if the conduct of the agent amounts to a tort, if it was not manifestly tortious, or tortious to his knowledge.[143] The question is sometimes raised as to whether it is possible to provide an indemnity against criminal liability. There is however the risk that the purported giving of such an indemnity would itself be illegal as it would apply to deliberate, negligent or innocent breaches of the criminal law. It might be regarded as incitement.

3.9 Relations between Universities and Third Parties when acts performed under Delegated Powers

If conditions or limitations[144] are imposed upon those exercising delegated powers, no act performed in excess of that authority is treated as the act of the principal as regards such persons who have,[145] or ought to have[146] notice of that limitation of authority. In the absence of notice of the limitation the principal cannot escape liability,[147] unless the act done by an agent falls outside the apparent scope of his authority, in which case the principal will not be liable for that act.[148] Thus a university would probably be bound by an offer made by an admissions officer acting with apparent authority even though he does not have actual authority, on the assumption that the candidate had placed reliance upon the offer by accepting it.[149] But if the candidate was aware that the admissions officer had made a mistake he cannot expect the university to be bound by the mistake.[150] Statutory provision may however make the principal liable.[151]

As a general rule, however, a principal, such as a university, is liable on any contract made by an agent, and that contract may be enforced by or against the principal.[152] Where a principal gives authority to his agent to make admissions on his behalf, the principal is bound as regards third persons, by any admission so made provided that the admission is within that authority.[153] Likewise with the disposition of property, no disposition made without the authority of the principal is binding upon the principal.[154]

3.10 Liabilities for Torts Committed Under Delegated Powers

There are certain senses in which the liability of a principal for the acts of his agent bears a close resemblance to the liability of a master for the acts of his servant, or the liability of a client for the acts of an independent contractor. The differences arise from the fact that only agents create legal relations between their principals and third parties.[155] The similarity is that all three can affect the legal position by creating liabilities.

In many cases the Courts have not found it necessary to decide whether the person committing the tort was an agent or an employee under a contract of service and have used the terminology of either relationship interchangeably. In such cases the "scope of authority" of an agent will be much the same as the "course of employment" of an employee. In Lloyd v Grace Smith Earl Loreburn said

> "It (the fraud complained of) was a breach by the defendant's agent of a contract made by him as defendant's agent to apply diligence and honesty in carrying through a business within his delegated powers and entrusted to him in that capacity. It was also a tortious act committed by the (solicitor's) clerk in conducting business which he had a right to conduct honestly, and was instructed to conduct, on behalf of his principal"

to which Lord MacNaughten added

> "The expressions 'acting within his authority', 'acting in the course of his employment' and the expression 'acting within the scope of his agency' as applied to the agent, speaking broadly, mean one and the same thing."[156]

An agent has a "usual authority" to act for his principal and the doctrine of usual authority is stated most clearly in s.5 of the Partnership Act 1890[157]:

> "Every partner is an agent for his firm and of his other partners for the business of the partnership, and the acts of every partner who does any act for the carrying on in the usual way business of the kind carried on by the firm of which he is a member bind the firm and his partners, unless the partner so acting has in fact no authority to act for the firm in the particular matter, and the person with whom he is dealing either knows that he has no authority or does not know or believe him to be a partner."

What is necessary to carry on the partnership in the usual way is the test of authority: it does not include a power to do what is unusual however urgent[158] and what is usual may vary from time to time.[159] The issue is determined by the facts of the case. The general rule is that a principal is responsible jointly and severally with his agent to third parties in respect of situations in which an agent is expressly authorised to perform a wrongful act,[160] or which necessarily results in a wrongful act.[161] Where the wrongful act is not expressly authorised but the agent is acting within the scope of his implied, apparent or ostensible authority, the principal is also liable.[162] When the principal has expressly prohibited the act complained of, liability will turn upon the apparent scope of authority and whether or not the third party had notice of the prohibition.[163]

The agent or delegate will, as a general rule, be liable personally for any wrongs committed under agency or delegated powers even with the authority of his principal, and for the benefit of the principal.[164] It does not matter that the agent was unaware that the act was tortious.[165] As both principal and agent are liable for the tort of the agent, either can, by virtue of the Law Reform (Married Women and Tortfeasor) Act 1935, be sued.[166] As between the principal and agent, any tort there is a claim for contribution. The Act also provides that "where damage is suffered by any person as a result of a tort, any tortfeasor liable in respect of that damage may recover contribution from any other tortfeasor who is, or would if sued, have been liable in respect of the same damage, whether as a joint tortfeasor, or otherwise".[167] This right to contribution is not unlimited. If the agent acted in breach of duty, either wilfully or negligently, he will not be able to recover from his principal. Thus, as already stated, it is principally in terms of action by delegation that a member of a university can render himself personally liable for "university" acts.[168]

Footnotes - Chapter 2

See generally Halsbury's Laws of England,Vol 1. Agency,Vol 9. Corporations

1. See Chapter 1 supra
2. Stewart Kyd, A Treatise on the Law of Corporations (Butterworth, London 1793, re-printed Garland, New York and London 1978) p. 107
3. Ibid
4. See, for example, The University of Hull, Statutes, Section 35

   "ACTS DURING VACANCIES

   No act or resolution of the Court, the Council or the Senate shall be invalid by reason only of any vacancy in the body doing or passing it or by reason of any want of qualification by or invalidity in the election or appointment of any appointment of any de facto Member of the body whether present or absent."

5. Kyd, op.cit. p. 424

6. See, for example, The University of Hull, Charter, Article 22

"22. The Court may at any time alter, amend or add to these Presents and their provisions by a Special Resolution in that behalf and such alteration, amendment or addition shall when allowed by Us Our Heirs or Successors by and with the advice of Our Privy Council become effectual so that these Presents shall thenceforward continue and operate as though they had been originally granted and made as so altered, amended or added to in manner aforesaid. This Article of these Presents shall apply to this Our Charter as altered, amended or added to in manner aforesaid.

A Special Resolution means a resolution passed at one meeting of the Court and confirmed at a subsequent meeting held not less than one calendar month nor more than three calendar months after the former provided that the Resolution be passed at each meeting by a majority of not less than three-fourths of those present and voting."

7. R v Gravesend Corpn, [1824] 4 Dow & Ry KB 117.
8. [1920] 3 KB 266 at 274
9. R v Sutton [1711] 10 Mod. Rep. 74 at 76
10. See, for example, The University of Hull, Statutes, Section 14 Clause 6

> "No Officer or Member of the academic staff who is also a member of the Court shall vote on any matter relating to his own salary or conditions of service."

11. R v Saddlers' Co [1863] 10 HL Cas 404
12. Gaiman v National Association for Mental Health [1971] Ch 317 at 338 (1970) 2 All ER 362 at 381, 382
13. R v Westwood [1830] 4 Bligh N S 213 H.L.
14. R v Bunstoad [1831] 2 B & Ad 699; Bentham v Hoyle [1878] 3 QBD 289
15. R v Governors of Darlington School [1844] 6 QB 682 at 717, Ex Ch
16. Chilton v London and Croydon Rly Co. [1847] 16 M & W 212 at 228, per Parker,B.
17. Re State of Wyoming Syndicate [1901] 2 Ch 431
18. Mayor etc., and Co. of Merchants of the Staple of England v Governor and Co. of the Bank of England [1887] 21 QBD 160 at 165 CA, per Wills J.
19. R v Langhorn [1836] 4 Ad. & El. 538
20. Companies Act, 1948 Table A, Art. 131, cited in V. Powell Smith, Blackwell's Law of Meetings, 9th Edition (London, Butterworths 1967) p. 99-100

21. Re West Canadian Collieries, Ltd., [1962] Ch 370
22. Re Oxted Motor Co. Ltd. [1921] 3 KB 32, cited in V. Powell Smith, op. cit. 99
23. Vide R v Langhorne, n.19 supra
24. R v Liverpool Corporation [1759] 2 Burr 723 at 731
25. Peel v LNWR [1907] Ch 5 at 14, CA per Vaughan Williams LJ
26. Kaye v Croydon Tramways Co. [1898] 1 Ch 358 CA
27. Ibid, at p.370 per Lindley MR
28. [1915] 1 Ch 503 at 514
29. Torbock v Lord Westbury [1902] 2 Ch 871
30. Sir Sebag Shaw and Smith, D. The Law of Meetings - Their Conduct and Procedure (Macdonald and Evans, London, 1974) P. 149 and Wright's Case [1871] LR 12 Eq, 331
31. Young v Ladies Imperial Club Ltd [1920] 2 KB 523
32. Re Hector Whaling Ltd [1936] Ch 208
33. Shaw and Smith op.cit. p.65
34. Pugh v Duke of Leeds 2 Cowp 714, 720
35. Re Railway Sleepers Supply Co. [1885] 29 Ch D 204
36. Vide n.31 supra
37. County of Gloucester v Rudry Merthyr Steam and House Coal Colliery [1895] 1 Ch 269
38. In re Imperial Chemical Industries [1936] 1 Ch 587 at pp. 614, 615
39. Leary v National Union of Vehicle Builders [1971] Ch 34; [1970] 2 All E.R. 713. Some passages in the judgment of Megarry J in this case have been criticised by the Privy Council in Calvin v Carr and others [1980] AC 574 (PC). Lord Wilberforce (at p.594B) expressed the rights of someone in Leary's position as having "..a fair deal of the kind that he bargained for" and that domestic disputes of this kind should be left to be settled by the agreed methods "without requiring the formalities of the judicial processes to be introduced."(at p.593A)
40. Re Graymouth Point Elizabeth Rly & Coal Co. Ltd [1904] 1 Ch 32
41. See, for example, The University of Hull, Statutes, Section 30, RESERVED MATTERS Clause 1

"1. Any student member or members of a statutory body of the University or a committee thereof shall be required to withdraw from a meeting when it is declared by the Chairman of the meeting that the meeting is about to discuss a reserved area of business and shall not return to the meeting until the discussion on the reserved area of business is concluded."

42. For the general rule vide Re Romford Canal Co [1883], 24 Ch D 85. For the quorum at the commencement of business only, vide In re Hartley Baird Ltd [1955] 1 Ch 143

43. Newhaven Local Board v Newhaven School Board [1885] 30 Ch D 350
44. Re Horbury Bridge Coal Iron & Waggon Co [1879] 11 Ch D 109 at 115 CA, per Jessel MR
45. Ernest v Lorna Gold Mines Ltd [1897] 1 Ch 1 at 6 CA, per Lindley LJ
46. Anon [1773] Lofft 315, per Lord Mansfield CJ
47. R v Ginever [1796] 6 Term Rep 797
48. Ibid. 798
49. Harben v Phillips [1883] 23 Ch D 14
50. Re Prain and Sons Ltd [1947] S C 325
51. R v Tralee Urban District Council [1913] 2 I R 59
52. Sebag Shaw and Smith op. cit., p. 52
53. R v Owens [1858] 28 LJQB 316
54. Cornwall v Woods [1846] 4 Notes of Cases, 555
55. Booth v Arnold [1895] 1 QB 571 at p. 579 per Lopes LJ cited in Sebag Shaw and Smith, op. cit. p. 60

    "It is a power essential to the good order and management of a corporation, and without it I do not see how the business of a corporation could be carried on."

56. Sebag Shaw and Smith op.cit. pp 54-5
57. See $$ 2.2 - 2.3 supra
58. See, for example, The University of Hull, Statutes, Section 32 REMOVAL OF CERTAIN OFFICERS AND MEMBERS AND VACATION OF OFFICE AND MEMBERSHIP, Clause 1:

    "The Chancellor, Pro-Chancellors, the Treasurer and any Member of the Court or of the Council (other than ex officio Members) may be removed for good cause by the Court."

59. Powell-Smith, op. cit., p.48
60. Foss v Harbottle [1843] 2 Hare 461
61. Browne v La Trinidad [1887] 37 Ch D 1 at 17 CA per Lindley LJ
62. Menier v Hopper's Telegraph Works [1874] 9 Ch App
63. $ 2.5.2, supra
64. Breay v Browne [1896] 41 Sol J 159
65. The other limits on freedom of speech at Common Law: sedition and blasphemy are not discussed. The position is discussed in Sebag Shaw & Smith op. cit. p.29. For further information on the statutory restrictions on free speech in relation to public order, race relations and official secrets, ibid pp.29-30
66. Powell-Smith, op. cit. pp.29-33
67. Lawless v Anglo-Egyptian Cotton Co [1869] LR 4 QB 262
68. Defamation Act 1952 s.57 and Schedule Part II s.8

69. In Re Horbury Bridge Coal, Iron and Waggon Co [1879] 11 Ch D 109 at p.118
70. Henderson v Bank of Australasia [1890] Ch D 330
71. Sebag Shaw and Smith, op. cit. p.73
72. Ibid.
73. Powell-Smith, op. cit. p.50
74. Sebag Shaw and Smith, op. cit. p.92
75. Ibid. pp.81-91
76. Ibid. p.81
77. Stoughton v Reynolds [1737] Fortescue's Rep 168
78. R v D'Oyley [1840] 12 A & E 139 at p.159, per Lord Denman CJ
79. Salisbury Gold Mining Co v Hathorn [1897] A C 268
80. See, for example, The University of Hull, Statutes, Section 15, Clause 1
81. Sebag Shaw and Smith, op. cit. p.101
82. Ibid. pp.101-2
83. Ibid. p.101
84. Re Jennings [1851] 11 Ch Rep 236
85. Sebag Shaw and Smith op. cit. p.102
86. Southampton Dock Co v Richards [1840] 1 Man & G 448
87. Re Fireproof Doors Ltd [1916] 2 Ch 142
88. Kerr v J Mottram Ltd [1940] Ch 657
89. Betts and Co v Macnaghten [1910] 1 Ch 430
90. [1906] 2 Ch 34. In that case a general meeting of the Company instructed, by simple resolution, the Board of Directors to sell the company's assets. The Board of Directors declined. It was held that as the management of the business and control of the company was vested in the Board of Directors, who were not removable save by a special (three- fourths majority) resolution, a simple resolution of the general meeting of shareholders could not overrule the Board of Directors. It would require a special resolution to change the powers of the Board.
91. See, for example, The University of Hull, Statutes Section 14, Clause 2
92. Ibid. Section 15, Clause 4
93. Re State of Wyoming Syndicate [1901] 2 Ch 431
94. Re British Sugar Refining Co [1857] 3 K & J 408
95. Re Haycraft Gold Reduction and Mining Co [1900] 2 Ch 230
96. Browne v La Trinidad [1887] 37 Ch D 1
97. Smith v Paringa Mines Ltd [1906] 2 Ch. 193
98. [1889] 22 QBD 470 at p.480
99. Young v Naval Military & Civil Service Co-operative Society of South Africa [1905] 1 KB 687
100. See $ 3.10 infra
101. For example, The Health & Safety at Work Act 1974, and see Chapter 7,$ 14 Licensing,infra

102. Flood's Case [1616] Hob 136; Bene't (or Corpus Christi) College, Cambridge v Bishop of London [1778] 2 Wm Bl 1182
103. Lydiatt v Foach [1700] 2 Vern 410
104. See, for example, The University of Hull Charter, Article 14 (T)
105. A-G v Caius College [1837] 2 Keen 150
106. Ibid. at p.169
107. See Glynn v Keele University, Chapter 3, $ 5.7 infra
108. [1967] 2 All ER 152
109. [1937] 2 KB 309 at 342
110. [1924] 1 KB 256
111. [1933] 2 KB 696
112. [1986] 1 All ER 272
113. R v Liverpool City Justices,ex.p. Topping [1983] 1 All ER 490 at 494 per Ackner LJ
114. [1971] 2 QB 662
115. R v Gravesend Corporation [1824] 4 Dow & Ry KB 117
116. Jones v Williams [1825] 3 B & C 762 at 771, per Holroyd J.
117. Committee of Vice-Chancellors and Principals,1985
118. S.203 (1)
119. Words and Phrases Legally Defined (London Butterworths 1969) pp.35-6
120. [1890] 25 QBD 391 at p.395
121. [1952] 2 All ER 747 CA at p.750
122. Lore v Mack [1905] 93 LT 352
123. Shackleton Aviation Ltd. v Maitland Drewery Aviation Ltd. [1964] 1 Lloyd's Rep 293
124. Parker v McKenna [1874] 10 Ch App 96 at 119
125. Lilley v Doubleday [1881] 7 QBD 510
126. Chown v Parrott [1863] 14 CBNS 74
127. Chadburn v Moore [1892] 61 LJ Ch 674
128. See, for example - The University of Hull, Statutes Section 36
129. Beal v South Devon Rly. Co [1864] 3 H & C 337 at 341, per Crompton J
130. Beauchamp v Powley [1831] 1 M & Rob 38
131. Moffatt v Bateman [1869] LR 3 PC 115
132. Donaldson v Haldane [1846] 7 Cl & Fin 762
133. Bullen v Swan Electric Engraving Co.[1907] 23 TLR 258 CA
134. Markesinis BS & Munday RJC, An Outline of the Law of Agency (London, Butterworth 1986) p.75
135. Osman v J.Ralph Moss Ltd. [1970] 1 Lloyd's Rep 313
136. Lucas v Fitzgerald [1903] 20 TLR 16
137. Cargill v Bower [1878] 10 ChD 502
138. Adamson v Jarvis [1827] 4 Bing 66
139. Lacey v Hill, Crowley's Claim [1874] LR 18 Eq 182
140. Duncan v Hill [1873] LR 8 Exch 242

141. Ellis v Pond [1898] 1 QB 426; Bowlby v Bell [1846] 3 CB 284
142. Herman v Jeachner [1885] 15 QBD 561 CA
143. Betts v Cribbins [1834] 2 Ad & El 57
144. Jacobs v Morris [1902] 1 Ch 816 CA
145. Cuthbert v Robarts, Lubbock & Co. [1909] 2 Ch 226
146. Reckitt v Barnett, Pembroke & Slater Ltd [1929] AC 176
147. Davy v Waller [1899] 8L LT 107
148. Wright v Glyn [1902] 1 KB 745, CA
149. On the basis of the rule in Freeman & Lockyer v Buckhurst Park Properties [1964] 2 QB 480 cited in Milman D Educational Conflict and the Law (London, Croom Helm 1986) p.104
150. Langlois v Laval University [1974] 47 DLR (3d) 674; Milman op.cit. p.120
151. For example, the Race Relations Act, 1976 s.32
152. Sadler v Leigh [1815] 4 Camp 195; Camillo Tank S.S. Co. Ltd. v Alexandria Engrr Works [1921] 38 TLR 134 HL
153. Tustin v Arnold & Sons [1915] 84 LJKB 221
154. Farquharson Bros & Co. v King & Co [1902] AC 325
155. Fridman, The Law of Agency (London Butterworths 1971) p.228
156. [1912] AC 716 CA
157. 53 & 54 Vict c.39
158. Cox v Midland Counties Ry. Co. [1849] 3 Ex 268
159. Mann v D'Arcy [1968] 1 WLR 893 cited in Scamell E H Lindley on the Law of Partnership (London,Sweet & Maxwell 1971) p.162
160. Schuster v McKellor [1857] 7 E & B 704
161. Glynn v Houston [1841] 2 Man & G 337
162. Morriss v C.W. Martins & Sons Ltd [1966] 1 QB 716
163. Norano v Moregrand [1915] 2 TLR 674
164. Stephens v Elwall [1815] 4 M & S 259
165. Baschet v London Illustrated Standard Co. [1900] 1 Ch 73
166. 25 & 26 Geo 5 c.30 s.6(1)(a)
167. ibid s.6(1)(c), cited in Fridman, op.cit. P.249
168. See $ 3.5, supra

CHAPTER 3

THE LAW GOVERNING STUDENTS

1. INTRODUCTION

1.1 The scope of the chapter

The student is the raison d'etre of the university and it is therefore of crucial importance that the relationship with the institution at all stages from application to graduation or other termination of his course be clearly understood. This chapter is divided into four substantive sections dealing with the prospective student, academic matters, discipline and fees. These will give the reader a general flavour of the subject, but it must be stressed at the outset that every institution has its own set of domestic legislation. In a chartered corporation there is the Charter itself, Statutes normally made with the approval of the Privy Council and therefore having some measure of consistency, and Ordinances and other regulations peculiar to the institution. No sensible legal analysis of an individual university's relationship to its students can be made without an in-depth study of that domestic legislation. As will be seen, cases in the courts have turned upon the precise wording of regulations drafted by university administrators and approved by the responsible authority.

1.2 The Visitor

In England, Wales and Northern Ireland (but not in Scotland) the domestic activities of chartered institutions are subject to the exclusive jurisdiction of the institution's Visitor. It will become clear to the reader that a number of important decisions in the courts affecting the status of students, academic progress and discipline were arguably in excess of the court's jurisdiction given the role of the Visitor, which is unaffected in this context by the provisions of the Education Reform Act 1988.

2. THE PROSPECTIVE STUDENT

2.1 Introduction

The legal relationship between an individual prospective student, or applicant, and a university is formed when a contract is entered into between legally competent parties (the university and the applicant) for the admission of the applicant either unconditionally or on satisfaction of certain conditions, whether to the University itself, or a Faculty or Department thereof. Prospective undergraduate students[1] use the procedure of the Universities' Central Council on Admissions (UCCA); postgraduate applications are made to and processed by individual institutions. There are also provisions at most universities for non-graduating and occasional students: the extent to which they enjoy the rights and owe the duties of students will depend upon the nature and terms of the contract with the institution.

2.2 The contractual relationship

The relationship between the university and the applicant who is not yet a member of the university can only be founded on contract which in English law is an agreement giving rise to obligations which are enforced or recognised by law. The university-applicant contract is formed when an offer of a place is accepted by the applicant.[2] Disputes arising under the contract fall within the jurisdiction of the ordinary courts.[3]

2.3 Applications through agencies

According to the UCCA Handbook,[4] the Council has a

> "duty...to enable the business of admission to undergraduate courses in all the constituent United Kingdom universities to be dealt with in an orderly manner and, equally important, in a way which allows each candidate freedom to make a responsible choice and each university freedom to select its own students."

UCCA holds itself out as the

> "agent of the universities and colleges whose courses are listed in this Handbook" but

> "accepts no liability for the outcome of decisions based on information about university courses contained herein..[it is] essential that candidates consult up to date university and college prospectuses and handbooks.."

The Handbook refers to "offers" by universities being "accepted" by applicants; the "conditions of acceptance"[5] include an undertaking to observe the Charter, Statutes, Ordinances etc.

UCCA is in effect an administrative device; the relationship between the applicant and UCCA, which is assumed to be contractual, in that there is an intention to create legal relations, is confined to the service which UCCA advertises: that is that the applicant will have his/her application forwarded to each of the universities listed on the UCCA application form. If the procedures are not followed according to the information supplied to the applicant by UCCA it is possible that an action might lie for breach of contract or negligence, but there are no recorded instances. According to legal advice tendered to the UCCA Council of Management in 1981, UCCA as an agent is not liable for the acts or omissions of its principals (the constituent universities) unless it expressly or implicity warrants that it has authority to make decisions on behalf of them. In practice, UCCA takes appropriate steps to avoid this impression by publishing disclaimers in its Handbook and by referring potential applicants to university and college publications.

Universities employ a variety of agencies to help in the recruitment of overseas students, normally on a fee commission basis. Such arrangements are the subject of a contract between the institution and agency concerned and in all cases it is the University, not the agency, which has the power to decide whether or not to admit a particular applicant.

2.4 Applications and the prospectus

Whether as an undergraduate applicant through UCCA or as a candidate making direct application for undergraduate or postgraduate study, the applicant makes an approach to individual universities on the basis of information contained in the university's prospectus and supplied to him/her directly or indirectly through, for example, the school. This document sets out the courses offered by the university and the conditions for admission and is often supplemented with detailed pamphlets or leaflets produced by departments or Faculties. The entry requirements of universities are summarised in the Compendium of University Entrance Requirements produced annually

> "by and for the Universities as the recognised source of information on entrance requirements to first degree courses".[6]

There are other official and unofficial guides to university entrance, including for Scotland that produced by the Scottish Universities' Council on Entrance. Prospectuses also contain information about such non-academic matters as accommodation and welfare facilities. The extent to which the contract between the university and the applicant may import the content of prospectuses and other documents will be considered later in this section[7]: no legal duty arises merely as a result of the potential applicant having received the university prospectus. In fact between publication of the prospectus and an offer of admission being made, it is quite possible for course details to change, so that an applicant may find that a course is offered other than that applied for.

2.5 Offers of admission

Applications to universities are received from UCCA (or directly from candidates not applying through UCCA) by the university administration and processed by academic selectors. It is an essential element of the UCCA procedure and good administrative practice that all applications are considered fairly on their merits. "Offers of admission" may be made on the basis of formal application alone, or on formal application supplemented by interview or examination. They may be either unconditional, in which case a contract of admission is made when the unconditional offer is accepted by the applicant, or conditional (e.g. on the acquisition of a specified number and grade of passes at Advanced Level of the General Certificate of Education or a specified class of degree), in which case the contract is made when the conditions are fulfilled and the offer then accepted by the applicant. The conditions of offer, not of acceptance (a term used both by UCCA and the Compendium of University Entrance Requirements to describe the formation of the contract of admission) include an undertaking on acceptance to abide by the Charter, etc. This term is implied from the UCCA Handbook or, where direct application is made, expressly from the application form.

2.6 Rejection of applications

At present nothing in English law obliges a university to give reasons for rejecting an application for admission. A university may decide to do so as a matter of policy and if so the reasons should be given in simple terms. The admissions procedure is founded in contract and thus it is arguable that the applicant cannot seek judicial review of the rejection. One 19th century[8] and three 20th century cases[9-11] have progressively established the reluctance of the courts to interfere in questions of admission to an essentially private organisation: to an Inn of Court,[8] to the Stock Exchange,[9] to a trainer's licence for horse racing from the Jockey Club[10] and to a manager's licence by the British Boxing Board of Control.[11] Each of the circumstances concerned the effective deprivation of a perceived "right" or "liberty" to work and admission to the status was essential to professional practice. The "right" of an unsuccesful candidate for admission probably lies somewhere between an application to join a club:

> "If a man applies to join a social club and is blackballed he has no cause of action"

per Lord Denning MR in Nagle v Fielden[10] at p.693, and an application for a licence to practice.

In R v The Benchers of Lincoln's Inn[8] both Abbott C.J. and Bayley J. (at p.1279) adverted to the concept of an inchoate right to be admitted a member of a college "in either of the universities". Bayley J.'s obiter dictum that

> "..[these societies]...make their own rules as to the admission of members, and even if they act capriciously upon the subject, this Court can give no remedy..."

was disapproved by both Lord Denning MR (at p.644) and Salmon LJ (at p.654) in Nagle v Fielden[10] and apparently also by Lord Atkinson (at p.631), Lord Parmoor (at p.636) and Lord Wrenbury (at p.642) in Weinberger v Inglis,[9] described as "astonishing" by Salmon LJ. However, his later statement that

> "...an individual has no inchoate right to be admitted as a member of a college and there is no obligation upon the college to admit him..."

has survived criticism. In a review of the "admission" cases by Megarry VC in McInnes v Onslow Fane and another[11] it was clearly established that no reasons for rejection of an applicant need be given, for to do otherwise would supply the applicant with material which would assist him/her in engaging the organisation in litigation. Megarry VC asked (at p.222):

> "Is a university when selecting candidates for admission acting unfairly when it gives no reasons to the unsuccessful?"

Indeed there is no requirement to comply with the rules of natural justice although in the polytechnic case CCETSW v Edwards[12] where the provision of a diploma was vital to the potential student's career, it was held that where an interview is given it must be conducted fairly. And Blain J.'s dictum at p.556 in R v University of Aston Senate ex.p. Roffey,[13] where he stresses the significance of possession of a degree to the job market, might possibly influence a court in the future. The acquisition of graduate status is no doubt of economic and social significance, but an individual university is not a monopoly supplier. It is argued therefore that the only "right" is to be dealt with fairly and for the application to be determined honestly, without bias and caprice. A rejection would not cast a slur upon the applicant.

Despite the anti-discriminatory provisions of most university Charters, applicants do not have the status necessary to bring an action before the Visitor. The scope of the anti-discrimination provisions of Articles 7 and 128 of the Treaty of Rome in respect of universities in the United Kingdom has yet to be clarified, but section 17 of the Race Relations Act 1976 and s.22 of the Sex Discrimination Act 1975 make it unlawful for the governing body of a university to refuse applications for admission on grounds of nationality or sex. There has recently been an investigation by the Commission for Racial Equality into the recruiting practices of one university institution where racial bias was shown to exist through use of an excessively mechanical selection process. Apart from these special provisions, there is no legal redress for the rejected applicant, other than perhaps an appeal to the European Court of Human Rights.

2.7 Withdrawal of accepted offers

When offers are accepted the University and the applicant are committed either conditionally or unconditionally (except where an "insurance" offer is held in accordance with UCCA procedures) and, although it is not unusual for the committed applicant to withdraw for a variety of reasons without penalty, the university which attempts to withdraw at this stage or to offer an alternative which is not acceptable to the applicant faces the possibility of action for breach of contract. So far as UCCA is concerned, once an applicant has been "admitted" i.e. has accepted a place unconditionally or has satisfied the conditions precedent he/she is outside UCCA's sphere.

Problems can arise when for strategic reasons, mainly due to changes in financing of the institution, a university seeks to make major changes in its academic programme, for example the elimination of a subject. This may occur either before or after admission. Two questions arise: (i) to what extent the institution is compelled by the operation of law to offer the course for which a potential student has applied and been unconditionally or conditionally accepted; and (ii) where an existing student has already embarked on a course with reasonable expectation of being able to complete a specified programme of study, what are the university's obligations?

In Casson v University of Aston in Birmingham[14] the university denied the existence of a contract to provide instruction in accordance with the terms of the original prospectus. Admission to a course in one subject having been offered and accepted, it was open to the applicants to sue for breach of contract when the University subsequently withdrew the offer, replacing it by an offer of a place to read a related subject, which the applicants accepted. Being unhappy with the new course, the students then sued in the county court, which ruled that it had no jurisdiction in disputes of this kind which were matters for the Visitor.

The Visitor held that the county court was wrong, as the dispute arose before the applicants achieved the status of corporator, despite a suggestion by Bridge that the jurisdiction of the Visitor might extend to persons who claim to be corporators, as rejected candidates for fellowships and scholarships had been held to be within that jurisdiction.[15] The contractual issue remained undecided: no further cases of this nature have received the attention of the courts. It seems to be clear from this case and Thomson v University of London[16] that, so far as students are concerned, the jurisdiction of the courts in matters of contract relating to chartered universities in England, Wales and Northern Ireland is limited to contracts which do not relate to the internal management of the institution.

2.8 Prospectuses and Calendars

The documents commonly issued by universities include:

(i) prospectuses for the information of and use by applicants <u>and</u>

(ii) calendars for the use of the university, its members and for general information, which commonly, but not always, set out the rules and regulations of the institution governing academic and non-academic matters.

Both types of document often carry disclaimer notices. These indicate that the institution reserves the right to modify or cancel, without notice, any information or statement contained in the document and accepts no liability for the consequences of that action. Another disclaimer may state that the contents of a particular document are not to be regarded as incorporated in the documents which record the formal relationship between a student and the University. On the other hand, the appearance in a university prospectus of an insurance disclaimer is clearly intended to be so incorporated. (See e.g. University of East Anglia undergraduate prospectus, 1990-1, p.5; cf. Heriot-Watt University Guide to Postgraduate Study and Research 1988, p.iii).[17] The position varies from university to university, prospectus to prospectus and each case must be considered on its own facts.[18]

2.9 Summary of the terms of the contract of admission

(a) On the part of the University:

(i) that the applicant will be admitted on payment of fees and otherwise complying with the relevant rules of the University;

(ii) that the applicant will be admitted on the basis of the offer of admission i.e. for the course or programme of study specified;

(iii) that the University will provide proper instruction and facilities to enable that course to be followed, subject to any proviso in the University's rules which may allow variation in the availability of certain subjects or courses from year to year.

(b) On the part of the applicant:

(i) that he/she will abide by the University's rules;

(ii) that he/she will pay or cause to be paid all relevant fees at the appropriate time.

2.10 Matriculation

A new contractual relationship is formed, sometimes called matriculation or enrolment, when the applicant completes the university's registration procedures and becomes a student.[19] This stage generally requires the production of proof that the applicant has satisfied any conditions attaching to the offer of admission, the payment of any fees and charges due on registration and the formal subscription by the applicant to the rules of the institution (although, as noted above,[20] the contract of admission through UCCA contains an implied term which presumably remains in force). When this contract has been entered into, the applicant becomes a registered student, normally a corporator in a chartered institution with all the associated rights, privileges and obligations attaching to that status. It is at this point that the individual concerned acquires two distinct but related relationships with the institution, contractual and status-derived.[21]

3. THE STATUS OF STUDENTS

3.1 Students - Contract and Status

There has been much academic debate about the legal relationship between individual students and universities largely in the context of disciplinary proceeedings.[22] It seems to be agreed that in chartered institutions where students enjoy the privileges of corporator, their status as members gives them rights independent of any contractual rights against the institution. The position in institutions established by statute is less clear cut.

According to one leading authority,[23] students have contracts of membership: it is implied that in return for their fees they will be treated in accordance with the university's rules. As most UK/EC students do not pay fees personally, it is assumed that payment of fees by the local education authority or other third party on behalf of the student does not invalidate the general rule of English law that consideration must move from the promisee.[24]

In R v University of Aston Senate ex.p. Roffey and Another[13] it was held that the University's regulations only took effect by way of contract. The students' status was

> "akin to membership of a social body, a club with perhaps something more than mere social status attached to it."[25]

Of course the parties to the contract are unequal. Bridge[15] suggests that the contract of membership of a student is closer to a contrat d'adhesion[26] ("take it or leave it") than to a contract based on consensus ad idem (where the parties negotiate an agreement). But as long ago as 1692 it was clear that whatever the respective strengths of the parties, the student was bound to accept the situation:

> "I am far from being a judge as shall lay any intolerable yoke upon anyone's neck: but I must say, if the head and members of a college will receive a charity with a yoke tied to it by the founder, they must be contented to enjoy it in the manner they received it from him. If they will have one, they must submit to the other."[27]

Christie's[28] view that the student-university contract is in law a contract of licence for consideration (i.e. that the student, subject to the terms of the university's regulations, is given permission to enter the university's premises and to use its facilities) seems unnecessarily narrow and appropriate only to a discussion of the legality of "direct action".

3.2 Registration

There is of course a wide variety of practice among institutions as to the precise nature of registration and for what the student has registered. This is dictated by the academic structure and ethos of the institution. In some the student registers to take subject A for the entire 3-4 years of his undergraduate course, normally in stages each of which must be completed successfully in order to proceed to the next. These may or may not involve the additional study of subjects B, C etc as an essential or optional element in the course.

In others the student has a wide, not usually completely unfettered, choice or "menu" from which to choose his own degree programme. That "menu", and the optional elements in courses of the first type, may change from year to year as the subject develops or as there is turnover in teaching staff. The prospect of such changes is as indicated earlier normally made clear to students at an early stage, both in the prospectus before admission and in the Calendar or similar document after admission.[29] There is no apparent legal obligation to consult those who might be affected by such changes before putting them into effect.

It is arguable that on registration at the beginning of each session a new contract is entered into, the consideration being the fee paid directly or indirectly by the student.[30] There is no apparent legal obligation to renew the contract from year to year unless this can be implied as a condition of the initial contract of admission which has been incorporated in the subsequent contract of membership.

3.3 Miscellaneous

There are a number of miscellaneous points related to status. Although there are no reported English or Scots cases, there is Canadian authority to the effect that a university is not liable for the actions of a student.[31] The university may be liable in some circumstances for securing according to normal legal principles the safety of its students[32] and the quiet enjoyment of residential accommodation.[33] Head leasing of property to accommodate students has been held to be a "business tenancy" within the meaning of the Landlord and Tenant Act 1954 and thus protected[34] but a dwelling let to a college on condition that it should be occupied by one student per room is not a protected tenancy within the meaning of the Rent Act 1974.[35] A student has been held to be an occupier of premises for the purposes of the Misuse of Drugs Act 1971.[36]

4. ACADEMIC MATTERS

4.1 Progress and failure

Once matriculated, a student's progress is governed by the regulations pertaining to the course or degree programme which is being followed. These are often complex, and universities differ as to the extent to which they expect students to find their way round the system unaided or offer advice or direction. There are no reported cases of students taking legal action against a university or a member of its staff for "bad" advice or professional negligence but the more complex the system, the more necessary it becomes for administrators and others to maintain a checking system to try to avoid a student going too far astray. Even if strict legal liability could be denied, a situation in which a student could demonstrate a reasonable case might lead to a university recognising some right to compensation.

Clearly the area in which legal action is most likely is that of academic failure. University regulations will spell out what a student is required to do should he fall ill or suffer some other extraneous mishap at a crucial stage in his assessment or examination and generally speaking there should be no problem if these regulations are adhered to. But where there is failure which is not for disciplinary reasons such as plagiarism or cheating[37] the student will almost certainly have a right of appeal on specified grounds.

In recent years there have been a number of appeals by failed postgraduates based on alleged bias by examiners, failure by the university to provide adequate supervision or procedural irregularity and these have received the attention of Visitors. Appeals procedures at postgraduate research degree level have also been the subject of a Code of Practice issued by the CVCP[38] which puts forward "clear general principles" while emphasising that it is for individual institutions to "formulate their own regulations in the light of these and of their particular circumstances."

It may fairly be argued that in an academic community there can be no "right of appeal" against an examination result. The findings of examiners, where examinations are properly conducted, are final. There may, however, be grounds for review of the examiners' findings if the board of examiners has not been properly constituted or where the examination has not been properly conducted.[39] In this case the examiners' finding is a nullity, any review committee will consider it to be quashed and a new, properly constituted board of examiners will have to be established to undertake the proper conduct of the examination. Neither the Visitor nor the courts will interfere with the exercise of an expert judgment.[40]

4.2 Roffey and its aftermath

In R v Aston University Senate ex.p. Roffey and Another[13] the court was invited to intervene in a case of academic failure. It did not do so, on procedural grounds: in the words of Blain J at p.556

> "This court should not be used for the creation of a real life counterpart to Checkhov's perpetual student..".

The case is curious since it dismisses the jurisdiction of the Visitor in one sentence:

> "The charter reserves a power of appointment of a Visitor, but no such appointment has yet been made" (per Donaldson J at p.543).

It has been criticised on this ground in Patel v University of Bradford Senate[41] which reconfirmed the sole jurisdiction of the Visitor in academic matters as explained in Thorne v University of London[42] and R v Dunsheath ex.p. Meredith.[43] The fact that a Visitor had not been appointed was irrelevant, since the visitatorial jurisdiction then vested in the Crown and

> "at common law the court has no jurisdiction to deal with the internal affairs or government of the University [of London], because these have been confided by law to the exclusive jurisdiction of the Visitor" (per Diplock LJ in Thorne v University of London[42] at p.240).

Nevertheless, Roffey's case does provide some insights into the working of the judicial mind in such cases, and would certainly be of persuasive authority in cases involving non-chartered corporations or those in Scotland where there is no equivalent of the visitatorial jurisdiction. Patel lays down the limits of the visitatorial power: Megarry, V.C., citing much earlier authority,[44] confirmed that the following matters listed in the applicant's submissions were exclusively within that power:

(i) withholding examination results:

(ii) appointments to university committees:

(iii) dismissal of a student from the university:

(iv) readmission to the university.

At p.849 he set out the following principle:

> "..that one of the functions of the Visitor is to decide all questions of disputed membership. Each corporation has its own peculiar system of laws, and these will provide how membership of the corporation is obtained as well as how it is lost. The interpretation of the statutes of the corporation has long been established as being part of the Visitor's functions..."

4.3 The wording of regulations

In Roffey's case,[13] which is then merely indicative of judicial attitudes, the view taken by Donaldson, J. was that the students concerned should have been given the opportunity to be heard, orally or in writing, before examiners reached a final decision on the termination of their course, particularly since the examiners took into consideration matters other than the mere examination results. In this view he was supported by Blain J. Lord Parker CJ had "considerable doubts" and reached the conclusion that there had been a breach of natural justice only on the particular facts of the case: the precise wording of special regulations and the fact that the examiners, in exercising discretion given to them by the regulations, were prepared to take into consideration the personal difficulties and problems of each student.

The special regulation which gave rise to the complaint stated:

> "Students who fail in more than one major subject, or who fail in a referred examination, may at the discretion of the examiners, re-sit the whole examination or may be required to withdraw from the course. Students who are successful in such re-sit examinations shall normally be eligible to proceed to the pass degree only."

The fact that the examiners could require withdrawal in the circumstances described persuaded the court that natural justice required an opportunity to be given to the students to put forward a statement in explanation or mitigation.

All such regulations clearly have to be interpreted as they stand and obviously should be expressed in clear and unambiguous terms. If a right of appeal against withdrawal is allowed, the reasoning in Roffey is that a student should be given the right to make a submission in his own defence.[45] Some institutions allow the appeal in person, others in writing, others at the student's choice.

5. DISCIPLINE

5.1 Introduction

The subject of student discipline has occupied more pages of text, in books, articles and law reports, than any other relating to the law applicable to universities. Much of this relates directly to the rapid development of administrative law from the mid-1960's onwards. Here the application of principles of justice and fairness in student disciplinary matters was seen to be of importance, just as in other areas of interaction between the citizen and public or quasi-public bodies. Once "natural justice" principles were seen to be satisfied, there was little more for administrative law to contribute and there is little of real substance in the legal literature, other than the continuing saga of the jurisdiction of the Visitor, since the early 1970's. In fact the relevance of administrative law in this area, and hence much of the material from that period, has been questioned on the basis that the relationship of the student to the university is contractual. While this section is concerned only with the legal aspects of student discipline, it is important to note that these interact strongly with operational issues.

5.2 Individual and collective issues

Disciplinary issues have to be considered in the individual and the collective context. There has always been, and will continue to be, the student who falls foul of university regulations, whether by cheating in examinations, parking a car incorrectly or failing to return a library book. But the period between 1968 and 1974 saw student mass action causing disruption and wholesale breach of regulations on a large scale for the first time; universities' disciplinary procedures drawn up rather like the rules of a gentlemen's club were unable to cope, and the general law relating to the occupation of property and the disruption of an institution's normal work was found to be procedurally cumbersome and in some cases (for example within the Scottish jurisdiction) wholly ineffective.

Lord Devlin echoed the feeling of the time when he reported[46]:

> "It is really only the threat of Direct Action that keeps university discipline going. It has to be remembered that most societies when they find themselves in peril from groups organised to disrupt, have had to resort to sterner procedures."

Revisions were carried out, some more hastily than others, and the legacy of that period is a set of usually lengthy Codes of Discipline which attempt to preserve a balance between the rights of individuals and those of the community, incorporating the rules of natural justice and rights of appeal. The status of universities as in some way similar to schools in loco parentis (if such a concept ever existed) was finally extinguished with the lowering of the age of majority from 21 to 18 by the Family Law Reform Act 1969;[47] students became fully-fledged enfranchised adults and demanded to be treated as such by university authorities. A number of notable incidents of violence and disruption occurred; there has been sporadic re-emergence of mass action since that time, with the focus in the mid-80's on the effects of public expenditure cuts on higher education and their consequences for students, rather than on the call for revolution and worker control. Less radically, the persistent demand for representation on university bodies is now largely conceded.

5.3 The legal basis of disciplinary power

As described earlier in this chapter,[48] the student in a chartered institution enjoys a dual relationship with the institution, derived from the contract of matriculation and from his status as a corporator (i.e. a member). (In non-chartered institutions, the status of member may be achieved by statute or in the Articles of Association, with the same effect.) In registering for admission and achieving a change of status from applicant to student an individual is normally expressly or by necessary implication required to subscribe to the rules of the institution. A form of undertaking to observe the Charter, Statutes, Ordinances, rules and regulations of the University from time to time is commonly executed, and often separate undertakings are given in respect of admission to university accommodation, use of the library and computing facilities and safety requirements of laboratories. Such undertakings form part of the contracts, whether of matriculation, of lease or licence or of membership of the library, etc. They are unaffected by the status of the student as corporator; this becomes of importance when considering the means of enforcing the terms of the contract and the penalties for breach of those terms.

5.4 Codes of discipline and procedural fairness

The essential elements of a Code of Discipline, which may take the form of an Ordinance or regulation, are that it should be expressed in clear language, enable the speedy determination of cases arising under it, be procedurally fair - which means that the rules of natural justice should be followed - and ensure that any findings of guilt and penalties imposed should be subject to appeal.

The reasons for having a fair disciplinary procedure are obvious without recourse to administrative law. As Lewis[49] says, the interests of a student lie in membership of the university and in obtaining an academic qualification. In the 1980's, it is an understatement to repeat Blain J.'s observation[25] that students are

> "potential graduates and potential holders of degrees which could prove advantageous in professional or commercial life".

The message of the 1969 Report on Student Relations[50] thus assumes even greater importance:

> "Disciplinary matters have in one sense assumed increasing importance as the value of a degree as a starting point has grown, and a decision to suspend or even in some cases to send down a student is regarded in a much more serious light than it would be a generation ago".

There is, as Lewis[49] points out, nothing inherently different about student discipline for non-academic offences than discipline in any other organisation or in society in general. It may be argued that theft, assault, traffic offences are not related to the academic nature of a university whereas cheating, plagiarism and general conduct in a hall of residence are.

One problem facing universities in applying the rules of natural justice is that of university members potentially being, at different stages in the hierarchy of committees and tribunals, prosecutor, judge and jury. There is no independent prosecution service and in some cases it is very difficult for university administrations to find persons qualified under the university's rules who are both willing and able to act as "judge and jury" and are not disqualified by some previous connection with the accused. This is obviously particularly difficult in cases of mass disruption of a Senate meeting, for example. (See chapter 2, $3.3, supra.)

5.5 Academic discipline

The law in general is much less suited to intervention in cases which are wholly related to the academic nature of a university. To quote the Annan Report[51]:

> "There are actions, such as cheating in examinations...which destroy...the relationship between teachers and students on which good teaching depends. They are not crimes but they cannot be tolerated because they destroy the raison d'etre of a university."

There is likely to be a considerable element of subjective judgment, particularly where charges such as plagiarism are invoked. Nevertheless, by analogy with cases of academic failure, such as Roffey[13] where counsel for the University of Aston conceded the applicability of the rules of natural justice, the possibility of judicial control cannot be ruled out. In a chartered institution, these matters will lie within the jurisdiction of the Visitor.

5.6 The role of the Visitor in disciplinary proceedings

As stated in the introduction and mentioned already in connection with the Casson[14] and Roffey[13] cases, the visitatorial jurisdiction in chartered institutions has recently experienced something of a revival, culminating in a landmark decision of the House of Lords in Thomas v University of Bradford and its subsequent attenuation by the Education Reform Act 1988.[52] The exclusive jurisdiction of the Visitor in disputes involving students is unaffected by the Act. Bridge[53] supported it in terms both of case law[54] and in terms of its "suitability, cheapness, expedition and informality" comparing the Visitor to an administrative tribunal. He saw it as satisfying the need for university disciplinary proceedings to avoid excessive formalism quoting the Hart Report,[55] de Smith[56] and Holland[57] in support. This advocacy of the Visitor over the courts has been seen by some as an effective denial of the right of recourse to law,[58] which is not denied to someone in a normal contractual dispute. However, there seems now to be no dispute about the exclusivity of the Visitor's unique jurisdiction.[59]

5.7 The attitude of the courts

Despite the clear jurisdiction of the Visitor in chartered institutions, some cases of alleged procedural irregularity have reached the courts, based on arguably misguided applications for judicial review. The attitude generally has been that while the principles of natural justice should be observed, unduly strict standards will not be applied. In particular, in a number of cases of which the best known is Glynn v Keele University[60] the courts have, while accepting jurisdiction and that procedural unfairness has occurred, declined to act, an attitude which has been criticised.[61] Assuming that the courts had jurisdiction, the reason for it in non-academic offences is not readily apparent. In fact, the recourse to law by students as by other members of society has been seen as the only way to secure "rights" against a system that was both paternalistic and tied by archaic procedure. A quotation from the Hart Report[55] exemplifies the former characteristic:

> "To turn the hearing of every disciplinary charge into a formal public trial would be, at the best, time wasting and, at the worst, might damage young mens' (sic) careers, and might sharpen and harden what has been a generally mild and even friendly attitude to those faced with disciplinary charges."

In fact it may be argued that the actions of a chartered institution do not fall within the scope of administrative law at all and that there can be no judicial review of actions based on contract. In Roffey's case,[13] detailed in s.4.2 supra, counsel for the university conceded that the rules of natural justice were applicable, bringing the case within the ambit of administrative law. In the event certiorari (a discretionary remedy which would have had the effect of removing the decision into the High Court and quashing it) was refused by the Divisional Court in exercise of its discretion because of delays by the plaintiffs in bringing the case before the courts. Surprisingly, the jurisdiction of the Visitor was not alluded to. As the University of Aston was founded by Royal Charter, then it is argued that only contractual remedies were appropriate. A Royal Charter confers the powers of a natural person only. Certiorari would not issue to enforce a contract of employment with a university: in Vidodaya University Council v Silva[62] the Privy Council refused the remedy to a university lecturer who had been dismissed from his post without a hearing, since the law will not restore employment specifically in a relationship which the Board judged to be purely contractual. The same must be true of the contract of membership - in support of which proposition may be cited the decision in Fekete v The Royal Institution for the Advancement of Learning.[63] In accepting that natural justice was applicable to another disciplinary case, the Privy Council in Ceylon University v Fernando[64] refused a declaration (a remedy suited to both statutory and contractual cases in which the court states the rights or legal position of the parties). It may be argued, however, that this case arose before the rise of administrative law later in the decade and as de Smith[56] points out, there are doubts about the procedure employed in the original hearing of the complaint.

In Glynn's case[60] the student concerned had appeared naked on campus and the Vice-Chancellor had, in the exercise of his disciplinary authority, excluded him from residence. The court held that the Vice-Chancellor's powers were so fundamental that they were quasi-judicial in nature rather than merely matters of internal discipline. The Vice-Chancellor failed in his duty by not giving Glynn an opportunity of being heard; an injunction was refused in discretion (the judge commenting that discretion should be very sparingly exercised against a plaintiff in these circumstances) since Glynn did not dispute the facts, there could have been no more than a plea in mitigation and the penalty inflicted was intrinsically a perfectly proper one for a serious offence. However, the undergraduate had failed to make the necessary arrangements to enable him to attend the hearing of his appeal. He had therefore not been deprived of his right to appeal and, as he had not applied for a re-hearing the decision of the appeal committee was still effective.

An undergraduate has a right to a fair hearing. In Bolchover's case[65] Lord Parker CJ said:

"At the end of the day we remain unconvinced that the conduct of the hearing before the Proctors offended against such rules of natural justice as were applicable in the circumstances. To put it more simply we are not satisfied that the hearing was unfair."

But even if it was it would not necessarily help the complainant:

"But it is only right to add that even if the court felt there might be something to be enquired into, nevertheless as a matter of discretion they would, having regard to the appeal, refuse you leave."

One response to the Glynn case was:

"Once more the university authorities have failed to observe the principles of natural justice and once again, the student has been sent away without remedy because the court's discretion has been exercised against him."[66]

Yet, as the University of Keele was a chartered institution, it was not possible to identify the legal source of the Vice-Chancellor's "obligation" to act in accordance with the rules of natural justice. After all, contractual rights are outside the scope of judicial review altogether.

In Roffey's[13] case the court ignored both the possibility of an appeal to the Visitor and the possibility that prerogative remedies (e.g. certiorari) might not be appropriate. Matters might have taken a different course if Aston had not conceded the relevance of administrative law at the start of the proceedings. In R v Post Office ex.p. Byrne, a case concerned with the dismissal of a Post Office employee, Bridge J[67] commented on this fact and that the majority judgments of Donaldson J and Blain J in Roffey had been the subject of criticism by Wade,[68]

"not least by reason of the fact that the relationship between the [students] and the university was one of contract."

In Herring v Templeman, Russell LJ[69] supported this view:

"..no-one appears to have examined what the precise contractual relationship between the [students] and the university was...".

The argument advanced by counsel in Byrne's case appeared to turn on whether the Senate of the University of Aston in Birmingham could be held to be a public body, to which certiorari might lie. In view of the criticisms of the Roffey case the court in Byrne felt that the case could not be of assistance.

However, a recent New Zealand case[70] suggests that a relationship founded upon contract and indeed in that case on a rather indirect chain of contracts would admit of judicial review, provided that the issue went to fundamentals and was not a matter solely of internal management or administration. If there is a right there has to be a remedy.

5.8 Statutory institutions

Universities founded by statute may be in much the same position. While in Re Schabas and Caput of University of Toronto,[71] a Canadian case, the court held that judicial review would lie to a body exercising disciplinary powers under statute, recent English cases point to the opposite conclusion. In these cases, concerned with the disciplinary powers over staff of statutory bodies, the courts have confirmed that an applicant for judicial review has to show that a public law right which he enjoyed has been infringed. Where a public body is controlled by statute, its employees (and by extension to a university founded by statute, its students) might have rights in both public and private law. A distinction must be made between an infringement of statutory provisions giving rise to public law rights and those arising from breach of a contract of employment. It is difficult to see what public law right a student could invoke.

Sir John Donaldson M.R. in R v East Berkshire Health Authority ex.p. Walsh[72] said at p.164 that employment by a public body does not per se inject any element of public law. Purchas L.J. at p.179 said that there has to be something more than a mere private contractual right upon which the court's supervisory functions can be focussed. In R v BBC ex.p. Lavelle,[73] Woolf J. held that certiorari and the other prerogative remedies were only available to impugn a decision of a tribunal which was performing a public duty; this did not extend to an employer's disciplinary tribunal. Similarly judicial review by way of injunction or declaration was confined to the review of activities of a public nature as opposed to those of a purely private or domestic character.[74]

It could be argued that the rights of students arising from their contract of membership are purely "private or domestic" in character and thus there is no entitlement to judicial review.

5.9 Discipline - Conclusion

It is clear that students are entitled to expect a fair disciplinary procedure and few disputes about procedural matters should now reach the courts. If as seems to be accepted the university-student relationship is founded on contract, then a student alleging breach of that contract must pursue a claim through the ordinary courts, seeking the appropriate contractual remedy. As an alternative, in a chartered institution with a Visitor, a student might seek review of a decision as a corporator.

6. FINANCIAL ASPECTS

6.1 Fees

Matriculation or enrolment normally requires the payment of tuition fees which for the great majority of home students are paid automatically by the LEA or equivalent. For most overseas students the position is different and universities have devised schemes of payment by instalments, provisional registration pending payment, deposit taking on acceptance of offer of admission, etc. to ensure that the considerably larger fees paid by this group are forthcoming.

In all cases the fee regulations, whether Ordinance or otherwise, will form part of the contract of matriculation and should therefore spell out clearly what will happen to a person (one cannot call him/her a student at this stage) who does not pay the fees by the time required. For obvious reasons universities are anxious to do everything in their power to avoid expulsion of a non-registered student; although other reasons can be adduced, one natural consequence is that the substantial overseas fee is lost with little prospect at that stage of filling the vacant place.

The exercise of discretion by the Vice-Chancellor, Registrar or Finance Officer as spelt out in the regulations has to be reasonably consistent if potential legal problems are to be avoided. Claims of discrimination on grounds of race or nationality are possible where a more liberal approach is taken with certain groups of potential students. While the non-matriculated student in a chartered corporation would appear to have no redress before the Visitor,[75] a claim of discrimination could be brought before the ordinary courts.

Where some time has been granted for late payment of fees, the non-matriculated student in a chartered corporation is in a curious position. By definition this person is not a member of the University unless the domestic legislation of the institution confers that status. It is possible to envisage an overseas student passing through a one year Masters' course or a nine month

Diploma course without ever having attained the status of matriculated student at all. Most universities provide that such a person may not have a degree or diploma formally conferred but that may be insufficient threat to produce payment at a time to suit the institution's cashflow.

Here there is an important interaction between law and practice. Powers do exist, in a number of universities, for the responsible administrative authority to refuse to allow a person who has failed to complete registration to sit examinations on a course, to impound the examination papers written and not release them to the examiners until the fees are paid, or for the examiners to be instructed not to disclose a result to a person who has not completed registration.

6.2 Determination of eligibility to pay home/EC fees

In accordance with The Education (Fees and Awards) Regulations,[76] higher (overseas) levels of fee are payable by students who do not have a "relevant connection" with the United Kingdom, the Channel Islands or the Isle of Man. "Relevant connection" requires firstly that the student has been ordinarily resident throughout the three-year period preceding 1st September, 1st January or 1st April closest to the beginning of the first term of the course and secondly that the student has not been resident therein, during any part of the three year period, wholly or mainly for the purpose of receiving full-time education.

There are also certain categories of excepted students, including nationals and children of nationals of the European Community, certain persons granted asylum or refugee status, students on fully-reciprocal exchanges, and recently-arrived immigrants who are also liable to pay only the lower (home) fee.

These categories are fixed by the general law and the question of racial discrimination should not now arise.[77] There is of course some discretion as regards the level of the overseas fee. University Calendars and similar publications differ very greatly in the extent of the detail which they give about overseas fees.

6.3 European Law

Recent judgments of the European Court of Justice,[78] ruling on the interpretation of Article 7 of Council Regulation (EEC) No. 1612/68 on freedom of movement of workers within the European Community, have further extended the categories of student who are eligible for mandatory awards under the annual Education (Mandatory Awards) Regulations.

7. SCOTLAND AND NORTHERN IRELAND

7.1 The visitatorial jurisdiction

The Visitatorial jurisdiction is unknown in Scotland; the ordinary civil courts have jurisdiction in all matters which would be subject to that jurisdiction in England and Wales. In Northern Ireland, the University of Ulster has a Visitor, while The Queen's University of Belfast has a Board of Visitors with equivalent jurisdiction.

7.2 Registration for the Community Charge

At time of writing only full time students attending universities in Scotland are liable to pay the reduced community charge or poll tax instituted by the Abolition of Domestic Rates Etc (Scotland) Act 1987.[79] A number of issues of interpretation of the relevant Regulations[80] remain unresolved, including elements of the definition of a "full-time student" and the extent and form of information which universities may be required to provide to the Community Charge Registration Officers or to the Regional Council Finance Directors who collect the tax.

7.3 Other matters

Although there is some difference in terminology and in some matters of detail, the basic principles set out here in relation to the formation of contracts of admission and matriculation apply in both Scotland and Northern Ireland. Questions of procedure are beyond the scope of this work and should be addressed to a legal practitioner.

Footnotes - Chapter 3

1. There is a separate procedure for entry to the University of Buckingham and additional procedures for entry to the Universities of Oxford and Cambridge.
2. It appears that in other Commonwealth jurisdictions, in cases turning on the existence of a contractual relationship with a student, it has been suggested that the applicant makes an offer on the basis of an invitation to treat set out in the prospectus and that the contract is concluded by acceptance by the institution.See e.g. Pecover v Bowker 8DLR(2d) 20 [1957]; Re University of Sydney ex. p. Forster [1963] 63 SR(NSW) 723; Sutcliffe v Governors of Acadia University 95 DLR(3d) 95 [1978]. This view has not been advocated in the United Kingdom and the discussion that follows is based on the premise that the university makes the offer for acceptance by the applicant. The necessary consideration for the existence of the contract is the promise by the applicant, in making his application, to pay the appropriate fee. The fact that an applicant may be a minor (under the age of 18) does not make the contract invalid since education may be regarded as a necessary (e.g. Roberts v Gray [1913] 1 KB 520).
3. See discussion of Casson v University of Aston in Birmingham, $.2.7, infra.
4. Published annually by UCCA, Cheltenham.
5. In view of the contractual position a better expression would be "conditions of offer".
6. Published annually by the Association of Commonwealth Universities for the Committee of Vice-Chancellors and Principals of the Universities of the United Kingdom (CVCP).
7. See $.2.8 infra.
8. R v The Benchers of Lincoln's Inn [1825] 4 B & C 859; ER v.107,1277
9. Weinberger v Inglis [1919] AC 606
10. Nagle v Fielden [1966] 2 QB 633
11. McInnes v Onslow Fane and another [1978] 3 All ER 211
12. CCETSW v Edwards "Times" 5 May 1978 (Ch.D.) cited in Milman D Educational Conflict and the Law London,Croom Helm 1986 p.105
13. [1969] 2 QB 538
14. [1983] 1 All ER 88.
15. 86 LQR [1970] 531. See St John's College Cambridge v Todington [1757] 1 Burr 158 and R v Hertford College Oxford [1878] 3 QBD 693 - in the latter case it was made clear that the Visitor would not interfere if the institution's discretion was exercised "honestly". Smith, PM, in "Visitation of the Universities: A Ghost from the Past" (Part III, New Law Journal 1986, p.568) holds that the cases establish the right of an applicant for admission to membership to appeal to the Visitor, his locus standi being based on his claim that the foundation has acted with respect to his application contrary to its internal rules. For a clear exposition of

the extent of the Visitatorial jurisdiction see the judgment of Hoffman J. in Hines v Birkbeck College and Another, loc.cit. n.47 infra.
16. [1864] 33 LJ Ch.
17. (i) University of East Anglia, Norwich 1989. This is intended to avoid the possibility of a finding as in D'Mello v Loughborough College of Technology (see n.29 infra) that the prospectus is a contractual document forming part of the contract between the parties. (ii) Heriot-Watt University, 1988.
18. See e.g. the Scottish case Cadells v Balfour [1890] 17 R 1138.
19. "Matriculation" is derived from "matricula" or roll of members of the institution. "Student" is not defined in general terms but may be for specific purposes, e.g. for social security or grant arrangements: see e.g. Social Security (Miscellaneous Provisions) Act 1977 s.14(1).
20. $.2.5 supra.
21. The relationship of a student to a non-chartered institution must be founded on contract alone; the student's contractual rights will be as set out in the statute or articles of association governing the constitution of the institution.
22. See e.g. Wade 85 LQR [1969] 468; Garner 90 LQR [1974] 6; and generally, Christie, D. "The Legal Basis of Student Tenure at Colleges and Universities" in "Academic Freedom and the Law" NUS/NCCL 1970, Ch.3; Lewis, CB "The Legal Nature of a University and the Student-University Relationship"15 Ottawa Law Review 11 [1983].
23. Wade n.22 supra and see the clear statement by Lord Fraser of Tullybelton in Orphanos v Queen Mary College [1985] 2 All E.R. 233 at 236.
24. See e.g. Cheshire, Fifoot and Furmston "Law of Contract" 11th edn, p.74 (Butterworths, 1986).
25. R v Aston Senate ex p. Roffey , n.13 supra, per Blain J at p.556.
26. i.e. "a prendre ou a laisser" - see Kessler, F. "Contracts of Adhesion: Some Thoughts about Freedom of Contract" [1943] 43 Columbia Law Review 629
27. per Holt CJ in Philips v Bury [1692] 2 TR 346 at 358.
28. loc.cit. n.22 supra.
29. See e.g. D'Mello v Loughborough College of Technology ("The Times", 17 June 1970); Sammy v Birkbeck College ("The Times", 3 November 1964).
30. The University of Stirling's semester system, with registration twice a year but only one fee payment, is anomalous.
31. See Re Newfoundland Telephone Co. and The Memorial University of Newfoundland [1984] 3 DLR (4d) 732
32. See Tuttle v University of Edinburgh [1984] SLT(OH) 172 (Forestry student fell from tree: compensation £112,400)

33. Smith v Nottinghamshire County Council "Times" 13 November 1981; a polytechnic case in which it was held that a student might restrain building works in the pre-examination revision period
34. 2 & 3 Eliz 2 c.56; Graveside Properties v Westminster Medical School [1983] 267 Estates Gazette 593
35. 1974 c.51; St Catherine's College v Dorling [1979] 76 Law Society Gazette 732
36. 1971 c.38 s.8 and R v Tao [1977] QB 141
37. See $.5 infra. At time of writing the case of Foecke v University of Bristol concerning allegations of cheating in an examination was before the University's Visitor; the University declined to make available any information about the case.
38. Appeals Procedures at Postgraduate Research Degree Level; CVCP 1986.
39. see Hollands v Canterbury CC [1966] unreported where a college was held liable for an error in adding up examination marks.
40. R v Her Majesty The Queen in Council ex.p. Vijayatunga [1989] 3 WLR 13
41. [1978] 3 All E.R. 841; if a Visitor has not been appointed, then the Visitatorial power is exercised by the Lord Chancellor or such other person as he may advise Her Majesty to nominate: Attorney-General v Dedham School [1857] 23 Beav. 350, 53 ER 138 and see the judgment of Megarry V-C in Patel v University of Bradford Senate, loc.cit. n.53 infra. and the comments of Kelly LJ in Re Wislang's Application [1984] CLY 2462
42. [1966] 2 QB 237
43. [1951] 1 KB 127
44. Dr Widdington's Case [1661] 1 Lev.23, T.Raym.31, 83 E.R. 278; [1663] T.Raym. 68, 83 E.R. 38; Parkinson's Case [1689] Carth.92, 90 E.R. 658; Philips v Bury [1694] Holt K.B. 715; Ex.p. Buller [1855] 3 W.R. 447;25 LTOS 102. Other early authority is discussed in Smith, P.M. "Visitation of the Universities: A Ghost from the Past" Parts I-IV in New Law Journal 1986 pp.484, 518, 567 and 665.
45. See for example Ordinance 19 University of Stirling, sections B7.1 and B7.2 viz:
"A student whose academic progress or record of attendance is unsatisfactory may be required by the Supervisory Board for Part One to withdraw from the University. A student who has been required to withdraw...has the right within a period of twelve months from the date of his withdrawal from the University, to make a submission to the Academic Council, or to a committee of its members appointed for the purpose, to have his case reconsidered with a view to his re-admission" and University of Bradford "Regulations governing the procedure to be followed in the Event of an Appeal by a Student Against an Aspect of his or her Academic Assessment" (Regulation 5) 1&2:

"Appeals by undergraduate students will be heard by the Student Progress Committee"

"Undergraduate students who, by reason of academic failure, are required to withdraw before completing their course, or to transfer to an Ordinary course without possibility for transfer back to Honours, or to delay their progress to the next period of their course, will be reviewed by the Student Progress Committee. The Registrar and Secretary will write to all students in the above categories, informing them of the review, their right to submit an appeal to the Committee in writing or in person, and the procedures for so doing."

46. Report of the Sit-In in February 1972 and its Consequences (Devlin Report), Vol. C111, Cambridge University Reporter, Special, No.12. 14 February 1972.P.54. See also Brown, L.N.: "Student Protest in England" [1969] 17 American Journal of Comparative Law 395; Sheridan, L.A.: "Sacking Professors and Sending Down Students: Legal Control" in Law, Justice and Equity 1967, p.43.
47. 1969 c.46
48. $.3 supra.
49. Lewis, C.B.: "Procedural Fairness and University Students: England and Canada Compared" 9 Dalhousie Law Journal 313 [1985]; Lewis, C.B.: "The Legal Nature of a University and the Student-University Relationship" 15 Ottawa Law Review 11 [1983].
50. Report of Vice-Chancellors and Principals and the National Union of Students, reproduced in Vol.11 of Report on Student Relations (Select Committee on Education and Science), 1969, p.83 para 13.
51. Annan Report, University of Essex 1974.
52. For a comprehensive account of the role of the Visitor prior to the House of Lords decision in Thomas v University of Bradford [1987] 1 All ER 834 and the Education Reform Act 1988 see Smith, P.M.: "Visitation of the Universities: A Ghost from the Past" loc.cit. n.44 supra. and chapter 2 of this work.
53. Bridge, J.W.:"Keeping Peace in the Universities: The Role of the Visitor" 86 LQR [1970] 531. In this view Bridge is supported by Sir Robert Megarry, V.C. in Patel v University of Bradford Senate [1978] 1 WLR 1488 at 1499 (a case approved by the Court of Appeal [1979] 2 All ER 582), apparently by Lloyd L.J. in Thomas v University of Bradford [1986] 1 All ER 217 at 233 and certainly by the judgments of the House of Lords in Thomas v University of Bradford [1987] 1 All ER 834.

54. Thomson v University of London [1864] 33 LJCh; Thorne v University of London [1966] 2 QB 237; Patel v University of Bradford Senate (loc.cit n.53 supra). In Thomson's case, the applicant was not a corporator (Smith, P.M. loc.cit n.45 supra p.568) but note that Hoffman J. in Hines v Birkbeck College and Another [1985] 3 All ER 156 at 163 makes it clear that the Visitatorial jurisdiction extends beyond corporators "to all persons who can be described as members of the institution or as being on the foundation."
55. Committee on Relations with Junior Members (The Hart Report) University Gazette, Supplement No VII, Oxford University Press [1969] at para.65.
56. de Smith, S.A. 23 MLR [1960] 428 at 431, 432.
57. Holland, D.C. "The Student and the Law" [1969] 22 Current Legal Problems 74
58. e.g. Lewis, C.B. loc.cit n.49 supra; cf.Bridge, J.W. loc.cit. n.53 supra.
59. From Wright, J. in R v Bishop of Chester [1747] 1 Wm.Bl. 22 at 26: "Visitors have an absolute power; the only absolute one I know of in England" through to Patel v University of Bradford Senate, loc.cit. n.53 supra, Re Wislang's Application [1984] CLY 2462 (a Northern Ireland case) and Thomas v University of Bradford, loc.cit. n.52 supra.
60. [1971] 1 WLR 487. Other relevant cases are Ward v Bradford Corporation [1971] 70 LGR 27; R v Oxford University ex. p Bolchover "Times" 7 October 1970; University of Essex v Ratcliffe "Times" 28 November 1969.
61. See Lewis, C.B. loc.cit n.49 supra and implicitly by Wade, H.R. 87 LQR [1971] 320.
62. [1965] 1 WLR 77
63. [1969] BR 1
64. [1960] 1 WLR 223
65. R v Oxford University ex.p. Bolchover loc.cit n.60,supra.
66. in Wade, H.R. (loc.cit n.61 supra); see also Hepple, B.A.:"Natural Justice for Rusticated Students" [1969] CLJ 169.
67. [1975] ICR 221 at 225.
68. 85 LQR [1969] 468
69. [1973] 3 All ER 569 at 585
70. Finnigan v New Zealand Rugby Football Union [1985] 2 NZLR 159
71. [1974] 52 DLR (3d) 495.
72. [1985] QB 154 (CA)
73. [1983] 1 All ER 241; see also the Northern Ireland case R(Snaith) v Ulster Polytechnic [1981] NI 28 where certiorari was granted to quash a decision of the Governors of the Polytechnic to make S. redundant and Re Ruiperez and Board of Governors of Lakehead University 130 DLR 427 where Galligan J (at p.428) justifies the intervention of the courts in an institution governed by a public statute
74. Under RSC Ord 53 and s.31 Supreme Court Act 1981 1981 c.54

75. See discussion of Casson v University of Aston in Birmingham n.14 supra.
76. See Education(Fees and Awards) Act 1983 (1983 c.40); Education (Fees and Awards) Regulations 1983 (S.I. 1983/973, as amended by S.I. 1984/201, 1985/1219, 1987/1364, 1988/1391. See also the annual Education (Mandatory Awards) Regulations e.g. SI 1988/1360 and the corresponding Scottish and Northern Irish regulations.
77. The case of Orphanos v Queen Mary College [1985] 2 All E.R. 233 deals with the situation in 1982. The unanimous view of the House of Lords was that the appellant had been the subject of unlawful racial discrimination but he was awarded no recompense. See also n.23 supra.
78. Le Centre Public d'Aide Social de Courcelle v Marie-Christine Lebon (Case No. 316/85; judgment given on 18 June 1987);Sylvie Lair v Universitat Hannover (Case No. 39/86; judgment given on 21 June 1988); Steven Brown v Secretary of State for Scotland (Case No. 197/86; judgment given on 21 June 1988);Education (Fees and Awards)(Amendment) Regulations 1988 (S.I. 1988/1391).
79. c.47

CHAPTER 4

UNIVERSITY STAFF AND EMPLOYMENT LAW

1. INTRODUCTION

1.1 The law of employment

The law of employment, which is an amalgam of common law principles and quite wide-ranging statutory overlays, does not leave Universities as substantially distinct from other employers. The most distinctive feature of university employment is academic staff tenure which is covered below and which in any case seems to be a characteristic of waning significance. The institution of Visitor also has a residual role in relation to staff employment.

1.2 Employer and employee

A less obvious, but perhaps more significant, feature of university arrangements is that as self-governing democratic institutions universities tend not to have as clear-cut a distinction in practice as other major employers between management and employees. The role of staff, in particular academic staff, in university government can blur the usual dichotomy and in union relations can sometimes lead, for example, to members of the AUT (Association of University Teachers) on either side negotiating with each other about their own interests. This potential difficulty is one good reason for maintaining a strong lay involvement in university Councils.

1.3 Staff Categories

Over the past 25 years there has evolved a fairly clear-cut categorisation of university employees, accepted at both local and national level, comprising in broad terms:

(1) academic staff (ie primarily teaching staff funded by the University)

(2) academic-related staff (ie graduate/professional staff in administration, library, computing service, etc and externally-funded research staff)

(3) technical staff

(4) clerical staff

(5) manual staff.

In the determination of salaries and conditions of service, categories (1) and (2) are grouped together, with the AUT (or for clinical academic staff, the British Medical Association/British Dental Association) normally recognised locally as the relevant trade union and with national negotiations being carried out under the umbrella of the CVCP, through the University Authorities Panel for non-clinical academic and academic-related staff and through the Clinical Academic Staff Committee for clinical staff. Similarly categories (3) to (5) are grouped together nationally through the UCNS which was established following a report by a joint working party of university and TUC members in 1970 which urged mechanisms for promoting good industrial relations and for providing satisfactory disputes procedures. UCNS from the outset has embraced subsidiary joint committees for each of the major groups of technical, clerical and manual staff.

Formal membership by a university binds it to implementation of all nationally negotiated changes in salary scales and conditions of service. In the case of UAP negotiations, the outcome is expressed as recommendations to universities (which however they can hardly reject) and the range of negotiations has been much more restricted, covering only salaries and certain major associated aspects such as probation but leaving most other conditions of service to be determined locally by individual institutions.

2. EMPLOYMENT LEGISLATION

2.1 Introduction

The statutory basis for modern employment law was commenced seriously in the 1960s, hiccupped through the notorious and now repealed Industrial Relations Act 1971[1] and is now provided in particular by the Employment Protection (Consolidation) Act 1978[2] and the Employment Acts 1980 to 1988.[3] The more political aspect of trade union and labour relations, which has been of less relevance to universities as employers, is governed by the Trade Union and Labour Relations Act 1974[4] (amended in 1976[5]) and the Trade Union Act 1984.[6] In addition there have been several statutes aimed at the eradication of discrimination in, inter alia, employment, most notably the Equal Pay Act 1970,[7] the Sex Discrimination Act 1975[8] and the Race Relations Act 1976.[9]

2.2 Institutions

2.2.1 ACAS

The Advisory Conciliation and Arbitration Service (ACAS) was set up on a statutory basis by the Employment Protection Act 1975[10] as a key element in the improvement of employment protection and collective bargaining. Its powers and duties, the key characteristic of which is persuasion rather than compulsion, include

(a) offering conciliation and other assistance to help settle any trades dispute

(b) providing conciliation officers to promote the settlement of complaints made to industrial tribunals

(c) offering and publishing advice on industrial relations and employment policies

(d) issuing Codes of Practice containing practical guidance for promoting good industrial relations, including Codes on specified matters.

ACAS has become a body of considerable influence in employment law. Many Universities specifically identify ACAS as an arbitration mechanism in local agreements with recognised unions, for example in relation to failure to agree on job gradings, while the role of ACAS as conciliator is firmly recognised in applications to industrial tribunals. Large numbers of unfair dismissal cases are settled by ACAS without a Tribunal hearing and such settlement bars further litigation.

Examples of Codes of Practice issued by ACAS are Disciplinary Practice and Procedures in Employment, Disclosure of Information to Trades Unions for Collective Bargaining Purposes, Time Off for Trade Union Duties and Activities. Such codes do not have the power of law but are required to be taken into account by tribunals and the CAC and in this way they have substantial influence and their recommendations on good practice are not likely to be disregarded.

2.2.2 The Central Arbitration Committee

A further independent body is the Central Arbitration Committee (CAC)[11] which not only provides arbitration at the parties' request but also has certain specific areas of operation in which its awards are binding (eg in relation to the implementation of equal pay in collective agreements). ACAS may refer a matter in dispute to the CAC.

2.2.3 Industrial Tribunals

Industrial tribunals, which date from 1964[12] and are now well established as the prime mechanism for dealing with employment issues, deal with questions, claims and complaints referred to them under various Employment Acts. A tribunal consists of a legally qualified chairman and two lay members drawn from employers, trades unions and others (usually one employer representative and one union representative). Hearings are semi-formal, normally held in public and reportable by the press. In many cases a complaint is referred first to an ACAS conciliation officer to try to promote a settlement before the tribunal hearing; where agreement between the employer and employee is reached in this way, the employee is precluded from pursuing the claim further. Tribunal decisions, normally given in summary form but on request with full detailed reasons, may be subject to appeal on a point of law only, to the Employment Appeal Tribunal[13] in the first instance and thereafter to the Court of Appeal and ultimately, if leave to do so is granted, to the House of Lords. The Employment Appeal Tribunal is also tripartite in composition, with a judge as chairman. In this way over the past 20 years a considerable body of "case law" of Industrial Tribunals has been built up and many solicitors have significant practice experience of tribunal work - despite the basic intention that tribunals should be relatively accessible to the claimant, informal, cheap and untechnical in their procedure.

The existence of industrial tribunals does not entirely preclude an employee from raising an action against the employer in the ordinary civil courts, but where the basis of the complaint is a statutory right rather than an item in the individual contract of employment, the tribunal route is normal. However the deciding line may be narrow - for example between an action for wrongful dismissal in breach of an individual contract of employment and a claim for unfair dismissal based on the provisions of employment protection legislation.

2.2.4 The Equal Opportunities Commission and the Commission for Racial Equality

The Equal Opportunities Commission (EOC) and the Commission for Racial Equality (CRE) are 2 major institutions created as a result of anti-discrimination legislation in the last 20 years. The EOC, which dates from 1976,[14] has the duty to work towards the elimination of sex discrimination, in particular but not solely in employment and related spheres. The EOC has published a Code of Practice on steps which are reasonably practicable for employers to take to promote equality of opportunity and eliminate discrimination in employment. The EOC has power itself to initiate action before a court (eg in relation to discriminatory advertisements) and it may assist a tribunal complainant with the preparation and conduct of a tribunal complainant's case. The CRE[15] has a very similar role in relation to racial discrimination.

As a result of the European Communities Act 1972,[16] UK courts are bound by decisions of the European Court of Justice which tends to act as a final court of appeal on certain aspects of employment law, most notably "social harmonisation" aspects such as equal pay and discrimination. A member state of the European Community is expected to introduce legislation to bring its law into consistency with decisions of the European Court of Justice or with related EEC Directives - a recent example was the ruling that the retirement age for women must be the same as for men, even if - permissibly under national law - there were different ages for commencing benefit from the State Pension.

2.2.5 The Visitor

An institution unique to universities, but not applicable to all universities, is the office of Visitor who is usually the Sovereign though the office will normally be exercised through the Lord President of the Council or possibly another appointed office holder.

The office of Visitor exists in most English and Welsh (but not Scottish) Universities for historical, legal reasons explained in detail in Chapter 1. The Visitor not only has complete powers of inspection of the University but also an appeal function on issues between members of the university. The Visitor's jurisdiction is such ("final and conclusive"[17]) that certain domestic issues, including some employment issues, cannot properly be raised in an ordinary court of law. In the most recent judgement to this effect, Thomas v University of Bradford[18] in which a lecturer had her contract of employment, and thereby her membership of the University, terminated and complained that in dismissing her the University had failed to follow the procedures set out in its Statutes, the ruling of the House of Lords was that the Visitor had exclusive jurisdiction and powers of reinstatement and compensation. It was also observed, however, that Parliament has by the Employment Protection (Consolidation) Act 1978 invaded the visitatorial jurisdiction and implicitly provided that industrial tribunals are to have concurrent jurisdiction with university Visitors in matters relating to unfair dismissal of university staff. If, in the course of tribunal proceedings, any question arises concerning the interpretation or application of the internal laws of the university it must be resolved by the tribunal hearing the case. Now s.206 of the Education Reform Act 1988[19] has had the effect of removing the exclusive jurisdiction of the Visitor in relation to wrongful dismissal so that university employees may henceforth bring actions in the courts in the same way as employees of other institutions - another step in the process of removing the special characteristics and privileges of the university in the sight of the law.

2.3 Natural Justice

The principles and rules of natural justice[20] are important in employment law and can lead to especial difficulties in an institution such as a university. The broad requirements of natural justice are that the "accused"

(i) has the right to be heard by an unbiased body;

(ii) has the right to have notice of the charges being faced; and

(iii) has the right to be heard in answer to these charges.

In a university context the term "accused" may on occasion be extended to include, for example, an aggrieved member of staff, an unsuccessful candidate for appointment or promotion, a member of staff appealing against disciplinary action or indeed a student appealing against an academic decision - though clearly not all the requirements stated above will apply in all circumstances.

In a university, requirement (i) offers particular difficulties because of the relatively closed nature of the institution and the difficulties tribunal members may have in excluding prior knowledge and bringing an open mind to an issue. The hierarchical nature of university government may also present problems in that certain key individuals may have and be entitled to have a significant involvement at several levels and since appeals necessarily move from level to level the question will arise whether an individual may properly be involved at more than one level.

The interpretation of the rules of natural justice is necessarily subjective to a considerable extent, though from cases in the area of exclusion and discipline of members of trades unions it seems clear that an organisation's own procedural rules, however plainly set out, are not in themselves sufficient to outweigh what may be described as the needs of society or public policy for natural justice. In practice, unless a university is willing to run the risk of having a decision, eg on dismissal, subsequently declared wrongful by a court or tribunal, it is advisable to go to what some might consider to be extreme lengths to ensure that the member of staff has a fair hearing before an unbiased tribunal, with full knowledge of the charges and ample opportunity to present his or her case including the unfettered submission and presentation of documents.

Another university situation where the natural inclination of a body like a university is perhaps at variance with the approach of lay members from industry and commerce is where a member of staff falls foul of the criminal law or more often the disciplinary rules of a professional body. While the initially dominant rule may be that the member of staff should be considered innocent until proved guilty - a process which with appeals may take a long time - the university may feel obliged to take some immediate action in order to preserve its reputation as a teaching body. In such a situation the rules of natural justice may be particularly hard to apply to everyone's satisfaction.

2.4 Discrimination

A major development in statutory law in relatively recent years has been legislation relating to various types of discrimination, in particular on grounds of:

(a) sex - Sex Discrimination Acts 1975[8] and 1986[21]

(b) race - Race Relations Act 1976[9] (s.3 "colour, race, nationality or ethnic or national origins)

(c) disablement - Disabled Persons (Employment) Acts 1944[22] and 1958.[23]

Discrimination on grounds of religion is not covered by UK legislation, though it is in the United States of America and indeed (along with political discrimination) in Northern Ireland; many Universities will also have provisions in their Charters and Statutes which outlaw discrimination on grounds of religious or political beliefs. Other forms of social discrimination, such as age discrimination, are not included in UK statutory provisions but there is a continuing trend in international (for example ILO and EC) codes towards wider coverage of discrimination in the cause of equal treatment in employment and in other spheres. EC law also provides for the free movement of all EC nationals and their equal rights to take up employment in other EC states (other than in the public service).

2.4.1 Sex Discrimination

The Sex Discrimination Act 1975[8] makes sex discrimination unlawful in full-time or part-time employment, as well as in training and various other fields. Most of the cases relate to discrimination against women - and for convenience that is how this description is written - but the Act for the most part applies equally to discrimination in the treatment of men. In addition to direct discrimination (ie on grounds of sex treating a woman less favourably than a man is or would be treated), the Act covers indirect discrimination where a person applies to a woman a requirement or condition which is applied or would apply equally to a man but

(i) which is such that the proportion of women who can comply with it is considerably smaller than the proportion of men who can comply with it, and

(ii) which cannot be shown to be justifiable irrespective of the sex of the person to whom it is applied, and

(iii) which is to her detriment because she cannot comply with it.

Unless being of a particular sex is a genuine occupational qualification (GOQ) for a job, it is unlawful for an employer to discriminate against a woman in advertising a post, in determining who should be offered employment, in the terms of employment offered, in affording access for promotion, transfer or training, or in dismissing her or subjecting her to any other detriment. An employer may, of course, lawfully discriminate against a woman on other grounds but may have to be prepared to satisfy a tribunal that the discrimination was not on grounds of sex.

Direct discrimination is a relatively simple concept with genuine occupational qualification being the main exception or defence to a claim. Some obvious examples of GOQ are in casting for dramatic performances or in residential or possibly other jobs in single sex establishments, cf Hugh-Jones v St John's College, Cambridge,[24] where the EAT held that refusal to consider a woman for the award of a research fellowship, which was prima facie unlawful under the Sex Discrimination Act 1975, was nevertheless rendered lawful by the earlier statutes of the College as a charitable body. Moreover the defence was not recognised in Greig v Community Industry and Ahern,[25] where a woman applicant for a post of painter and decorator who was excluded by the personnel officer because she would have been the only woman in the team and problems had arisen in similar circumstances in the past, was judged to have suffered discrimination, since sex was not a genuine occupational qualification.

Indirect discrimination is a more complex concept and there is a wide range of interesting cases which can be used to demonstrate the relevance to the practice of personnel management in Universities.

In Clarke v Eley (IMI) Kynoch Limited,[26] dismissals of part-time workers in redundancy, though agreed with the union as a specific breach of the normal "last in, first out" principle of seniority, were held to be sex discrimination because the part-time workforce included a much higher proportion of women than the total workforce. A university case with similar outcome was Dick v University of Dundee,[27] where the University was held by a tribunal to have indirectly discriminated on grounds of sex by reviewing part-time lecturers on fixed-term appointments for redundancy in advance of reviewing all relevant staff, full-time and part-time. In Huppert v University Grants Committee and University of Cambridge,[28] the UGC was held to have discriminated indirectly against a 39 year old female candidate for a "New Blood" lectureship in setting and adhering to an upper age limit of 35 for the appointment. Again a major part of the case hinged on the relevant comparator pool and the fact that a much smaller proportion of women than of men were able to satisfy the age limit of 35 because of the slowdown of their careers as a result of family and maternal duties.

In Home Office v Holmes,[29] the issue was the right of a member of staff to return to work after maternity leave to a part-time post instead of the full-time post she had previously occupied. Though stressing that the case rested very much on its own facts, the tribunal and the EAT both held that there had been unlawful indirect discrimination in that the requirement to work full-time was detrimental to women on whom the raising of children cast a greater burden than on men; the Home Office's counter-arguments that she had the right to return to work only on the same contractual terms as before, ie full-time, and that it was not departmental policy to allow part-time staff in her grade were not accepted.

Sexual harassment is not explicitly covered by the Sex Discrimination Acts, but in Strathclyde Regional Council v Porcelli,[30] the EAT and the Court of Appeal, reversing the original tribunal's decision, held that the sexual harassment (suggestive remarks and conduct by two male school laboratory technicians against a female colleague with the intention and result that she applied for a transfer to another school), while not in itself amounting to sex discrimination under the Act, in fact constituted a detriment within her contract of employment.

Tribunal hearings on discrimination have also thrown up a series of cases on discovery of documents (ie production to the tribunal or court). In Science Research Council v Nasse,[31] unsuccessful applicants for promotion sought the discovery and inspection of confidential documents about others considered by management for the same posts, one alleging sex discrimination, the other race discrimination. This case went eventually to the House of Lords, with the Court of Appeal setting aside orders for discovery, with the comment from Lord Denning that confidential documents should only rarely be subjected to such an order, but with the House of Lords taking a narrower view to the effect that the test should be whether the discovery was needed in order fairly to dispose of the proceedings and that accordingly the tribunal itself should look at the documents and decide whether confidential reports should be disclosed or perhaps partially disclosed.

In cases of indirect discrimination the employer has normally the task of showing justifiability but this of course is after the case has been presented by the claimant who may have difficulties in collecting, for example, sophisticated statistical evidence - though the EOC often assists claimants, particularly in what may prove to be test cases. Regulations under the Sex Discrimination Act[32] enable a complainant to serve a form on the employer asking certain standard and useful questions, the replies to be admissible evidence and a refusal or failure to reply being liable to be regarded adversely by the tribunal.

The structure for enforcement of discrimination legislation, encompassing both individual complaints and actions raised by the EOC (or the CRE in the case of racial discrimination), comprises industrial tribunals with appeals to the EAT and occasionally beyond to the Court of Appeal and House of Lords. The EOC, in addition to helping individuals in their claims and in raising actions itself (for example against discriminatory advertisements), has power to issue non-discrimination notices and to issue codes of practice. The main remedies available to tribunals are:

(a) a declaration of rights;

(b) compensation (to the same monetary limits as for unfair dismissal - revised from time to time);

(c) a recommendation to the employer to remove the discrimination, with unreasonable failure to do so allowing the tribunal to order compensation.

Where the complaint is of indirect discrimination, no compensation can be awarded if the employer proves he did not apply the requirement or condition with intention to discriminate.

The Sex Discrimination Act 1986,[21] which was intended to repair several gaps in the UK statutory provision, in particular in relation to European Court of Justice rulings, is a relatively minor piece of legislation. The provision of most relevance to universities is probably that employers will no longer be able to set out different compulsory retirement ages for men and women nor set discriminatory age limits for promotion, transfer and training (cf Huppert v UGC and University of Cambridge[28] supra). It may therefore be indirectly discriminatory to have an earlier retirement age for part-time staff. It will still be lawful, however, to discriminate in the provision of "benefits, facilities or services" - for example in occupational pension scheme benefits.

The Equal Pay Act 1970,[7] which inserted into contracts an implied right to equal pay for like or equivalent work, is not in general a problem to universities, but one case of some interest is Pointon v University of Sussex,[33] which determined that the "age-wage norm" for university lecturers, because it was not a contractual provision, but informal, was not covered by the Act.

2.4.2. Racial Discrimination

The provisions of the Race Relations Act 1976[9] are enforced by mechanisms parallel to those for sex discrimination, with tribunals as the first forum and similar further stages up to the House of Lords for appeals and with the Commission for Racial Equality having a very similar supportive and pro-active role to the EOC. Direct and indirect discrimination are again differentiated, and the case law dwells on very similar issues to those described in the previous section on sex discrimination.

S.1 of the Act defines direct and indirect discrimination in virtually identical terms, mutatis mutandis, to those used in s.1 of the Sex Discrimination Act 1975. "Racial grounds" is defined to include colour, race, nationality or ethnic or national origins. A person may fall into more than one racial group (for example, a black Scot) and for the purpose of the Act nationality includes citizenship (for example, it would be discrimination to accord less favourable treatment to a British national who is a French citizen). Religious discrimination is not expressly included, though it could give rise to indirect discrimination under the Act and the House of Lords has held that Sikhs may be counted as a separate racial group because of their long-shared history and separate cultural tradition including religion.

2.4.3 Disablement

An early development in the employment protection of exposed groups, very much arising from the Second World War, was the Disabled Persons (Employment) Acts 1944[22] and 1958.[23] Employers with 20 or more employees are normally required to give priority in recruitment to registered disabled persons up to a quota of 3% of their workforce unless a permit is obtained from the Manpower Services Commission excusing them from the quota. The statutory sanction is against the employer (criminal prosecution) and there is no specific civil remedy to the individual, though a claim may be made before a tribunal that dismissal was unfair with some hope of favourable treatment.

There is also a MSC Code of Practice (1984) which advises and encourages management on the employment of disabled persons, but even so the intended positive discrimination in favour of the disabled is not strongly applied, since the quota arrangements are very widely relaxed. In universities academic and academic-related staff are often excluded from quota calculations and even in non-academic staff categories permits are readily granted.

In disablement - as indeed in racial discrimination - there is a significant data collection and record-keeping problem for employers, since many staff who could register with the MSC as disabled fail or do not choose to do so.

2.4.4 Rehabilitation of Offenders Act 1974

This Act[34] made it improper to exclude a person from an office, profession, occupation or employment on the grounds of a previous criminal conviction deemed to be "spent". Failure to disclose a spent conviction is not a proper reason for dismissing or failing to employ a person. Not only is the employee or prospective employee thus protected for failing to disclose, but the protection extends also to, for example, a referee or previous employer.

Where and when a conviction has become spent and the person therefore rehabilitated for the purposes of the Act depends on the conviction and on the sentence and cannot be easily summarised. Certain professions and employments are excluded by Order from the provisions regarding spent convictions, including - of potential relevance to universities - doctors, dentists, barristers and solicitors.

3. CONTRACTS OF EMPLOYMENT

3.1 Introduction

The conditions of service of a member of University staff are an amalgam derived from

(a) the individual contract of employment

(b) the provisions of University statutes and subsidiary legislation

(c) collective agreements, national and local, for the relevant staff category and

(d) statutory rights under the Employment Acts and other employment legislation.

3.2 The contract of employment

Of these (a) is fundamental and in the absence of a contract of employment the other items have restricted force. Where a university engages a person on a "contract for services" basis, ie as an independent contractor rather than as an employee, many of the benefits and obligations of employment lapse. The employer for example no longer has the same common law liability for the actions of his "servant", while the independent contractor cannot benefit from such statutory rights as those granted to employees in relation to unfair dismissal or redundancy payments - though other statutory rights, for example under the Sex Discrimination Acts, apply equally to the employee and the independent contractor.

The law of master and servant has a long history with various tests being applied to distinguish between an employee and an independent contractor. Great emphasis was placed in earlier days on the right of the master to control the servant not only in what he did but also in how he should do it, and this test has survived many challenges (for example, in relation to an employer's vicarious liability for the negligence of a surgeon, despite the fact that the employer was in no position to dictate how a surgeon should use his skill) but alternative or supplementary tests have emerged, for example whether someone is employed to carry out work as an integral part of a business (contract of service) rather than in an accessory fashion (contract for services). The important point is that the courts will determine the matter by reference to the facts of the case and will not necessarily follow what is stated in the engagement documentation. In Market Investigations v Minister of Social

Security,[35] a market research interviewer engaged intermittently, determining her own hours of work, without sick pay or holiday benefits and not prevented from working for other companies, was nevertheless decided to be in insurable employment as an employee under a series of contracts of service, because she did not display such characteristics of being in business on her own account as providing tools or risking capital. In general, despite a social trend towards more part-time, temporary and casual workers, the courts have seemed reluctant to allow a growth in the numbers and categories of legally "self-employed", regardless of whether it is the employer or the employee who sees advantage in and tries to achieve that status.

The vast majority of university staff therefore must now be regarded as having contracts of service and the status of employee in relation to statutory rights, with only a few exceptions where the university has genuinely contracted for the provision of services - an example would be where the university contracts with a public relations firm which may nominate a specific individual to serve as the university's public relations officer.

3.3 Collective agreements and University Statutes

In theory an individual contract of employment, as a mutually agreed and signed document, may validly include any provision which is not inconsistent with public law. In practice in the university context the contract has to be considered not only with the statutory rights of an employee but also with the contents of relevant nationally and locally negotiated collective agreements and with the provisions of the employing university's statutes. A single comprehensive statement of all conditions of service is not practicable but there is a statutory requirement[36] on the employer as a minimum to give the employee, within 13 weeks of commencement of employment, a written statement of certain particulars of the contract covering

(i) the parties:

(ii) commencement date:

(iii) termination date (if fixed-term):

(iv) starting date of continuous service (ie if the new contract follows immediately a previous period of employment):

(v) remuneration:

(vi) hours, holidays, holiday pay, sickness pay:

(vii) pension arrangements:

(viii) length of notice required of both parties:

(ix) title of the job:

(x) disciplinary rules and disciplinary superior:

(xi) grievance procedure:

(xii) whether a contracting out certificate is in force for the State pension scheme.

It is permitted however not to include full details in the initial statement of particulars but to refer the employee to some reasonably accessible document, and that mechanism can also be used for subsequent changes in conditions, resulting for example from collective agreements for the relevant category of staff.

In university employment collective agreements with detailed provision are more common for the various categories of non-teaching staff than for academic and academic-related staff; maternity leave is a good example in the former category where there is a detailed nationally negotiated scheme which universities in membership of UCNS are obliged to observe. In the academic sector, however, subject to meeting the minimum statutory requirements, universities are free to determine their local provisions for maternity leave at their discretion. There may also be locally negotiated collective agreements with similar force, and there is a further category, now of declining importance, of "custom and practice" where detailed provisions are not set out in an agreed document between employer and employees or their union but are derived from established and understood precedents. Courts will enforce a custom if it is "reasonable, certain and notorious", the last term meaning well-known either in the industry or profession or in the geographical area.

3.4 Implied terms

"Custom and practice" is an example of an implied term in a contract. When necessary to determine a point, courts and tribunals will take into account other implied terms - even on occasion an implied term which both employer and employee declare they would not have agreed to had they turned their attention to it as part of the contract - but in the absence of a contrary express term a court or tribunal can assume such an implied term. There is a strong reluctance to declare a contract unworkable, since the basic presumption is that the parties intended it to be workable and therefore implied terms are readily introduced. The question of whether a particular implied term forms part of a contract is a question of law and therefore a decision by a tribunal to imply a term may be challenged before the EAT as an error of law.

Alteration in the terms of employment of existing employees may be achieved by means of collective agreements, if provision is so made in the original contract of employment or if the negotiating arrangements with unions are such that the terms of collective agreements are binding on both employer and current as well as prospective employees. This is essentially the situation with agreements reached through UCNS, though there is usually a "no detriment" provision expressly or by implication included. The alternative approach is to make an offer of varied terms to each individual current member of staff with the probable consequence of a mixed response - for example, many universities in the past sought to reduce the retirement age of academic staff in this way with the result that commonly there is an administratively confusing and perhaps inequitable mixture of age 65, 67 and 70 retirement ages. The extreme measure to achieve changes in conditions of service would be to terminate each contract of employment by giving due notice and to offer simultaneously re-engagement on new terms - this procedure has many legal pitfalls, perhaps especially for universities, and would not normally be recommended. It is not adequate to give the contractual period of notice of a compulsory change in conditions without explicitly terminating the employment, since this would be regarded, in the absence of agreement, as unilateral alteration of contract terms (cf Burden, Coutts and Others v Hertfordshire County Council).[37]

3.5 Termination of Employment

Even without the complication of academic staff tenure - which is separately treated later in the Chapter - the most interesting and significant aspects of employment law for universities relate to security and termination of employment.

The normal means of termination of an appointment is of course by the provision of due notice by the employee and acceptance of that notice by the employer. And by mutual agreement an appointment may be terminated without due notice, though both in this case and in the "normal" case a tribunal may wish to scrutinise very closely whether on the employee's part there was full and free agreement. There may also be agreement on an offer by an employee to be selected for redundancy, in which case however the position will not normally be regarded as termination by agreement but as dismissal on grounds of redundancy.

An irregular termination of contract is nonetheless a termination. In R v East Berkshire Health Authority ex.p. Walsh[38] Sir John Donaldson MR said

> "The ordinary employer is free to act in breach of his contracts of employment and if he does so his employee will acquire certain private law rights and remedies in damages for wrongful dismissal, compensation for unfair dismissal, an order for reinstatement or re-engagement, etc."

What an employee cannot secure is a legally enforceable right to continued employment. Where the employment was protected, however, by an undertaking by the employer to comply with certain procedural requirements outside the common law before dismissing the employee, the court did have jurisdiction if the employer failed to observe those requirements.[39]

3.6 Fixed-Term Contracts

Termination may also arise from the expiry of a fixed-term contract, without specific action by either party. If however an employee on a fixed-term contract is allowed to continue working and is paid by the employer on the previous contractual terms, then an indefinite contract of employment may be assumed terminable on a reasonable period of notice. It is important therefore that employees on fixed-term contracts should not be permitted to continue working beyond the expiry date save on expressly agreed terms.

Expiry of a fixed-term contract, however, is specified as a statutory dismissal under the Employment Protection (Consolidation) Act[2] [EPCA] s.55(2). In Dixon v BBC,[40] commissionaires were employed on fixed-term contracts which also contained a one-week's notice provision. The EAT and Court of Appeal, overruling a tribunal decision that the contracts were not "fixed-term" since there was a provision for notice, decided that the words "fixed-term" meant a specified period even though it was terminable by notice within that period and that failure to renew on expiry of the specified period constituted dismissal for the purpose of s.55(2).

It is possible for an employee on a fixed-term contract for one year or more (two years or more up to 1980) to waive the right to complain of unfair dismissal, and thus get access to a tribunal, on expiry of the contract (EPCA, s.142(1)). The waiver must be in writing, though not necessarily in the original contract, and must be made before the expiry date. In Open University v Triesman,[41] a lecturer appointed initially for a fixed period of 18 months and then for a further 7 months, with the latter contract including a waiving of rights to redundancy payments or to claim unfair dismissal, was ruled to be able to claim unfair dismissal because the relevant contract was for less than two years and therefore no exclusion from rights was effective. The fact that the cumulative period of employment exceeded two years was irrelevant.

There are two other interesting cases on the employment of casual, short-term staff. In Wiltshire County Council v NATFHE and Guy,[42] a lecturer was appointed part-time for each academic session but did not necessarily work until the end of the session since the principal of the college could decide that her course, if not well enough attended, would be cut short. When she complained of unfair dismissal when her contract was not renewed, the tribunal, EAT and Court of Appeal all agreed that the contract was for a fixed-term expiring at the end of the session even if her work ended earlier by decision of the principal, and that therefore there was a dismissal under s.55(2)(b). The Court of Appeal added, however, that had the employee been contracted to teach certain courses of uncertain duration and the employment ceased when the courses ceased, that could not have been a fixed-term contract for the purposes of s.55(2)(b).

In Brown v Nowsley,[43] the EAT accepted that a lecturer employed "so long as sufficient funds are provided" by the Manpower Services Commission was not dismissed when her appointment was not renewed because funding dried up, on the argument that the specific purpose of her employment had ceased and her job thereby disappeared.

A similar ability to waive rights is provided in relation to redundancy payments but in this case the qualifying period of fixed-term contract is two years or more entered into after 5 December 1965.

In practice many universities have now agreed not to require waiver clauses in relevant fixed-term contracts, in particular for research staff, accepting that statutory rights should not be unreasonably shut off from such staff and that the university (even if not the research funding bodies) should be prepared to pay out the additional sums involved in meeting redundancy payments.

3.7 Dismissal

3.7.1 Definition of "dismissal"

The meaning of dismissal is set out in s.55(2) EPCA, as follows,

> "an employee shall be treated as having been dismissed by his employer if, but only if,

(a) his contract is terminated by the employer with or without notice;

(b) where a fixed-term contract expires without being renewed under the same contract; or

(c) where the employee himself terminates the contract with or without notice in circumstances such that he is entitled to terminate it without notice by reason of the employer's conduct."

3.7.2. Normal and "constructive" dismissal

An employee has the right not to be unfairly dismissed but to pursue a claim for unfair dismissal before a tribunal he has to show that he was in fact dismissed in terms of s.55(2).

S.55(2)(a) covers both the "normal" case of dismissal on due notice, as provided for in the contract, and summary dismissal which can be carried out without breach of contract only if the employee has been guilty of repudiation of the contract or has fundamentally breached the contract in some way, for example by gross misconduct. A summary dismissal, whether or not justified, will always be a dismissal under s.55, but whether it is unfair or not will depend on the Act and not on whether the contract expressly entitled the employer to dismiss summarily.

S.55(2)(b) has been covered in the preceding section of this Chapter.

S.55(2)(c) covers what is normally termed constructive dismissal, that is to say where there is no actual dismissal - there may even be a resignation by the employee - but the Act treats certain acts of the employer as tantamount to dismissal. The leading case in this controversial area of law is Western Excavating (ECC) Limited v Sharp,[44] where the Court of Appeal firmly held that whether an employee is entitled to terminate the contract without notice by reason of the employer's conduct must be determined in accordance with the law of contract and that the alternative test of "unreasonable conduct" by the employer was not acceptable. As Lord Denning put it

> "an employee is entitled to treat himself as constructively dismissed if the employer is guilty of conduct which is a significant breach going to the root of the contract of employment or which shows that the employer no longer intends to be bound by one or more essential terms of the contract".

In this case an employee, who had had a dispute with the company over time off in lieu, was refused an advance on his holiday pay entitlement, resigned in order to obtain the holiday pay, and claimed constructive dismissal on grounds of unreasonable conduct by the employer - to the satisfaction of the tribunal and the EAT but not the Court of Appeal.

Many other cases relate to situations which might easily occur in university employment, and the following two examples are given. In British Aircraft Corporation v Austin,[45] an employee who used spectacles and who needed to wear eye protection for her work found she could not wear the goggles provided. She stopped using them and asked for safety glasses incorporating her own prescription, to be provided at the employer's expense. The safety officer undertook to investigate the employer's reaction to this request. When she heard nothing more, she left and successfully claimed constructive dismissal before the tribunal and the EAT which agreed that the employer's failure to investigate the employee's complaint was a fundamental breach of the contractual duty to take reasonable care for the safety of employees.

In Robson v Cambion Electric Products,[46] the secretary to the company accountant was promoted by being simultaneously appointed personnel officer with her own secretary. There was then a further reorganisation and she was told that she would revert to being only secretary to her initial superior (by then company secretary), at the same rate of pay, except that an expected 10% increase would not be implemented. She resigned and the tribunal accepted that there had been constructive dismissal.

If an employer acts within the entitlement of the contract of employment, there is no fundamental breach and therefore constructive dismissal is not proven, however unreasonable the employer's conduct may seem. For example, if there is a mobility clause explicitly or even implicitly in a contract, constructive dismissal will not arise merely because the employer, however unreasonably in the particular personal circumstances, decides to make use of the power to relocate.

A contract of employment may also be terminated without notice under the common law where the other party has repudiated the contract, that is shows that he no longer regards himself as bound by the contract. For example, an intimation by an employer that wages will be stopped or unilaterally reduced will usually amount to a repudiation.

The onus is on the employee to show that he has been constructively dismissed. Moreover he has to act reasonably promptly if he wishes to use a breach of contract as the basis of a claim for unfair dismissal; otherwise he will be regarded as having chosen not to treat the contract as terminated and therefore will not be able to claim constructive dismissal.

3.7.3 Unfair Dismissal

While the employee has to demonstrate to a tribunal that dismissal in the legal sense has taken place, the onus is on the employer to show that the dimissal was fair, though since 1980 tribunals no longer have to give the employee the benefit of the doubt (eg in the absence of a "defence" by the employer) but can proceed "in accordance with equity and the substantial merits of the case", while bearing in mind the size and administrative resources of the employer's undertaking (EPCA s.57(3)[47]). In other words did the employer act reasonably in all the described circumstances? The employer must show

(a) what was the reason or the principal reason for the dismissal and

(b) that it was a potentially fair reason or some other substantial reason justifying the dismissal of an employee holding the position which the employee held.

The potentially fair reasons are stated to be:

(a) a reason related to the capability or qualifications of the employee for performing work of the kind he was employed to do:

(b) a reason related to the conduct of the employee:

(c) that the employee was redundant:

(d) that the employee could not continue to work in the position that he held without contravention of an enactment.

In deciding on the reasonableness of a dismissal, a tribunal may also take into account Codes of Practice, not as rules of law but as evidence of good practice. The ACAS Code on Disciplinary Practice and Procedure is of particular weight, covering important aspects such as the right to warnings except in the case of gross misconduct, the right to be accompanied, and the right to appeal against disciplinary decisions.

It is important to realise in unfair dismissal cases that not only does the tribunal decide on the facts before it whether the dismissal has been for a substantial reason as defined in EPCA s.57 and, if it was, whether the employer acted reasonably in treating the reason for the dismissal as a sufficient reason for dismissing the employee, but also that an appeal against the tribunal's decision can only be on a point of law. Consequently precedents in tribunal decisions are not reliable indicators of likely outcomes even when the facts seem very similar, since different tribunals may legitimately reach different decisions on virtually the same facts. The EAT can change a tribunal decision only if there has been a mistake of law evident from the reasons given for the decision (eg using the wrong statutory provision) or, rarely, if the tribunal decision is such that no reasonable tribunal understanding the law could have reached it.

3.7.4 Capability and Qualifications

Although conduct can easily become entangled with capability as a reason for dismissal, capability should normally be a relatively straightforward test, and indeed a rarely invoked reason if one bears in mind that the qualifying period of employment for unfair dismissal claims is two years and one would normally expect lack of capability to be identified and remedied in some way within such a period. However jobs - and the people who do them, their health and motivation - can change over time and it may become apparent that even a long-serving employee is not matching up to the job. If so, a tribunal will expect the employer to have investigated the reason and if possible to have applied a remedy or sanction to retrieve the situation; if the remedy is adjudged by the employer to be partly or wholly within the employee's own control, a written warning will often be advisable. If dismissal thereafter follows, the employer will have been well advised to consult the employee (and his representative) to give him a chance to put his case before implementation of the dismissal. What the employer has to satisfy a tribunal about if there is an unfair dismissal claim is that he honestly and reasonably believed the employee failed to meet the standard of performance the employer required of the holder of that job. Lack of capability may be demonstrated by a series of incidents individually of small import, though there should have been prior warnings and urgings to improve. Occasionally a single incident with serious consequences for the employer (eg loss of a necessary licence) may be justification for dismissal on grounds of lack of capability.

Ill health is a special category of lack of capability. In the case of prolonged absences affecting the employer's business a tribunal is unlikely to find a dismissal unfair provided the employer has assessed the situation in a balanced way with the help of medical reports, has consulted the employee and has considered alternatives such as job transfer or early retirement.

3.7.5. Dismissal for Misconduct

There is a close link between disciplinary procedures and relating dismissal to the conduct of an employee. Underlying the whole issue is the concept of natural justice (described earlier in the Chapter) but it is the interaction of that concept with the tribunal's power and duty to reach an equitable decision on consideration of all the facts that provides the interesting diversity of decisions. In short, failure by an employer to observe all the rules of natural justice in reaching a decision to dismiss can be discounted by a tribunal in the light of the circumstances of the case. Nevertheless an employer would be well advised not to rely on this discretion but to promulgate and observe as punctiliously as possible a well drafted disciplinary procedure, even at the cost of some time. Disciplinary arrangements should also allow for a range of sanctions for misconduct - it is unfortunate to have no option between a warning and a dismissal, and this may well be the situation in many universities with good cause statutes. The other general consideration is the desirability of having a contemporaneously written record of disciplinary decisions taken, partly to guard against changes in personnel and partly to allow ready submission of documentation to a future tribunal.

Brief references can be made to a number of cases to illustrate the possible relationships of types of misconduct to the question of fairness of dismissal.

In Martin v Yorkshire Imperial Metals Ltd[48] a lathe operator tied down a safety lever which was designed to occupy his left hand during operation and thereby reduce the risk of accidents. His dismissal was held to be fair, on evidence that he knew that if he neglected safety procedures he would be dismissed.

In Meridian v Gomersall[49] an employee who five minutes before the end of a lunch break had clocked in not only herself but also three colleagues who were still smoking in the canteen was dismissed (and her three colleagues) because the factory rules provided that anyone committing a clocking offence was liable to instant dismissal. The tribunal, with the EAT refusing to interfere with its decision, deemed the dismissal unfair on the ground that the offence was not sufficiently serious for a reasonable employer to dismiss rather than adopt a lesser sanction.

In Hallett and Want v MAT Transport Ltd[50] two employees had received formal written warnings for lateness, following which one was late on 12 out of the next 80 days, while the latter was late on seven out of 77 days. The former dismissal was ruled fair but the latter was successful in his claim for unfair dismissal, the tribunal accepting that three of the seven occasions were due to industrial action on the railways and in general his timekeeping had considerably improved.

In Ahearn v National Coal Board[51] an employee was frequently absent on sickness grounds, producing medical certificates, but also absent for no specified reason. He had received several warnings over a period of 4 years and been downgraded as a disciplinary measure for a period. His dismissal was decided to be fair, the tribunal emphasising that where there are substantial periods of ill health absence, it is very important that there should be no unauthorised absences.

In Boychuk v H J Symons Holdings Ltd[52] an accounts clerkess, coming into contact with customers from time to time, was dismissed, after a warning, because she insisted on wearing a "Lesbians Ignite" badge. The dismissal was ruled fair by the tribunal and the EAT agreed, on the basis that while the right of an employer to impose standards of dress and appearance is not absolute, the tribunal is entitled on the facts of the case to strike a balance between the interests of the employee and of the employer. It was not necessary for the employer to demonstrate before dismissing that his business had actually suffered.

More complex is the relationship to the continuation of employment of criminal offences, which may be either connected or unconnected with the employment. There are dangers and difficulties in an employer conducting disciplinary proceedings while a criminal charge is still pending, but in certain circumstances some disciplinary action or at least suspension from work may have to be taken in advance of the court hearing. An offence within the business, such as theft from fellow employees, may come into this category, as may also a sexual offence even if committed outwith the business. If the employee is found guilty of the criminal offence, his employment position may be readily resolved by the imposition of a lengthy period of imprisonment involving frustration of the contract of employment, but a shorter period of imprisonment or a non-custodial sentence will not necessarily lead to this result and the employer will have to take a separate decision whether or not to dismiss. If the employee is acquitted, it may still be reasonable for the employer to dismiss, taking account of all the circumstances including the effect on the business, customers and fellow employees and bearing in mind that for a criminal offence the standard of proof is beyond reasonable doubt whereas for unfair dismissal it is only on the balance of probabilities.

In Norfolk County Council v Bernard[53] a drama teacher, convicted of possession and cultivation of cannabis, was ruled to have been unfairly dismissed on evidence that he was not an habitual cannabis smoker; there is no rule that a teacher so convicted must automatically be dismissed or that such a dismissal will be fair.

In British Home Stores v Burchell[54] an employee was dismissed for involvement with another employee in allegedly dishonest staff purchases. The tribunal declared the dismissal unfair, on the grounds that the employer had failed to confront both employees together and observe their reactions to each other's account and that the company's security officer had admitted there was insufficient evidence to prosecute. The EAT, however, reversed this decision stating that it was a correct and adequate test if the employer had a genuine belief in the employee's guilt, there were reasonable grounds to sustain this, and reasonable investigation into the incident had been carried out; it was not necessary to assess the position by reference to the criminal standard of beyond reasonable doubt.

3.7.6 Redundancy

The Redundancy Payments Act 1965[55] introduced a requirement on employers to make redundancy payments to employees dismissed on grounds of redundancy after not less than two years' continuous employment. If, however, the employer makes an offer of new employment and the employee unreasonably refuses that offer, then the statutory redundancy payments (which are related to length of service, current weekly pay and to some extent age) are forfeited, since he is no longer regarded as having been "dismissed". There was later introduced a four-week trial period for such a new job without forfeiture of rights of dismissal/redundancy, and indeed the trial period can be agreed in writing to be longer (for example to cover a retraining period). Disputes over redundancy, and in particular over whether an employee has unreasonably refused an alternative offer of employment, are referred to industrial tribunals.

A dismissal is by reason of redundancy if, wholly or mainly, it is attributable to the fact either

> that the employer "has ceased, or intends to cease, to carry on the business for the purposes of which the employee was employed by him or ... to carry on that business in the place in which the employee was so employed" (EPCA, s.81(2)(a))

or

"that the requirements of that business for employees to carry out work of a particular kind ... have ceased or diminished" (EPCA s.81(2)(b).

The Education Reform Act 1988,[19] which legislates for redundancy of academic staff, uses a definition of redundancy very closely based on the EPCA wording (s.203(5)).

On the whole courts have tended to accept redundancy arguments as legitimate reasons for dismissal, but there have been exceptions. For example, in Nelson v BBC,[56] a BBC producer working on the Caribbean Service but with a contract of employment as a producer to serve the BBC generally as required, successfully claimed unfair dismissal, since the court accepted there was no redundancy for producers generally. In this case the very general terms of the contract were the over riding factor but to a substantial extent decisions have favoured employers' arguments that employees to carry out work of a particular kind are no longer required.

Selection for redundancy is a controversial area. In certain situations there is a well-established principle of "last in, first out" (sometimes qualified by "other things being equal"), but it is not essential to select by length of service - another rational or fair method of selection may be adopted by the employer. Union concurrence, though not essential, is desirable and early consultation with unions is legally required in some situations (for details see Employment Protection Act 1975 s.99). Unions are sometimes unwilling to discuss agreements on redundancy selection, feeling it better to contest the individual cases as they arise.

It is not a legal requirement that an employer must look for, let alone find, alternative employment possibilities, but it may be useful in contesting any unfair dismissal claim to be able to show that some such effort has been made by the employer.

Compulsory, as opposed to voluntary, redundancies have to date been rare in the university situation in the United Kingdom and few universities will have negotiated detailed agreements with unions on selection criteria. The leading case of Williams and Others v Compair Maxam Ltd,[57] identifies five principles laid down by the EAT which cannot be lightly discarded, in summary:

(i) give as much warning as possible to employees and unions;

(ii) agree as fair as possible selection criteria with the union;

(iii) seek as high a degree of objectivity in selection as is possible;

(iv) consider union and employee representations on the selection;

(v) seek alternative employment for the employees wherever possible.

These principles, the EAT urged, should only be departed from where there was good reason to justify departure. It is not acceptable to argue that in the absence of a customary practice or agreement, the employer can have freedom of choice (cf Bessenden Properties v Corness,[58] where one of three negotiators in an estate agents was selected for redundancy, despite being the longest serving, on the grounds that she was married and had other means of support - this was judged inequitable under s.57(3) EPCA). There have been several cases ruling a selective redundancy as unfair on the grounds that the employer has not adequately searched out employment opportunities in associated companies but it seems improbable that a university in this context, even bearing in mind inter-university collaboration and UFC-directed rationalisation, need look beyond its own employed work force.

4. ACADEMIC STAFF TENURE

4.1 Introduction

Traditionally tenure has been held up as a strong distinguishing mark of university employment. Not only was it a feature of the older universities which were governed by Acts of Parliament but it was perpetuated in the newer Charter universities which commonly had and have "good cause" statutes specifying that dismissal or suspension of a member of academic staff can take place only on certain specified grounds - covering broadly:

(a) conviction of a crime or offence which is deemed to render him unfit to continue to hold office;

(b) immoral or disgraceful conduct;

(c) failure or inability to carry out the duties of office;

(d) physical or mental incapacity.

4.2 The development of policy towards tenure

Tenure as so defined was commended as preventing, or at least minimising the dangers of, dismissal from office of a member of academic staff with views that were not palatable to authority, whether within the university or in wider political circles. In the fairly small university sector that obtained until about 1960 and in the fast expanding post-Robbins era of 1962-1976, the protection of tenure was comfortably accepted on all sides, but when Universities became faced with the need to implement cutbacks, whether in total establishment or in selected subjects, tenure became perceived as an unreasonable obstacle to rationalisation and the introduction of new blood. Government perception to this effect led to the incorporation in the Education Reform Act 1988[19] of provisions designed to remove tenure from the university scene as quickly as seemed practicable. University opposition to these proposals eventually concentrated not on the need to retain pure tenure but on the desirability of getting built into the legislation a recognition of the right to freedom of speech and thought. The outcome is that, under s.204 of the Education Reform Act 1988, no new academic staff appointment made on or after 20 November 1987 has tenure nor from the same date does any promotion of an existing member of academic staff retain tenure as a condition of appointment. Moreover the jurisdiction of the Visitor in respect of a staff dispute or termination of appointment is removed by s.206 of the Act, though this provision will not be fully effective until the individual university's statutes are amended through Commissioners. Such academic staff will therefore no longer have any special position in the eyes of the law in regard to security of employment but will be exposed to the whole range of the statutory provision relating to dismissal and redundancy.

4.3 University Commissioners

S.203(4) of the Education Reform Act 1988 gives a detailed definition of good cause as

> "a reason which is related to his conduct or to his capability or qualifications for performing work of the kind which he was appointed to do", where "capability" is defined as "assessed by reference to skill, aptitude, health or any other physical or mental quality" and "qualifications" by "any degree, diploma or other academic, technical or professional qualification relevant to the office or position held by him".

University Commissioners have now taken on the task of modifying the statutes of each university so as to allow for dismissal of academic staff by reason of redundancy or on good cause. The same Commissioners will also deal with disciplinary procedures for complaints against and grievances by academic staff and with procedures for hearing appeals against dismissal or disciplinary decisions (s.203(1)). On academic freedom the Act circumscribes the powers of the Commissioners by specifying that (s.202(2)) "in exercising these functions, the Commissioners shall have regard to the need -

(a) to ensure that academic staff have freedom within the law to question and test received wisdom, and to put forward new ideas and controversial or unpopular opinions, without placing themselves in jeopardy of losing their jobs or privileges they may have at their institutions

(b) to enable qualifying institutions to provide education, promote learning and engage in research efficiently and economically, and

(c) to apply the principles of justice and fairness".

4.4 Individual universities and tenure

The validity of the tenure position in individual universities, particularly where the good cause statute was specifically linked with the terms of the individual contract, was in any case often a matter of some dubiety which had very infrequently been tested in the courts. In Birch v University of Liverpool[59] the normal basis of employment contract was considered even though the University statutes provided for removal only on good cause. The facts were that two employees, having applied for early retirement under a scheme which was expressly stated not to be a redundancy scheme, subsequently sought redundancy payments when their vacated posts were not filled. The EAT and the Court of Appeal, overruling the tribunal which had held that there had been a dismissal by the employer or at least a "consensual dismissal", decided that this had not been a dismissal within the meaning of s.83(2)(a), even though a redundancy situation existed, but a termination by mutual consent. Similarly in Vidyodaya University of Ceylon v Silva[60] a writ of certiorari to quash dismissal without a hearing by the University Council was refused on the grounds that the professor's appointment was governed by the law of master and servant and procedure by certiorari was not available where a master summarily terminated a servant's employment.

Many universities use contracts of employment for their academic and related staff that provide for termination of appointment by the giving of notice on either side as well as dismissal for good cause under provision in the statutes, with the relevant statute stating that "subject to the terms of his appointment" no member of the academic or related staff may be dismissed except under the provisions of the "good cause" statute. There does not appear to be a reported case on the subject, which is not surprising given the exclusive nature of the visitatorial jurisdiction in England, Wales and Northern

Ireland, but an analogous situation was pursued in the courts in Gunton v Richmond-upon-Thames LBC.[61] In that case Mr Gunton was Registrar of Twickenham College of Technology and his contract provided for two ways of termination: by the giving of notice and by the procedure prescribed in the Regulations as to staff discipline. One cause of the dispute was that the Council had "changed horses" and purported to terminate the contract by simple notice without properly pursuing the prescribed disciplinary procedure, but a judicial review of the two procedures was taken. Shaw L.J. said:

> "There was explicit provision for the termination of the appointment by one month's notice on either side...There was incorporated a disciplinary code.... It is manifest that the cause of the steps or stages to be taken will generally be prolonged beyond a month from the time when they are initiated. How is this code...to be reconciled with the express provision for termination...by one month's notice on either side? A possible solution is that the code extends or varies that express provision where the council purports to dismiss on disciplinary grounds, but that in any other circumstances the contract of service may be determined by reference to the express provision. This, however, would produce a grotesque result, for it would mean that the Council could, without assigning any reasons, terminate the contract by a month's notice, but could not, if they complained of misconduct on his part, determine that employment save by what might prove a long protracted process. As this apparent contractual anomaly lies at the root of the matters to be resolved in examining the judgment which is appealed, I think it as well to indicate at the outset the views which I have formed as to the interaction of the stated contractual term of notice and the procedure in relation to dismissal for breaches of discipline which it is accepted forms part of the plaintiff's contract of employment. For myself, I do not consider that the regulations as to staff discipline were designed to deprive the council of their contractual power to determine the contract of service by one month's notice; nor in my view did they have that result."[62]

This was supported by Buckley LJ:

> "The adoption of the disciplinary regulations does not appear to me to be in any respect inconsistent with the continued power of the council to dismiss the plaintiff on a month's notice upon grounds other than disciplinary grounds."[63]

On the other hand, at an earlier juncture,[64] the House of Lords had ruled by a majority that an employee in public service with a contract restricting the power of dismissal narrowly to misconduct, inefficiency, etc, could not be dismissed by notice in a redundancy. It was indeed by virtue of being an office holder rather than an employee that in the past the tenure of academic staff had been considered to be best defended but this line might have seemed increasingly unsure even before the passing of the Education Reform Act 1988. Since the employment of many academic staff with contracts antedating 20 November 1987 will continue for many years to be governed by the law which operated before the passing of the Education Reform Act, it is possible that there will now be a test case on tenure, as University managements acknowledge the inequities in the situation of staff holding pre-20 November 1987 and post-20 November 1987 contracts: if so the outcome will be interesting and of continuing relevance.[65]

4.5 Dismissal under the terms of the Education Reform Act

It is interesting to speculate whether the Education Reform Act 1988 - perhaps inadvertently - may have introduced a further legally valid basis for dismissal. S.131(6) gives the UFC power to make grants to universities "subject to such terms and conditions as they think fit" - a controversial phrase. S.203(7) states that "dismiss" is to be construed in accordance with s.55 EPCA 1978. The latter Act, however, goes on to set out the reasons which an employer can show to justify dismissal and s.57(2) specifies a reason which

> "was that the employee could not continue to work in the position which he held without contravention (either on his part or on that of his employer) of a duty or restriction imposed by or under an enactment".

A simple example of what was intended to be covered would be an employed driver losing his licence, but one wonders whether the UFC might ever impose a condition of grant to the effect that a university shall not employ academic staff in, for example, Chinese Language. It has to be admitted, however, that case law to date under EPCA, 1978, s.57(2)(d) is restricted to clear breaches of a specific statutory provision and it is doubtful whether breach of an administrative condition imposed by a public corporation, albeit under statutory authority, would be regarded as falling within the provision - and of course it might well be much more straightforward to justify any such forced dismissal as a redundancy.

5. REMEDIES AND DAMAGES

Where a tribunal decides a claim for unfair dismissal is well-founded, the outcome can be

(a) an order for reinstatement (ie to the same job):

(b) an order for re-engagement (ie to a comparable job): or

(c) an award for compensation.

The tribunal is required to ask the claimant whether he wishes an order for reinstatement or re-engagement made; if he does not, or if the tribunal decides not to make one - for example, if it is considered impracticable for the employer to comply or if it seems inequitable because there has been contributory fault on the part of the employee - then an award of compensation must be made.

If an employer fails to comply with an order for reinstatement or re-engagement, then the tribunal will award additional compensation, ie over and above the basic sum under (c). This is an option not infrequently taken by employers who prefer to pay more heavily in order to avoid taking an employee back into employment - to this extent the remedies open to tribunals may be regarded as ineffective.

An employer cannot demonstrate impracticability of reinstatement by quickly appointing a permanent replacement member of staff. A tribunal will ignore this fact unless the employer can show either that such a permanent replacement was essential to maintenance of the business or that a reasonable period had passed without the dismissed employee expressing a wish to be reinstated. Practicability is at the discretion of the tribunal on the facts of the individual case; in Nothman v Barnet London Borough Council (No 2)[66] where a teacher successfully claimed unfair dismissal on the basis of inadequate warnings about her peformance, the EAT and Court of Appeal, reversing the tribunal decision, decided reinstatement was unthinkable because of the allegations against other school staff advanced by the claimant.

The calculation of the basic compensation award is related to length of service and age and expressed in terms of a week's pay up to a maximum which is revised from time to time (in mid-1989, £172 per week). Where the employee is considered as having caused or significantly contributed to the dismissal, the tribunal may reduce the calculated award. There may also be a reduction in respect of a separate statutory redundancy payment. If a dismissal is unfair on grounds of trade union membership or activities, there is a minimum entitlement of £2,520 (mid-1989).

The basic award is of compensation for loss of job, not compensation of loss arising from the dismissal. There is therefore no obligation on the employee to mitigate his loss, though the award is reduced if the employee unreasonably refuses an offer of reinstatement. Additional compensatory awards are subject to a maximum (£8,925 in mid-1989) and in determining the "just and equitable" sum between zero and the maximum to compensate for the loss sustained, a tribunal will look to the employee having mitigated the loss.

The duty to mitigate one's loss is a common law principle. It is interesting to speculate what impact this would have on the level of damages awarded by a court if a university lecturer successfully claimed wrongful dismissal on the basis of academic staff tenure - in some subjects it might even be argued that such a dismissed lecturer could be expected to enjoy increased earnings outside the ivory tower!

6. TRADE DISPUTES

6.1 Introduction

The right to strike or to take other industrial action is well established as part of collective bargaining. Where there is a full-scale withdrawal of labour or alternatively a lockout by the employer, the position is relatively clear-cut. Where some more limited form of action is decided upon - in an industrial situation, a go-slow, work-to-rule or overtime ban but in the academic environment, more typically a selective withdrawal from duties, for example the 1989 refusal by AUT members to participate in examining - the legal position may be very uncertain and it may be more important to be able to point to a specific breach of an individual's contract - as probably most universities would be able to do in relation to examination duties. If there is a specific breach of contract - and that depends on the facts of the case and the terms of the individual contract - the employer has the ability to terminate the contract on the grounds of repudiation by the employee. For example, a refusal to work overtime would not normally be a breach of contract unless there were a contractual obligation to work overtime. EPCA s.62 clearly acknowledges that an employer may dismiss workers who take part in a strike or other industrial action, though it requires equality of treatment among all the workers concerned if the dismissal is to be adjudged fair by a tribunal - that is to say the employer cannot be selective in dismissing or in re-engaging.

6.2 Suspension without pay

At least under common law, a trade dispute should not lead to a suspension without pay - since that would be a unilateral suspension of the contract of employment - a collective agreement may in essence allow that course of action. Nor is industrial action made lawful by issue of a prior strike notice.

Case law does not give a clear picture of remedies applicable where employees have committed a partial breach of their contracts and are threatened with suspension or withholding of pay. Three examples will suffice: in Royle v Trafford BC,[67] a judgement of Solomon was that a teacher who on union instructions refused to add five extra pupils to his "normal" class of 31 was indeed in breach of contract but that the appropriate penalty was a 5/36 deduction in pay rather than a six months' pay deduction as "damages" imposed by the employer who had impliedly affirmed the contract by accepting partial performance over the period in question. In Henthorne v CEGB,[68] power station workers working-to-rule who had had pay stopped failed to recover it on application to the court, since it was held that the burden of proof was on them to show, as persons claiming money under a contract, that they were fully willing and able to affirm the contract. In Wiluszynski v Tower Hamlets LBC[69] an estate officer, in furtherance of a NALGO dispute with the Council, refused to answer one or two enquiries a week from Council members but otherwise performed his duties normally. The Court of Appeal, reversing the judge's decision that he was entitled to be paid, ruled that he was in breach of contractual conditions in a small but constitutionally important respect and, therefore, the Council was entitled to refuse to pay him.

In the first case the employer was in breach of its statutory duty as an education authority, since the five extra children had been sent home. In the context of university examinations, it is clear that the university will be exposed to a breach of a range of its obligations under Charter and Statutes and to individual students. It may not be easy, therefore, for a university to fail to take all appropriate and available action to enable it to meet its obligations.

7. MISCELLANEOUS

7.1 Coverage of this section

A chapter on employment law in relation to universities might well take in or refer to many other aspects of the law. Several of these are covered substantially in other chapters - for example, intellectual property rights

(Chapter 6), health, safety and welfare (Chapter 7), professional liability (Chapter 6), - and there is little point in repetition. This final section therefore is restricted to a small number of miscellaneous items which may deserve greater coverage than they have obtained either in other chapters or earlier in this chapter.

7.2 Restrictive Covenants

It is permissible, and occasionally desirable even in a University, to make an appointment subject to a restrictive covenant. For example, when a medical school wished to establish a Teaching Practice in an area where the local NHS committee responsible for appointing to principalships considered there was already a surfeit of general practitioners scraping a living, the compromise reached was that the senior lecturer who was to be one of the principals in the Practice signed a restrictive covenant preventing him practising as a general practitioner in that area for a period of three years following his future departure from university employment. In RS Components v Irwin,[70] a company distributing electrical components introduced a new service agreement with a restrictive covenant preventing employees from competing in the same business in the same geographical area for a period of 12 months after leaving the company's employment. Mr Irwin refused to sign and was dismissed. It was held that the dismissal was fair, since the employer had a substantial reason for the restrictive covenant and was entitled to seek protection against competition.

7.3 Employment of Non-UK Nationals

Work permits are not required for EC nationals who must be allowed access to employment on equal terms with UK nationals, except employment in public administration, and equal treatment in respect of remuneration, working conditions, social security rights, etc. The immediate family of an EC national so employed have the right to join him or her in the UK and to enjoy all rights, on a non-discriminatory basis, even after retirement from employment.

Commonwealth citizens and non-EC foreign nationals require work permits issued by the Department of Employment on application by the employer. In general terms, a permit will not be issued if the Department of Employment considers there is suitable resident labour to fill the vacant post offered. Overseas students need Department of Employment approval to take up vacation employment and are not permitted to remain in the UK for employment on completion of their studies, unless for training or work experience.

7.4 Time Off

An employee is entitled to take time off - not necessarily paid - to carry out certain public duties, for example as a local authority councillor or a member of a health authority or as a justice of the peace.[71] Similarly there is a right on the part of union officials to paid time off to carry out trade union duties, whether connected with industrial relations (but not participation in industrial action) between the employer and a recognised trade union or to undergo training in industrial relations or as a safety representative. All such time off must be "reasonable" in all the circumstances. An ACAS Code of Practice attempts to set out what might be regarded as reasonable in the case of union activities but clearly there is considerable scope for disagreement between employer and employee. A trade union official may complain to a tribunal that the employer has failed to allow time off or has failed to pay for the time off taken, and any perceived unreasonableness of an employer in relation to public duties may also be brought before a tribunal for a declaration or, exceptionally, compensation. A tribunal, while it may make a declaration on the number of days off, has no power in the case of public duties to state whether they should be paid or unpaid.

7.5 Disciplinary and Grievance Procedures

Disciplinary and grievance procedures are very closely related to contracts of employment. If the disciplinary procedure or grievance procedure is incorporated into the contract of employment, then failure to apply it may be a breach of contract by the employer allowing damages to be claimed.

More commonly disciplinary procedures are contained in a separate reference document and an ACAS Code of Practice sets out detailed recommendations on contents, with particular emphasis on the importance of including a right of appeal and generally applying natural justice; alleged defects in disciplinary procedure feature strongly in informal dismissal claims.

Grievance procedures in universities are sometimes separate documents, sometimes included in procedure agreements with recognised unions, and sometimes are included in individual contracts. Persistent failure to deal with a grievance according to a procedure agreement may not lead to a claim for damages but may greatly strengthen a claim for unfair dismissal. The essentials of a grievance procedure as set out in the Code of Practice issued under the Industrial Relations Act 1971[1] are: a written statement specifying, by description or name, the person to whom the employee should apply for redress of any grievance, the manner in which the application should be made and the procedure for pursuing the grievance. Universities have sometimes complicated their position by confusing grievances between employee and employer with more academic issues arising, for example, between a lecturer and a head of department which may or may not have significant employment implications; these academic issues may very sensibly be determined by procedures involving academic bodies of the university, such as a Faculty Board or Senate, but it is not so clear that strictly employment grievances are appropriately handled through such a procedure.

7.6 Hours of Work

Statutory control of hours of work is of little relevance to universities. The definition of the working week, however, is a potential source of difficulty in the case of categories of staff who have no specified contractual hours of work, most notably academic staff. When AUT members took industrial action in 1986 and withdrew their labour for a day, there were disputes in some universities over whether the appropriate pay deduction was 1/365 of annual salary or 1/260 on the assumption of a normal 5-day week or some other fraction. The definition of working week has a potential relevance also in the calculation of Statutory Sick Pay.

7.7 Maternity Rights

There is full statutory specification of rights to maternity leave and maternity pay,[72] the details of which cannot readily be summarised here and which in any case are often topped up by UCNS-negotiated provisions or by schemes adopted by individual institutions. One important point is that an employee who takes maternity leave has a right to return to work after confinement, subject to certain conditions, the most important of which is that she has at least 2 years' continuous service at the beginning of the eleventh week before the expected week of confinement. The primary right is to return to the same job or, if for example redundancy has intervened, to a suitable alternative vacancy on not less favourable terms and conditions. The right to return is enforced by allowing complaints of unfair dismissal to a tribunal.

7.8 Unfair Contract Terms

The Unfair Contract Terms Act 1977[73] was designed to restrict the extent to which persons, including employers, could contract out of liability for negligence. Its provisions override anything in individual contracts or collective agreements, on the basis that the weaker party, the employee, deserves protection. One major area of potential negligence in the employment context is of course safety. In the case of death or personal injury, employers are in any case required by statute to carry Employers' Liability Insurance. For damage other than death or personal injury liability can be excluded or restricted (eg by monetary limit) only if it is "reasonable". A court in judging reasonableness will bear in mind the resources of the employer and how far insurance cover might have been taken. The onus of proof of reasonableness rests on the party who is seeking to rely on the contract term restricting liaiblity. An employer should make expressly known to employees that liability is restricted or excluded, with advice that they should consider insuring personally against the risk.

There is some uncertainty how far a disclaimer of liability in a job reference would be effective in the light of the Unfair Contract Terms Act, though normally one could expect the test of reasonableness to remove risk in the absence of fraud (cf Lawton v BOC Transhield Ltd,[74] where it was held that an employer had a duty of care to a former employee to ensure that the facts stated in a reference were accurate and the opinions justified, though the more general question of whether a disclaimer would have fallen foul of the Unfair Contract Terms Act was not answered).

7.9 Copyright

The law of copyright is covered in some detail in Chapter 6. It might briefly be noted here, however, that the statutory presumption that ownership of work carried out by an employee in the course of employment belongs to the employer is commonly reversed in the university situation, either explicitly through a university Statute or Ordinance or the contract of employment or implicitly through custom and practice. This attitude developed, of course, in a period when copyright related primarily to literary work - the advent of computer software and other technical objects of copyright with considerable commercial value may encourage institutions to observe more closely the statutory presumption.

8. NORTHERN IRELAND

The "mainland" statutory provisions on employment protection, sex (but not racial) discrimination, health and safety and trade union control have been incorporated into the law of Northern Ireland by Orders at various times and agencies (e.g. the Health and Safety Agency, the Labour Relations Agency and the Equal Opportunities Commission) set up with powers similar to those of the mainland agencies.

Unique to Northern Ireland is the concept of fair employment first introduced in the Fair Employment (Northern Ireland) Act 1976.[75] A Fair Employment Agency, established under the Act, has the general function of promoting equality of opportunity and eliminating unlawful discrimination on the grounds of religious belief or political opinion.

Footnotes - Chapter 4

1. 1971 c.72
2. 1978 c.44
3. 1980 c.42; 1982 c.46; 1988 c.19
4. 1974 c.52
5. 1976 c.7
6. 1984 c.49
7. 1970 c.41
8. 1975 c.65
9. 1976 c.74
10. 1975 c.71 s.1
11. 1975 c.71 s.10
12. Industrial Training Act 1964, 1964 c. 16 s.12
13. Employment Protection Act 1975, 1975 c.71 s.88
14. Sex Discrimination Act 1975, 1975 c.65, Part VI
15. Race Relations Act 1976, 1976 c. 74 s.43
16. 1972 c.68
17. Attorney-General v Talbot [1747] 3 Atk
18. [1987] 1 All ER 834 (HL)
19. 1988 c.40
20. For a full account of the operation of the principles of natural justice see any leading textbook on Administrative Law.
21. 1986 c.59
22. 7 & 8 Geo 6 c.10
23. 6 & 7 Eliz 2 c.33
24. [1979] ICR 848
25. [1979] IRLR 158
26. [1983] ICR 165
27. [1982] unreported
28. [1986] unreported
29. [1984] ICR 678 (EAT)
30. [1986] IRLR 134
31. [1979] ICR 921
32. SI 1975/2048

33. [1979] IRLR 119 (CA)
34. 1974 c.53
35. [1969] 2 QB 173
36. 1978 c.44 ss. 1-11
37. [1984] IRLR 91
38. [1985] QB 152
39. R v British Broadcasting Corporation,ex.p. Lavelle [1983] 1 All ER 241; see also R (Snaith) v Ulster Polytechnic [1981] NI 28 and in particular the comments of Hutton J. at p.38
40. [1979] ICR 281
41. [1978] IRLR 114
42. [1980] IRLR 198
43. [1986] IRLR 102
44. [1978] IRLR 27
45. [1978] IRLR 332
46. [1976] IRLR 109
47. Employment Protection (Consolidation) Act 1978, 1978 c.44, s.57(3) as amended by Employment Act 1980, 1980 c.42 s.6
48. [1978] IRLR 140
49. [1977] ICR 597 (EAT)
50. [1976] IRLR 5
51. [1974] IRLR 372
52. [1977] IRLR 395
53. [1979] IRLR 220
54. [1978] IRLR 379
55. 1965 c.62
56. [1977] ICR 649
57. [1982] IRLR 83
58. [1977] ICR 821
59. [1985] IRLR 165 (CA)
60. [1965] 1 WLR 77
61. [1981] 1 Ch 448
62. Ibid. at p.457
63. Ibid. at p.462
64. McClelland v Northern Ireland General Health Services Board [1957] 2 All ER 129 (HL)
65. As this book goes to press, there are newspaper reports that the University of Aston's plans to dismiss tenured academic staff on grounds of financial stringency but in contravention of the University's Charter and Statutes have been ruled unlawful by the University Visitor. The University's argument had apparently been that the Charter and Statutes protected the rights of staff to remain as members of the University but that the University had power to breach, with compensation, the separate contracts of employment in a situation of financial need. The Visitor ruled this

argument inadmissible and reaffirmed that no member of academic staff could be dismissed other than for good cause as defined in the University's Statutes.

66. [1980] IRLR 65
67. [1984] IRLR 184
68. [1980] IRLR 361 (EAT)
69. [1989] IRLR 259 (CA)
70. [1973] IRLR 239
71. Employment Protection (Consolidation) Act 1978, c.44 ss.27-32
72. ibid. ss. 31-48 (as amended by Employment Acts 1980 and 1982
73. 1977 c.50
74. [1987] ICR 7
75. 1976 c.25

CHAPTER 5

ORGANISATIONS OF STUDENTS AND STAFF

1. STUDENTS' UNIONS

1.1 Introduction

In spite of recurring interest in some aspect or other of organised student life, there has never been a systematic analysis of the divergent provisions for student representation among our universities. This part of the discussion of Organisations of Students and Staff contains such an analysis for the first time and attempts to draw out some general themes. The analysis is based on material supplied in 1987 by the Registrars/Secretaries or equivalent of all the institutions surveyed.[1]

Students' unions have developed to their present, easily recognizable form from diverse historical origins. Some started as and constitutionally still technically are representative councils with direct participation in the government of their institutions (see particularly the ancient Scottish universities under an Act of 1889,[2] and the "Scottish influence" that led some of the then new English universities of the early 20th century to accord recognition to the student body). Some started life as social and/or athletic clubs and their current constitutions reflect that origin. In its Report for 1923-24[3] the University Grants Committee encouraged universities to establish unions to develop

> "athletic and social clubs and societies and to foster the growth of a corporate life"

when many students lived at home. Following the development of students' unions as political pressure groups in the 1950's and 60's, the "Robbins" universities experimented with new constitutional forms. "Student representation" has been widened from catering, accommodation, etc. questions into academic areas. The result is fascinating diversity.

1.2 A definition of "Students' Union"

For simplicity the phrase "Students' Union" will be used to describe the students' organisation in each institution.[4] There is however, a range of names including Union, Guild, Association and Assembly. Sometimes the "Union" is a building or the social part of a larger organization, particularly in Scotland where the Union is often a club within the meaning of the licensing laws: it is important not to confuse the terminology. For the purposes of this part of the chapter, the relevant body in the ancient Scottish universities is the Students'

Representative Council (SRC), which may be part of a larger Association or Assembly. In one case the officially-established body (the SRC) is part of the Students' Union. On occasion the constitutional provisions for the name of the students' organisation are inconsistent.[5]

1.3 <u>Analysis of provision for Students' Unions</u>

The analysis is conducted under the following general headings:

(i) status of the Students' Union or equivalent in the institution of which it forms part ($$4-6)

(ii) objectives and charitable status ($$7-8)

(iii) relationship with the institution ($9)

(iv) internal government and discipline ($$10-11)

(v) freedom of speech and disruptive activity ($$12-13).

1.4 <u>Status of the Students' Union in the institution</u>

Constitutionally, we may group students' unions in two ways:

(i) by the form of their establishment ($1.5);

(ii) by the controls which the institution exercises over their government and management ($1.6).

1.5 <u>Form of establishment</u>

A total of 54 institutions have been examined, including most colleges of the University of London but excluding the University of Wales itself, UWCM and the Open University. Apart from the ancient Scottish universities and the University of Newcastle-upon-Tyne, where the relevant body is established under Act of Parliament,[6] almost all unions are established either by the Charter itself (31, including both Northern Irish and the four remaining Scottish universities) or by Statute (15). The exceptions are Cambridge[7] and Essex and York where the relevant instrument is an Ordinance. The practical effect of the difference is that if established by Ordinance the Union's existence could be terminated by act of the institution. Changes to Charters and Statutes require the consent of the Privy Council, changes to Acts of Parliament can only be made by Parliament itself.

In the majority of cases in which the union is constituted by Charter or Statute, detailed provision is then made by Ordinance. In one case (Brunel) the Charter makes no provision for Statute or Ordinance and alternative arrangements have been made.

1.6 Controls

The position in 51 of the 54 institutions surveyed is clear. Either the Council (Court in Scotland) or the Senate (or equivalent) must approve the constitution of the union (or at least regulations/rules of major significance). The former route is chosen in 31 of the 41 English and Welsh institutions, all eight Scottish universities and one of the two Northern Irish universities. In many cases Council/Court approval depends on a recommendation of the Senate or equivalent.

The extent to which the rules/regulations are spelt out in the Ordinances or similar instruments varies considerably, reflecting local circumstances and problems which have arisen in past years: in most cases only the principal rules are set out and the union is permitted to adopt subsidiary rules which do not conflict with the principal rules. Some ten universities have adopted a more detailed approach than is the norm: in five institutions amendments to the constitution of the students' union may only be made on the motion of the union itself or with its agreement. The position is under review in a number of cases.

The question of control is complicated to some extent by the existence of joint university-union boards, e.g. the Aston Guild Board, established by the Council of the University "to have general oversight of the affairs of the Guild" with power inter alia to approve the constitution of the Guild of Students, approve estimates and authorise expenditure and the Liverpool Joint Union Management Committee which is responsible to the University for the good order and management of the Union, i.e. the building.

In some cases (e.g. Bristol, Liverpool) the University participates in the financial control of the union either by the appointment of a Senior Treasurer or a Financial Adviser. In Baldry v Feintuck[8] the court noted that the University of Sussex Union had a Treasurer nominated by the Senate, but the office was vacant at the time.

1.7 Objectives

The list of objects or functions of unions ranges in size from one sentence (e.g. the University of East Anglia: "to promote the development of the corporate life of members of the Union") to a page of detailed clauses (e.g. the University of Durham with ten lengthy objects). Several include among their objectives or as an overriding clause the requirement for equal treatment of members, etc., in terms of sex, race, political belief, etc. but only one has a specific objective to uphold freedom of speech.

The most common objectives of students' unions are:

(i) to act as a recognised means of communication between students and the University/College authorities;

(ii) to foster and develop a corporate spirit, including athletic, cultural and social activities;

(iii) to support student societies;

(iv) to liaise with other student unions, locally and nationally;

(v) to represent the interests of students.

Others reflect the origins of the union or its trading/commercial activities e.g.

(i) "to provide alcoholic and other refreshment in the premises known as the Union.."(Hull)

(ii) "the running of the Union as club premises for the members of the Association" (Strathclyde)

(iii) "to work for an Education system which is open to all, which is relevant to the needs of the country and truly serves the interests of the country" (Queen's, Belfast).

1.8 Charitable Status

As the Attorney-General's (Lord Advocate's in Scotland) guidance on expenditure by student unions states,

".. a student union has charitable objects if it exists to represent and foster the interests of the students at an educational establishment in such a way as to further the educational purposes of the establishment itself. It is not open to a union to adopt objectives which conflict with the charitable educational purposes of the university."

In the words of Brightman J in Baldry v Feintuck[8] (at p.84)

"The union [of the University of Sussex] is, clearly, an educational charity and the officers of the union who have power to dispose of the union's funds are, clearly, trustees of those funds for charitable educational purposes."

In the letter covering the Attorney-General's guidance, the Solicitor-General asked universities to ensure that the guidance was drawn to the attention of the "leaders of your student body" in each succeeding year and it is now normal practice to do so.

1.9 Relationship of Students' Unions to their institutions

A number of constitutional documents refer to students' unions or their equivalents as "part of [the] University"[9] while others seek to distance them by expressing disclaimers of liability for debts and other obligations.[10] In practice where unions are constituted by Charter, Statute or Ordinance they are likely to be treated as creatures of the University. As Lord Annan said in his report[11] (p.16)

"The Students' Union, like any other constituent part of a university, is subject to the Statutes, Ordinances and Regulations of that university. Lord Devlin made this clear in his Report" (p.55).[12]

This was also assumed in the one substantive English case on the status of students unions: Baldry v Feintuck[8] where Brightman J at p.84 held that the constitution of the relevant union

"...must by necessary implication, be construed in the context of the educational purposes of [the] University..".

This treatment of students' unions is important in two aspects:

(i) in the internal relationship between the University and the union;

(ii) in contractual relationships with third parties and in breaches of statutory obligations.

Even in cases where the union is expressed to be part of the university, it is at law an unincorporated association of persons; it is not a legal entity.[13] The relevant officers or committee have power to sue and be sued and to enter into contracts as representatives of the membership, but the union itself has no legal personality. In the Reference to the Visitor of the University of Hull,[14] a case concerned with a dispute over the levying of an "amenity fee", Lord Roskill appeared (at p.7 of his advice) to countenance the prospect of a legally binding agreement between the University and the Union. It is difficult to imagine a situation in which one part of a corporation can enter into a legally binding agreement with another. How could the terms of such an agreement be enforced? It can only be argued that some form of legal identity has been created for Student Unions by the practice of naming their officers in representative actions but there is no authority to this effect.

This should not be confused with the right to petition the Visitor on "domestic" matters: in In the Matter of the Students' Union of Brunel University, John Flanagan, Andrew Gale and Brunel University[15] Lord Hailsham LC, the Visitor, found it unnecessary to decide on a challenge by the University to the locus standi of the union in a case concerning the termination of a course. He went on to say:

> "But I must make it clear that I do not necessarily consider that the Students' Union has a locus standi except in cases which actually or potentially involve existing students."

This, then, would probably exclude the union from making valid representations to the Visitor about changes in the academic structure of the University which did not affect existing students.

A number of universities have from time to time taken steps in the courts to restrain students from disruptive activity of various kinds or to regain possession of buildings unlawfully occupied, usually following a resolution of the students' union.[16] Such actions are normally taken against named officers of the union as representative of the students. The union itself, as an unincorporated association and as part of the university, cannot be sued.

The question of status is equally important in relation to third party contracts for the employment of staff or for the supply of goods or in cases involving torts or breach of statutory liability. A third party might reasonably expect for example that he would have redress against the university for failure to meet lawfully-incurred debts or for wrongful or unfair dismissal. If a "stand-alone" unincorporated association, a students' union could not itself be sued by those aggrieved. Equally, an aggrieved member of the union might attempt redress against the university for alleged invalid acts by the union. The action in Baldry v Feintuck[8] against the Chairman of the Council and a university employee was withdrawn, it being accepted by counsel for the plaintiff student that neither was responsible for disputed payments

> ".. since .... [the payments]...were the subject-matter of a resolution of the union in general meeting." (at p.85).

The position of union staff varies but generally speaking they are appointed by and are responsible to the relevant officers or committee of the Union: they owe no direct allegiance to the university. As mentioned above, at least three universities have sought to exclude these possibilities in their legislation but it remains a matter for decision whether such a provision would have the desired effect. The only certain way for the university to avoid the prospect of suit for damages for breach of contract by the union would appear to be to incorporate the union itself.

1.10 Internal government

The General Meeting of members or similar body often exercises supreme power. The result can be, of course, that a minority of interested or activated students can effectively prescribe the policy for the majority. The position can best be demonstrated by an analysis of the constitutional provision for the quorum for meetings with power to authorise "direct action" (i.e. occupations, disruptive activity, etc.). This has been interpreted, where there is no specific provision, to mean the quorum for a Special or Emergency General Meeting called to discuss particular issues. In some instances the position is unclear. The information relates to 1987.

In one case there is no quorum. Otherwise the quorum for General Meetings ranges from 1.3% to 15% of the full membership, provision for Special or Emergency meetings being made in five cases, with an increased quorum (up to 5%) in four cases. The absolute number of students needed for special meetings (ordinary meetings where there is no special quorum) is remarkably similar, thirty out of forty-five lying in the range 200-300, excluding very small institutions, with only two large institutions requiring a quorum in excess of 500. There is no direct correlation between size of institution and number of students able to authorise "direct action". Although there seems to be a tradition that students will not entertain "direct action" unless this has been "legitimised" in some way by a quorate meeting, there is in fact no possibility of action which is otherwise unlawful being rendered lawful simply by reason of approval by a quorate meeting. This is a political rather than a legal advantage.

Below the level of General Meeting it is common to find two further tiers of government and numerous sub-committees of various kinds. Depending on the nature, size and geographical layout of the university, it is common to find a representative Council with policy-making powers (often subject to the direction of a General Meeting) and an Executive Committee with day-to-day control of the union's affairs, including the appointment of staff. The Executive Committee normally includes among its members a number of full-time sabbatical student officers as well as permanent staff. The number of sabbatical officers allowed by the university depends on its size and in some cases on its geographical layout.

1.11 Disciplinary powers

Most unions reserve the right to discipline members, generally in relation to misconduct on union premises, in union meetings or in relation to elections. Some appoint a special Judicial or Disciplinary Committee, others act by the Executive Committee or its equivalent. In all cases the rules of natural justice apply, and in some cases are spelt out in elaborate detail. Typical penalties would include suspension from the use of union facilities for a period, restoration of damaged property or moderate fines. Universities generally have by the act of approval of the unions' constitutions delegated such disciplinary power in respect of union offences although the position varies considerably between institutions.

As a consequence of the status of unions as unincorporated associations, any member with a grievance which could not be settled otherwise would have to sue the committee and could bring a representative action.

1.12 Freedom of Speech

S.43 Education (No.2) Act 1986,[17] which does not extend to Scotland or Northern Ireland, imposes certain duties on individuals and bodies concerned in the government of universities ("establishments") in relation to freedom of speech on their premises. Ss.8 brings the premises of students' unions which are not premises of the university within the definition of "premises of the establishment".

The Act does not define "student union" nor does it tackle the problem of the wholly independent union, one occupying its own property or a "conglomerate" union such as that of Loughborough or Aberystwyth. According to the CVCP in a letter to the Secretary of State for Education and Science[18]

> "The practical difficulties...[of the legislation]...are greatly increased by ss.8 which brings into the net the premises of students' unions."

Is a students' union a body "concerned in the government" of a university? The DES view is that it is, where it is part of the institution under the Charter and Statutes, etc.

> "The purpose of subsection (8) was to bring the premises of a legally separate students' union within the scope of subsection (2) which seeks to prevent discrimination in the use of university..premises. Given that in most cases the premises of a students' union would be 'premises of the establishment' within the meaning of subsection (2), it was not considered that the definition of a students' union was critical".

The provisions were drafted

> "in such a way as to avoid the risk of accidentally excluding any bodies we wished to include."[19]

The original <u>Freedom of Speech (Universities and Institutions of Higher Education) Bill</u>[20] would have imposed a duty on every "member, union, guild or association" and would have compelled the university to "forbid its student union, guild or association...to discriminate.." among speakers on political grounds. The Act has approached the matter from a different direction.

The Act imposes on universities and other institutions of higher education in England and Wales the duty to prepare a code of practice relating to free speech. Universities have approached this duty in a number of ways; there has as yet been no judicial interpretation of the Act. It is of course, only one weapon in the armoury of an institution facing disruptive behaviour against unpopular speakers by students or other groups on its premises. For example the common law provides a remedy against actions likely to cause a breach of the peace and the <u>Race Relations Act</u> 1976[21] amended the <u>Public Order Act</u> 1936[22] in respect of incitement to racial hatred.

1.13 Other disruptive activity

If a union general meeting authorises "direct action" this may take many forms, e.g. sit-in, work-in, lobby, picket. The consequences of disruptive activity may be dealt with under the university's disciplinary code[23] but the university may seek to forestall the activity by an application to a judge of the High Court for an interlocutory injunction ex parte[24] (or interdict in Scotland) or if unlawful occupation has taken place, for an order of repossession. Such applications are well-documented and part of the general law. In some cases, depending on the nature of the disruptive activity in relation to the criminal law, the police may be prepared to assist; whether or not they are prepared to do so depends on the particular circumstances.

2. TRADES UNIONS AND OTHER STAFF ASSOCIATIONS

2.1 Introduction

Since the passing of the Industrial Relations Act 1971,[25] which led to proliferation of procedure agreements between universities and recognised trades unions, it has been rare for a more informal local staff association to retain significant standing in a university's governance. Individual members of academic, and increasingly non-academic, staff are of course elected to membership of Councils/Courts and Senates but for the most part these elections are not dependent on the existence of a staff association separate from the trades unions.

2.2 The pattern of representation

Chapter 4 has described the evolved categorisation of university staff and how these categories are represented, at both national and local level, by trades unions, in particular in negotiations on salaries and conditions of service. In summary the normal pattern is:-

Academic and Related Staff

Non-clinical: Association of University Teachers (AUT)
Clinical - Medical: British Medical Association (BMA)
Clinical - Dental: British Dental Association (BDA).

Frequently however there are local concordats between AUT and the BMA/BDA whereby the AUT is recognised as representing all academic staff in relation to local conditions of service.

<u>Non-Academic Staff</u>

Clerical: National and Local Government Officers' Association (NALGO)
Technical: Manufacturing Science Finance (MSF) (formerly ASTMS)
Manual: National Union of Public Employees (NUPE) and/or other public service and craft unions.

2.3 Procedure Agreements

Most AUT local branches have entered into formal procedure agreements with the governing bodies of their universities, usually based on the "negotiation" and "consultation" promulgated by but not adequately defined in the <u>Industrial Relations Act</u> 1971. The interpretation of "negotiation" has proved particularly troublesome; for example, where a trade union has pressed the import of negotiation as being that the formal agreement of the union must be obtained before a university introduces any change in conditions of service (often very widely defined) and that in the absence of agreement on any matter there must be arbitration, preferably binding, by some external authority, the university has understandably felt itself restricted in its freedom to manage. In practice, where procedure agreements seem to work, either there has been some blurring of the distinction between negotiation and consultation or the institution and the union have openly or tacitly agreed to a quite restricted list of matters for negotiation.

2.4 Inter-Union collaboration

There has also been in many universities a movement towards inter-union collaboration, resulting often in the development of a joint union campus committee. To what extent recognition is granted to such a committee is for the individual university to decide. It should be noted, however, that at the national level, while the various non-teaching staff unions come together in the operations of the Universities' Committee for Non-Teaching Staff (UCNS) there is currently no wider forum which takes in the academic staff unions.

2.5 The role of Trades Unions in Health and Safety

Regulations under the <u>Health and Safety at Work Etc Act</u> 1974 legislate for the appointment of safety representatives from among employees, describe their functions and make provision for time off with pay to carry out these functions and to undergo training. Recognised trades unions have the right to appoint safety representatives (and to terminate their appointments), generally to consult with the employer to promote health and safety but more specifically:

(a) to investigate potential hazards, dangerous occurrences and the causes of accidents at the workplace;

(b) to look into employees' complaints relating to health and safety at work;

(c) to make representations to the employer both on specific matters and more generally on health, safety and welfare;

(d) to represent employees in consultations with inspectors of the Health and Safety Executive;

(e) to attend meetings of safety committees.

Safety representatives are entitled to inspect the work place or part of it, on reasonable written notice to the employer and provided they have not inspected it in the previous three months; more frequent inspections may be carried out with the agreement of the employer and the three months' qualifying period is dispensed with, for example if there has been a substantial change in conditions of work, such as the installation of new machinery, or new Health and Safety regulations introduced. Safety representatives, however, have no duties under the law to carry out their functions properly and therefore face no liabilities.

Requirements on employers to allow safety representatives time off with pay during working hours to enable them to carry out their functions and to receive appropriate training are related to a Code of Practice approved by the Health and Safety Commission. A safety representative may complain to an industrial tribunal that the employer has not allowed time off or has not made the appropriate wages payment for such time off.

An employer is required to establish a safety committee not later than three months after a proper written request by two or more safety representatives. Consultation with those and other recognised trade union representatives is required and a notice on the establishment and composition of the committee must be displayed at the workplace where it may be easily read by the employees. Typically a university would have a Safety Committee, as a committee of Council or Court, on which safety representatives nominated by the recognised trades unions would be entitled to serve.

Footnotes to Chapter 5

1. Throughout this section references to individual institutions have been avoided where notification has been made that matters are controversial within the institutions concerned. In April 1988 the Government announced its intention, as part of an investigation into the role of the National Union of Students, to gather on a sample basis up-to-date information on inter alia, the organisation and legal status of students' unions in universities and other institutions of higher and further education. On the basis of this and other information the Government would "reach conclusions and consult all concerned on the best action to take in relation to the present arrangements whereby institutional student unions affiliate to and fund the NUS." A questionnaire was issued to 70 institutions in July 1988, with replies required by the end of October 1988. A summary of the survey's findings was published in May 1989: there is no significant inconsistency between those findings and the material in this Chapter. It was not possible to incorporate the results of the Government's consideration of this matter into the current volume.
2. Universities (Scotland) Act 1889: 52&53 Vict.c.55
3. HMSO, 1924.
4. Some unions are conglomerate with functions ranging outside the university. For example Loughborough Students' Union serves also the Loughborough Technical College and the College of Art and Design; Aberystwyth Guild of Students serves also The College of Librarianship Wales, the Welsh Agricultural College and the Aberystwyth College of Further Education. This obviously requires complex constitutional provision. The remainder of the text ignores this particular complication except in the context of freedom of speech ($.12 infra).
5. e.g. Kent at Canterbury, where the Charter names the organisation of students "the University of Kent at Canterbury Students' Union" and the Ordinance names it "The Students' Union of the University of Kent at Canterbury." At Hull the title is the "Hull University Union of the University of Hull" (Ordinance XIII) which is the "Union of Students" prescribed in the Charter (Article 12).
6. Universities of Durham and Newcastle-Upon-Tyne Act 1963.
7. Grace 1 of 16 May 1984; amended by Graces 2 of 30 January and 9 of 24 April 1985.
8. [1972] 2 All ER 81; see also Harrison v Hearn [1972] 1 NSWLR 428
9. e.g. Hull, Ordinance XIII; Nottingham, Ordinance X.
10. e.g. Stirling, Charter clause 15(3); Dundee, Charter clause 11(3); Kent at Canterbury, Ordinance XXVIII(VIII).
11. Annan Report, University of Essex, 1974.

12. Report of the Sit-In in February 1972 and its Consequences (Devlin Report), Vol.C111, Cambridge University Reporter, Special, No.12. 14 February 1972.P.54.
13. Such bodies apparently exist and carry on their activities as separate units, but are not incorporated: common examples outside universities are members' clubs , friendly societies and trades unions.
14. May 1983.
15. 1985
16. The procedure used in England and Wales depends upon whether disruptive activity is apprehended, in which case an interlocutory injunction may be sought ex parte from a judge of the High Court, or when repossession of premises unlawfully occupied is sought, in which case the university may proceed under RSC Order 113. The position in Scotland is entirely different.
17. 1986 c.61
18. Attachment to letter of 15 October 1986.
19. Letter dated 19 August 1987 to the author from Further and Higher Education Branch III, DES.
20. 11 February 1986
21. 1976, c.74, s.70
22. 1 Edw 8 and 1 Geo 6 c.6 s.5A
23. See chapter 3, $5 supra
24. n.16 supra
25. 1971 c.72

CHAPTER 6

UNIVERSITY TRADING AND ENTREPRENEURIAL ACTIVITIES

1. LEGAL POWERS TO ENTER INTO VENTURES IN THE NATURE OF TRADE

1.1 Origins of the powers to trade

An earlier chapter dealt with the legal powers of chartered corporations such as universities as distinct from the legal powers of other types of corporations. If it is accepted that chartered corporations, unlike statutory or registered corporations, have all the powers of natural legal persons then it follows that they do not need to have the power to trade vested in them by their constitutions. By trade is meant for the purposes of this work the provision of teaching, research and related activities for profit. This is otherwise than in the nature of teaching and examining under degree schemes or carrying out research. By trade is also meant a venture in the nature of trade which carries some measure of risk, financial or otherwise. It may very well be, however, that some of a university's activities, particularly in the field of continuing education and in the provision of research, consultancy and advisory services will nevertheless involve some degree of financial or other risk which, on the test of the contents of the contract, might be held to be ventures in the nature of trade.

1.2 Express powers to trade

The point to consider is that if the law of corporations or the constitution of the relevant university or college does not confer a power to enter into ventures in the nature of trade then, as between the university and the third party, it might be held under the doctrine of ultra vires that there is no enforceable contract. However, looking at a typical new university, it will be seen that the university's Charter confers a miscellaneous power

> "to do all such other acts and things whether incidental to the powers aforesaid or not as may be requisite in order to further the objects of the University".[1]

Since the Charter also stipulates a power on the part of the university to provide courses of lectures and other instruction for non-members, and also to make provision for research and advisory services, more particularly in relation to the applied sciences and technologies and the allied industries, then it can be assumed that there is a general power for the university to enter into ventures in the nature of trade. To argue otherwise would be to say that the university was not empowered to make appropriate charges for the provision of such research and teaching services.

Chapter 1, $4.8 supra deals with charitable status and the controls exercised by the Charity Commissioners in respect of universities in England and Wales.

1.3 The formation of contracts

Typically, in a university Charter, one of the functions of the University Council is

"to enter into, vary, carry out and cancel contracts on behalf of the University".

The Statutes may typically also contain a section dealing specifically with contracts as follows:

Contracts made by or on behalf of the University shall be validly made and binding on the University if made as follows:

(i) Any contract which if made between private persons would be by law required to be in writing and, if made according to English law to be under seal may be made on behalf of the University in writing under its common seal and such contract may in the same manner be varied or discharged.

(ii) Any contract which if made between private persons would be by law required to be in writing and signed by the parties to be charged therewith may be made on behalf of the University in writing signed by any person acting under the express or implied authority of the Council and such contract may in the same manner be varied or discharged.

(iii) Any contract which if made between private persons would by law be valid although made orally only and not reduced into writing may be made either in writing or orally on behalf of the University by any person acting under the express or implied authority of the Council and such contract may in the same manner be varied or discharged.[2]

2. UNIVERSITY STAFF AS AGENTS OF THE UNIVERSITY

2.1 Introduction

The issue of agency has already been discussed in Chapter 2, supra. A contract made under the authority of the Council of the university or its equivalent, whether executed under seal or under the hand of an authorised agent, will clearly be a contract made by the university. However, the majority of contracts will not be brought to the attention of the university Council and therefore the university will be made a contracting party through some mechanism of agency. General discussions of this matter can be found in most books on the law of contract. However, many of these refer to the position of companies incorporated by registration under the Companies Acts[3] where the doctrine of ultra vires (as modified by s.9 of the European Communities Act 1972[4]) will apply. In the case of chartered corporations, which have the full range of legal powers available to a natural human person, questions of agency may be more complex.

2.2 How agency arises

The essence of agency is that B gives A the power to alter B's legal relations with C. The relationship of principal and agent may arise in any one of five ways:

by express appointment:

by virtue of the doctrine of estoppel:

by the subsequent ratification by the principal of a contract made on his behalf without any authorisation from him:

by implication of law in cases where it is urgently necessary that one person should act on behalf of another:

by presumption of law in the case of cohabitation.

On express appointments, except in one specific case concerning the execution of a deed, no formality such as writing is required for the valid appointment of an agent. An oral appointment is effective. This is so even though the contract which the agent is authorised to make is one that is required by law to be evidenced by writing, such as a contract to buy or to take a lease of land.

A set of procedures followed, if not written down expressly, can constitute certain persons within the university as its agents for making contracts of one or of many classes. Agency by estoppel is probably the most general way in which people are appointed to be agents of another. This would arise where a person is understood to represent and act for the person who has so placed him in that position. Thus, if the University Council generally accepts that, say, the Bursar or the Registrar signs contracts for the supply or provision of services or goods and knows that other persons outside the university act on that belief, then, in general, the Council will be estopped from disputing that the officer is its agent.

2.3 Relationship to third parties

A question requiring careful consideration is whether it is the principal or the agent who is capable of suing or being sued by the third party with whom the agent has completed the contract. The position of the agent with regard to such a third party varies according to the circumstances. Assuming the agent has the power to make the contract, there are three possibilities -

(a) The agent may disclose to a third party the fact that he is a mere agent and he may also say who is his principal.

(b) He may say that he is an agent but withhold the name of the principal.

(c) He may conceal both facts, in which case the third party will believe, contrary to the truth, that the agent is himself the principal and that nobody else is interested in the contract.

The courts have developed certain general rules which vary with each of these three cases. The general rule is that if the contract is made prima facie for a named principal then the principal alone can sue or be sued. These rules are, however, of a purely general character and are presumptions which can be displaced by proof that the parties intended something else. The question whether the agent or the principal is competent to sue or be sued may depend on the construction of the form of the contract between the agent and the third party.

2.4 Actual or ostensible authority

The relevance of the above analysis and what follows can be seen in the context, for example, of a member of staff who receives a letter or telephone call to him at his university department asking him to undertake a piece of consultancy or testing work for an industrial company. The question of legal liability on research contracts and consultancies was dealt with in advice from the Committee of Vice-Chancellors and Principals[5] of April 1979. It will be appreciated that different consequences can flow from the determination of the essential fundamental question who is the contracting party - is it the university acting through the agency of the member of staff or is it the member of staff acting in a purely personal capacity? The internal rules and regulations of the university concerning this type of activity may not enable the university to rely on the doctrine of ultra vires, as it might (subject to s.9 of the European Communities Act 1972) in the case of a limited company whose Memorandum and Articles of Association are available for inspection at Companies House. Although a university Charter is a public document it may not in sufficient detail describe who has the power to enter into contracts on behalf of the university. It therefore may be difficult for a university to defend an action for damages on a consultancy contract by attempting to demonstrate that a member of staff was not in fact the agent of the university in agreeing to carry out a piece of work and in performing the contract. Even if the university had issued instructions to academic departments by which members of staff were enjoined to declare to such outside organisations as require their services that they were not acting as agents of the university but only in their private capacities that would not protect the university if the caveat was not entered by the member of staff. The third party will almost certainly be entitled to rely upon the doctrine that the member of staff was acting with the actual or ostensible authority of the university. This doctrine would have to be examined on the basis of the facts of the particular case.

To take an extreme example, a professor who telephoned an outside supplier to order large quantities of food for the university catering service would probably not be held, on the doctrine of ostensible authority, to be an agent of the university because the category of contract which he purported to be authorised to make was not one which would usually be associated with the office of a professor in the university. However, since university Ordinances, together with other regulations in the university, might impose on the head of a department the duty to organise and implement research programmes, then it could be argued that a contract for the provision of research services could be made by a professor with a third party which would be entitled to believe that he was acting with the authority of the university.[6] Recent years have seen new procedures adopted by universities in relation to research contracts (as opposed to grants) particularly because of the deployment of university resources which are involved, not to mention the need to ensure that there is professional scrutiny of contract documents. Nevertheless, there will be many occasions in which heads of departments or academic staff will deal directly with outside bodies and effectively commit the university to a contract. As the CVCP guidance of 1979 indicates,[7] it is therefore in the interests of the university to ensure that members of staff dealing directly with third parties are aware of the position in which they may place the university and that they are encouraged to seek advice from the Administration on contractual matters.

In this connection it is often helpful to be able to provide to members of staff a 'DIY kit' for short-term consultancy and testing services, which has been approved by the university's administration and is in accordance with its various insurance policies, in particular professional negligence indemnity. However, even the best insurance cover in modern times is not capable of protecting the university in every eventuality. Accordingly, there is a burden of responsibility on the administration to ensure that contracts made in the name of the university, quite often in a fairly informal way, are acceptable. It is salutary to recall that the nature of chartered corporations is such that their liability in law for damages is theoretically unlimited.

3. GENERAL LEGAL ISSUES ON TYPICAL TRADING ACTIVITIES

3.1 Scholarly Publishing

3.1.1 Introduction

Given that a major primary object of a university is to advance learning and knowledge by teaching and research and given that a requirement for charitable status is that new knowledge is not simply stored but is disseminated, it is a necessary implication of that object that research work conducted in the university shall be published. In many cases, of course, this will be undertaken by means of manuscripts submitted to the journals of, and presentations to, learned societies. The Charter of a typical modern university may also include a specific power

> "to provide for the printing and publication of educational, research and other works which may be issued by the University".[8]

There is unlikely to be any obligation on a university to secure the publications of scholarly works through any particular means. Many universities have a well established publishing activity carried out by their own presses and printing units.

3.1.2 The scope for publishing

The scope available to a chartered corporation for carrying out activities in the nature of scholarly publishing is extremely wide. The right, for example, of the University of Cambridge to print and sell all manner of books was granted by Henry VIII in royal letters patent of July 1534. The publishing activities are under the control of the Syndicate of the Press of the University of Cambridge on behalf of the "Chancellor, Masters and Scholars of the University of Cambridge". A similar arrangement prevails at Oxford. It is on this simple legal basis that an internationally renowned multi-million pound venture is carried on. The basic principles are equally applicable in more modest circumstances.

Subject to the general laws concerning copyright, and in this connection the international character of copyright should not be overlooked, there are no particular requirements in law for publishing activities. In the British book publishing industry there are over 500 separate publishing houses responsible for over 50,000 separate titles each year. The trade's turnover is measured in hundreds of millions of pounds. The Society of Authors and the Writers' Guild represent authors of all types and can offer assistance in the negotiation of publishing contracts. The power of large publishing houses to impose contracts on authors is well known.

3.1.3 Ownership of copyright and licence to publish

The contractual arrangements between members of the university and its own publishing organisation are usually much more informal. However, the key point to cover in any correspondence, which could be construed as a contract, relates to the ownership of copyright in the work to be published and in the various rights which the university's publisher will need to obtain. It is usually the case that academic staff in the universities, under the doctrine supporting academic freedom, own the legal title to the copyright in works which they produce unless there is some agreement to the contrary. This reverses the statutory provision[9] whereby the copyright of any work produced by an employee in the course of his employment belongs to the employer.

It is not, of course, necessary for a publisher to own the copyright in order to publish any work. The minimum which the publisher requires is a licence to do so. Most universities offering publication opportunities would wish to have at least an exclusive licence to publish and may even prefer to have an assignment of all the rights in the work. The contents of the contract for either a licence or an assignment will of course depend upon the negotiations between the author and the university. It is particularly important, if the

Ordinances of the university, which may be incorporated into a contract of employment, reverse the statutory presumption, to ensure that the University has the right of publication. It is also desirable to set out in formal terms the arrangements between the author and the university in respect of the various subsidiary rights and also to make provision for the sharing of income either on a profit sharing basis or on a straight royalty basis.

In a university publishing venture it may not always be the case that a work is commissioned in advance. Usually an author will present a draft of a work to those responsible for the publishing function. If, however, the work is commissioned in advance it is important for the contract to indicate the length of the text together with other details such as the number and title of illustrations, the index and whether these are to be provided by the author. Clarification of such points at the outset can often prevent misunderstandings and consequent disputes at a later stage. It is also important to ensure in the contract who is responsible for obtaining permission for the reproduction of any material not produced by the author.

3.1.4 The publishing agreement

The nature of the contract between a publisher and an author is personal in the sense that the rights and obligations of the parties cannot be assigned to others without the written consent of the other. This is because the contract is for the provision of services and the exercise of skills which a publisher has specifically identified by his choice of author.

The contents of a publishing agreement might very well include the following main heads.

(i) The preamble. This gives the date of the contract, lists the parties and the title, or provisional title, of the book with an indication of its minimum and maximum length.

(ii) Delivery of type script. Publication schedules need to be prepared in advance since late delivery of a book can have serious consequences for the flow of work through the publishing unit.

(iii) Warranty and indemnification. The author is expected to indemnify the publishers against the risks of actions by third parties alleging libel and infringement of copyright.

(iv) Volume form English language rights. The main licence agreement will cover the publication of books in other markets. The question of abridgements or adaptations of the work should also be dealt with.

(v) Publisher's undertaking to publish. The publisher may reserve the right to reject a draft but having accepted it should undertake to publish the work within a specified time from delivery of the typescript.

(vi) Author's correction proofs. It is normal for the author to undertake to read, correct and return proofs within a specified time of receipt. It is also normal practice for the author to bear the cost of proof corrections, other than printer's errors, over and above a specified allowance (10% or 15% of the cost of composition). Any costs incurred by the publisher for proof corrections may be deducted from royalty payments.

(vii) Production and distribution. The publishers insist as a rule on having the final say on all matters concerning the manufacture, advertisement and distribution of the book. This may be reasonable since they are invariably responsible for all of the costs involved.

(viii) Author's copies. The provision of a number of free copies to the author is a tradition.

(ix) Payments to the author for volume form publication. These are normally calculated on the UK published price for home sales. The contract may also provide for cheap editions and remainders and for the distribution of overseas royalties. Book club and condensed book rights often feature in publishing contracts from major publishing houses together with provision for paperback rights and advances on royalties.

(x) Translation rights. These may produce a large proportion of the income from a book.

(xi) Other so called subsidiary rights. In general publishing these can often be more valuable than the basic publication rights and can cover film, dramatic, television or radio rights together with sound and video recording rights. Publishers may also attempt to obtain rights to include the work in collective licensing and distribution arrangements. It is a matter for negotiation whether authors reserve these rights for later negotiations.

(xii) Accounts. The contract should provide for royalty statements to the author on a regular basis and a right to send in an independent accountant to verify statements.

(xiii) Competing works. In view of the economic interest of the publisher in ensuring that the exclusive licence or assignment produces a good yield, it is often the case that the author is asked to refrain from publishing any later work which might compete with the work which is the subject of the publishing agreement. It is a matter for local negotiation whether such a clause is included in an agreement between a member of academic staff and his University.

(xiv) Revised editions. The question of future editions of a work should always be dealt with. It is obviously desirable to have clear arrangements for keeping a work up-to-date. Whereas the publishers might wish to have the right to ask the author they will also wish to reserve the right to ask somebody else if he declines and to take the cost of that extra work out of future royalties. On the other hand, to protect his reputation the author would usually insist on the right to revise the work himself.

(xv) Options. A publisher will often wish to take out an option on the future works of an author. This does not oblige the author to produce other works but governs the situation should he do so.

(xvi) Termination. Every publishing contract must have a clause setting out the contingencies which might bring it to an end.

(xvii) Copyright notice. The publishers usually undertake to print a copyright notice in all copies of the book consisting of the symbol C in a circle followed by the author's name and the year of first publication or by the name of the publisher if the copyright has been assigned.

It should be noted that the Society of Authors in its advice to its members states that there are three essential points to be checked before an author finally signs a contract:

(a) that there is a firm commitment to publish the book

(b) that there is a proper termination clause and

(c) that the option clause will not unduly fetter him in his future work.

Not discussed in this work are questions of the right of an author to expect the university to publish his work, questions of academic censorship and freedom, questions of appeal against a decision of the university to reject an author's work and its implications for his reputation, nor the moral rights of authors.[10]

3.2 Contracts Research and the Provision of Academic Services

3.2.1 Introduction

In the great majority of universities arrangements for the administration of research grants and contracts are well developed and provide mechanisms for the scrutiny of arrangements before the work begins. This is particularly important given the need to ensure that the background resources of the "wellfound laboratory" are available to underpin the grant or contract project, particularly where hard pressed resources, such as additional accommodation for research staff, are required. However, there will be a significant number of occasions when the work under discussion may be perceived as being short term and not requiring detailed scrutiny of contract terms. In either case, it is important to be clear whether the funds or resources provided to the University are to be held on trust for research into general or specific areas, or whether the work is a commission which will be based in contract. Grants from the Research Councils are clearly set in contractual terms. Grants from a large number of charitable organisations may be either trusts or grants. Funds coming from public and commercial organisations will prima facie be the subject of contractual arrangements whether or not these are comprehensively detailed in a formal agreement. It is, as a general rule, not necessary to evidence a contract in writing for it to be enforceable by or against the university. There is, of course, the problem of evidence which may lie in a combination of written or parole material but the basic principle is clear. To avoid this problem a written contract is always desirable even if it consists of an exchange of simple letters.

3.2.2 Preliminary negotiations "subject to contract"

Referring back to the above sections dealing with the problems of agency, it is obvious that great care must be taken by all academic and research staff who are involved in preliminary negotiations with external sponsors seeking access to the resources and services of the university for their commissioned work. The simplest form of advice is to ensure that all such discussions are clearly made 'subject to contract'. It is often the case, however, that the external sponsor is anxious for the work to begin and the academic department is anxious to oblige and not to threaten the contract by drawn out contractual negotiations involving the central administration. However, should the project not proceed well or come to an unsatisfactory end or give rise to subsequent disputes then it will be invariably the university which will have to resolve the contractual problems which have arisen.

3.2.3. Implied terms of contracts - The Supply of Goods and Services Act 1982

A contract may arise not as a separate, isolated act but as an incident in the general course of business or in the framework of some more general relationship. It may be set in the context of the usage, custom and practice familiar to all who engage in work of that kind and which may be taken to import into the contract, whether written or not, certain implied terms.

Whereas contracts for the sale of goods and hire-purchase agreements were for many years the subject of statutory controls, contracts for the transfer of goods which do not amount to either a sale or a hire-purchase contract were not. The Supply of Goods and Services Act 1982[11] now brings contracts for the supply of work and materials within the statutory scheme. Part I of the Act deals with contracts for the transfer of hire of goods made after 4 January 1983. Part II with contracts for the supply of services made after 4 July 1983.

Implied terms relate to conditions or warranties which can have far-reaching implications should the contract give rise to disputes. Because many of the smaller contracts will not be fully documented, it is particularly important to take account of terms which will be implied by the statute in contracts for the provision of services. The most important relates to the implied term under the 1982 Act that suppliers of services will carry out the work with reasonable skill and care (s.12) and carry out the services in a reasonable time (s.13). These implied terms are made the more onerous if the university, or its agents, have made representations about, or held out the university or individual members of staff as having, particular expertise. Given the highly expert nature of university staff this is not difficult to allege. The plaintiff in any situation would, of course, have to prove on a balance of probabilities that the standard of care and skill devoted to a particular project fell below an objective standard which would be expected of an institution of university standard. Taking into account the difficult nature of much of the work which could be expected to be carried out in the university, the plaintiff may have a difficult burden to discharge. This is one of the possible arguments in favour of including a clause for the settlement of disputes of a technical character by means of arbitration rather than by litigation. It is important to note that if an arbitration clause is not included in the contract ab initio it can only be effected at a later date with the agreement of both parties.

Where a contract, especially an oral contract, for the supply of a service fails to fix the price or any method for determining the price and where there is no previous course of dealing from which either could be deemed, then the 1982 Act provides that a reasonable charge is payable (s.15). What is reasonable for the purposes of s.14 (time) and s.15 (price) is a matter of fact for the courts to decide ultimately. The question of exclusion by a supplier of liability for breach of the terms implied by the 1982 Act is dealt with below.

3.2.4 Scope of the work and misrepresentation

It is important that the extent and scope of the work to be carried out under the contract is clearly delineated. This must obviously take account of the resources in terms of time, expertise and equipment available to the university to do the work. Both sides should be quite clear about the extent of the obligations and benefits to be contained in the contract. Contract research is therefore considerably different from research which an individual member of staff may carry out for his own intellectual curiosity and as part of his general academic duties. It is, therefore, necessary to take into account the reasonable expectations of the sponsor of a particular project and agree the scope of the basic work to be undertaken. Care should be taken to avoid making claims about the quality of work which can be produced.

There are dangers in making claims beyond a reasonable description of what an individual investigator or a piece of equipment in a university laboratory, for example, can do. Firstly the results may be alleged to fall short of those which the sponsor may claim he was induced to believe would be produced. This might be held to be either a misrepresentation about the type and quality of services which the University holds itself out as being competent to provide and, depending on the circumstances, a misrepresentation on which a sponsor was intended to rely, and on which he did rely, to induce him to enter into the contract. The Misrepresentation Act 1967[12] is exceptionally difficult law but basically provides a remedy to a party suffering loss or injury by reason of an innocent misrepresentation, that is, in the absence of fraud.

3.2.5 Remedies for misrepresentation

Another serious problem may arise for the university because the law has provided a number of remedies for negligence and innocent or other misrepresentation which can have far reaching consequences. Dependent upon the circumstances, the aggrieved party may have a choice between rescission of the contract or damages. If the contract is rescinded then all monies had and received must be returned and the parties must be put in the position they were in before the contract existed. The Misrepresentation Act 1967 gives the court a general power to grant damages in lieu of rescission. In contract the general principle governing damages is that the injured party should be put, as nearly as may be, in the position he would have enjoyed if the contract had been performed. This may involve damages not only for the recovery of money laid out for the research but also for the loss of the bargain.

The extent of the damages recoverable are governed by what is reasonably foreseeable at the time of making the contract. If a sponsor loses general business because of the ending of the contract through no fault of his then he may be able to claim general damages for loss of profits. If, however, the sponsor made it plain before entering into the contract that he is depending upon the results of the research project or the services sought for some particular purpose, such as a special overseas contract, then he may be able to claim special damages in that regard. The extent to which the university is able to insure against such claims is discussed below in the context of professional negligence indemnity insurance.

3.2.6 Confidentiality

An important term which may be implied by common law relates to the question of confidentiality. Here the main requirements of industry and commerce will tend toward keeping the results of a project confidential to protect commercial interests. Given that a primary object of the university is the advancement of education by publication and dissemination of knowledge, the natural instincts of academic staff will veer towards disclosure by publication in the open literature. It is vitally important, therefore, that this question is addressed at an early stage in negotiations on contract work, otherwise both sides may proceed on totally different assumptions which could lead to accusations of breach of contract.

3.2.7 Ownership of intellectual property

Following on from the issue in a contract of confidentiality of the results of a project there should be a clear statement relating to the vesting of intellectual property rights in the results. The basic question is to ask what does a sponsor think he is getting for his money? There is no easy answer to the question how does the law decide who owns the results of a project if there are no express terms in a contract for services. This is because the law relating to different types of intellectual property is not drawn up in a consistent code. In general terms, the ownership of patent rights in an invention will belong to the inventor. This is not to say, however, that the sponsor may not have an interest in the beneficial ownership of the invention or at least a licence, whether exclusive or non-exclusive, to use the results for commercial purposes. In copyright the legal ownership of literary, dramatic and musical work will usually lie with the author but even so a sponsor may again be able to claim some or all of the beneficial interest. Clearly, both the university and the sponsor of research or the seeker of services have a considerable freedom in contract to determine these questions at the outset.

Of importance in negotiating contracts with third parties are the implications of the contract of employment between the member of academic or research staff who carries out the work and the university which will invariably be the contracting party with a sponsor. The Patents Act 1977[13] introduced a number of important features in this area. The first is that the university as employer cannot oblige an employee-inventor to sign away his rights. Whereas first ownership of the rights in an invention lie with an employer as opposed to the employee, the employee has the right to a compensation award if the employer receives any outstanding benefit from the exploitation of the invention. Any term in a contract between the employer and the sponsor which purports to reduce or eliminate that right is unenforceable. Any term in an agreement between an employee and a third party inserted at the behest of the employer is similarly unenforceable.

In a typical modern university, in order to protect academic freedom to publish, the Ordinances dealing with copyright, as mentioned above, will reverse the statutory provision of s.4(4) of the Copyright Act 1956[9] whereby ownership of copyright lies with the employer in any work produced during the course of employment. The Ordinance may provide that it does not apply in any agreement to the contrary. Clearly, if a member of academic staff, having the benefit of this Ordinance, agrees to take part in a contract between the university and an outside sponsor to do a particular piece of work in which the contract provides for the vesting in the sponsor of the copyright in the results, then he must be taken to have made an agreement with the university contrary to the benefit provided by the Ordinance. The copyright will thus vest firstly in the university, not the member of academic staff, and secondly in the Research Sponsor.

3.2.8 Use of University Equipment

In contracts providing for services which go beyond purely intellectual activities the University will utilise equipment of many different types.

Whether this equipment is owned by the university, or made available on loan, or by other arrangement, the university will be held on an implied term of the contract to use equipment which is capable of meeting the objectives described in the contract. Since the equipment will be under the control of the university it must accept responsibility for the quality of its output. If, however, the equipment is of an experimental nature then care should be taken to exclude or limit liability to the maximum price of the contract (see below on exclusion clauses in general). This is important where the sponsor supplies material which will be subject to test or examination by the equipment in which case care should be taken to agree the value of the item. The basic principles here are no different to those applicable to the provision of commercial services for example dry cleaning and development and printing of photographic films.

3.3 Sale of Manufactured Goods

3.3.1 Introduction

Whereas universities have been very large purchasers of goods and thus increasingly expert in the law of procurement of goods, it is only relatively recently that they have taken on the role of vendor to any significant extent. As entrepreneurial activities develop in universities it is likely that the experience gained as purchasers will be reflected in activities as sellers. Extended treatment of the law of the sale of goods is not appropriate in this work but the general features should be noted to encourage those responsible for selling activities to consider the many issues raised and to seek appropriate expert advice.

3.3.2 The Sale of Goods Act 1979

The Sale of Goods Act 1979[14] consolidated with some amendments the 1893 Act of the same title. There is a mass of pre- and post-1983 case-law which is relevant to the 1979 Act. It does not attempt to codify the general principles of contract law -

> "The rules of the common law, including the law merchant, except in so far as they are inconsistent with the provisions of this Act, and in particular the law of principal and agent and the effect of fraud, misrepresentation, duress or coercion, mistake or other invalidating cause, apply to contracts for the sale of goods".

As P.S. Atiyah observes in "The Sale of Goods",[15] the Act was originally passed in the last century to govern transactions between businessmen or organisations. However, in this century a large proportion of cases coming to the Courts relate to sales by retailers to the consuming public. Very different and economic implications arise from these transactions. Recent legislation has tended to discriminate, as the Unfair Contract Terms Act 1977[16] does, between consumer and non-consumer transactions.

3.3.3 Contract

The Sale of Goods Act 1979 provides for certain terms to be implied on a contract for the sale of goods. These relate for example, to the seller's title to the goods, their description, merchantable quality and fitness for purpose. Liability for breach is effectively "strict" and the seller's innocence or fault is irrelevant. Under the law of contract, therefore, the seller has no defence if he knew or could reasonably have known that the product was not of merchantable quality or fit for the purpose for which it was sold. The ability of the seller to limit liability by means of exclusion clauses in the sale agreement has been dramatically cut down by the Unfair Contract Terms Act 1977, especially in so called consumer sales.

3.3.4 Negligence

In many cases contractual remedies will not be available because there was no contract between a seller and a purchaser, the seller has gone out of business or the purchaser may have passed the product to someone else who in turn suffers loss or injury. In the latter case the injured person must prove negligence to claim damages. This task is more difficult than seeking contractual remedies because the plaintiff will have to establish that the manufacturer was in breach of a duty of care owed to him. That duty in general terms is measured by what a reasonable manufacturer would have done to avoid the injury suffered by the plaintiff.

In the well-known Scots case of McAlister (or Donaghue) v Stevenson,[17] the House of Lords (per Lord Atkins) affirmed

> "the proposition ..... that a manufacturer of products, which he sells in such a form as to show that he intends them to reach the ultimate consumer in the form in which they left him with no reasonable possibility of intermediate examination, and with the knowledge that the absence of reasonable care in the preparation or putting up of the products will result in an injury to the consumer's life or property, owes a duty to the consumer to take reasonable care."

Where a product is defective through no fault of the manufacturer there can be no claim against him. This is the area of law which will be affected by Part I of the Consumer Protection Act 1987[18] referred to below.

3.3.5 Criminal penalties and breach of statutory duty

If the law of contract deals with quality and fitness of goods and the law of negligence with product safety, then the criminal law could be said to deal with safety regulations to ensure that goods are safe or to ensure that unsafe goods are not put on the market. The principal consumer safety legislation consists of the following:

a) The Consumer Protection Act 1961[19] (powers to introduce regulations improving safety requirements on products and to prohibit the sale of products not complying with such regulations);

b) The Consumer Safety Act 1978[20] (extension of powers under the 1961 Act, and introduction of prohibition Orders and Notices);

c) The Consumer Safety (Amendment) Act 1986[21] (enables Customs Officers to seize and detain unsafe goods at the point of entering into the UK).

The criminal liability imposed by these Acts is not strict since manufacturers may offer a defence that all reasonable steps were taken and all due diligence was exercised to avoid committing an offence. In the case of the 1961 and 1978 Acts a proven breach of statutory duty would give rise to a civil claim for damages by the person suffering from the failure to perform that duty.

3.3.6 The Consumer Protection Act 1987

The impact of Britain's membership of the European Community on domestic legislation has been evident in this area also. The Consumer Protection Act 1987 will have far reaching consequences in many areas of industry. Part I implements the EC Directive on Product Liability by imposing "strict" or "no fault" liability on producers and certain others for defective products. Part II introduces a general safety requirement for consumer goods and when in force will replace the existing safety legislation.

The remainder of the Act relates to misleading price indications, enforcement of new provisions and miscellaneous matters. It is to be noted that the Act supplements rather than supplants existing law on product liability and consumer safety. Accordingly existing areas of law should be examined in determining the basis of liability for defective products.

Part I of the Act came into force on 1 March 1988 and provides that a producer of a defective product will be liable for injury to a person or damage to property whether or not he was negligent or at fault. A producer will not be able to contract out of his obligations under the Act. Producer is comprehensively defined in the Act to include not only the "final" manufacturer or processor but also manufacturers of component parts and suppliers of raw materials. Other parties can attract liability under the Act, for example a person putting his trade or other distinguishing mark on the product, an importer and a supplier who cannot give the name of the producer or the person who supplied him. Thus, in theory, more than one person may be sued. The definition of "product" is very wide and will include computer software. Under s.3(1) there is a defect in a product "if the safety of the product is not such as persons generally are entitled to expect", an extremely widely drawn concept. S.5(1) broadly defines damages as "death or personal injury or any loss of or damage to property (including land)".

S.4 provides defences as follows:-

a) that the defect is attributable to any requirement imposed by Government or EEC enactment or obligations

b) that the defendant did not at any time "supply" the product (i.e. did not sell, hire or lend it)

c) that the supply was otherwise than in the course of business

d) that the defect did not exist at the time the product was supplied by the defendant

e) that the state of scientific and technical knowledge at the time of supply was not such that a producer of products of the same description as the product in question might be expected to have discovered the defect if it had existed in his products while they were under his control.

f) that the product was comprised in another product and that the defect was wholly attributable to the design of the other product.

S.4(e) provides the "development risks" or "state of the art" defence which aroused controversy during the Bill's passage through Parliament. This will clearly be an important defence for manufacturers at the "leading edge" of science and technology and has implications for university research contract where principal or component products may result. There is, furthermore, a ten year limitation period so that all rights will expire ten years after the product was supplied. The usual limitation period of three years for personal injury claims applies, running from the date on which the injured person became aware of the cause of action.

Many insurance brokers, solicitors and other professional advisers are now urging companies to take practical steps to identify and eliminate the greater risks of legal action for defective products. Such strategies will include transferring the risk to third parties who supply components or services or to subsidiary companies with minimal capital put at risk. Insurance cover will be an obvious requirement. However, just as the market for professional negligence indemnity insurance has been badly affected by the increasing volume of claims and size of damages, so the product liability market may see very severe increases in premiums. The additional costs of such cover will clearly be passed on to purchasers.

Whereas a professional negligence indemnity insurance policy will typically exclude products, it may cover prototypes. If a research contract relates not only to the design of a product but also to the creation of a prototype it is alarmingly easy to see how a short production run could be started by the university at the sponsor's request. Such an activity will, however, change significantly the scope of the University's liabilities and this should be examined very carefully.

3.3.7 The Health and Safety at Work Act 1974[22]

S.6(1) of the Act provides that it shall be the duty of "any person who designs, manufactures, imports or supplies any article for use at work"

a) to ensure so far as is reasonably practicable, that the article is so designed and constructed as to be safe and without risks to health when properly used;

b) to carry out or arrange for the carrying out of such testing and examination as may be necessary for the performance of the duty imposed on him by the preceding paragraph;

c) to take such steps as are necessary to secure that there will be available in connection with the use of the article at work adequate information about the use for which it is designed and has been tested, and about any conditions necessary to ensure that, when put to that use, it will be safe and without risks to health.

S.6(2) imposes a duty

"to carry out or arrange for the carrying out of any necessary research with a view to the discovery, and, so far as is reasonably practicable, the elimination or minimisation of any risks to health or safety to which the design or article may give rise."

The Act thus provides a chain of responsibility from the retailer to the wholesaler to the manufacturer to the designer.

3.3.8 Exclusion of Liability - Unfair Contract Terms Act 1977

As indicated above there are a significant number of ways in which common law and statute can cut down the freedom to contract enjoyed by various parties. A further restriction is included in the Unfair Contract Terms Act 1977 which has the effect of either outlawing or severely cutting down the effect of exclusion clauses and indemnity clauses. Its main purpose is to control the exclusion or restriction of liability in contract or for negligence which arises in the course of business. The Act would therefore have application beyond the entrepreneurial trading activities of the university and could equally apply to the provision of teaching and non-commercial research. A detailed examination of the Act is outside the scope of this work but the general features are described below.

Ss.2-4 of the Act cover negligence liability, liability arising in contract and unreasonable indemnity clauses. For the purpose of these sections negligence means the breach

(a) of any obligation, arising from the express or implied terms of a contract, to take reasonable care or exercise reasonable skill in the performance of the contract;

(b) of any common law duty to take reasonable care or exercise reasonable skill (but not any stricter duty);

(c) of the common law duty of care imposed by the Occupier's Liability Act 1957.[23]

Liability arising from the sale or supply of goods is also dealt with in Ss.5, 6 and 7.

Ss.2-7 of the Act, therefore, apply only to business liability, that is, liability for breach of obligations or duties arising

(a) from things done or to be done by a person in the course of a business (whether his own business or another's) or

(b) from the occupation of premises used for business purposes of the occupier.

S.2 provides that a person cannot by reference to any contract term or to a notice given to persons generally or to particular persons exclude or restrict his liability for death or personal injury resulting from negligence. In the case of other loss or damage a person cannot so exclude or restrict his liability for negligence except in so far as the term or notice satisfies the requirement of reasonableness. A term in a contract purporting to exclude or restrict liability is not of itself to be taken as indicating voluntary acceptance of any risk.

S.3 deals with liability arising in contract as between contracting parties where one of them deals as consumer or on the other's written standard terms of business. The Act defines consumer as a person who neither makes the contract in the course of a business nor holds himself out as doing so where the other party does make the contract in the course of business, and, in the case of a contract governed by the law of sale of goods or hire purchase, goods passing under or in pursuance of the contract are of a type ordinarily supplied for private use or consumption. S.3, therefore, imposes controls on exclusion or restriction of liability for breach of contract or lack of contractual performance.

S.4 of the Act provides that a person dealing as consumer cannot by reference to any contract term be made to indemnify another person, whether a party to the contract or not, in respect of liability that may be incurred by the other for negligence or breach of contract except in so far as the contract term satisfies the requirement of reasonableness. The rest of this commentary will not deal with the supply of goods of a type ordinarily supplied for private use or consumption.

Schedule 2 of the Act provides guidelines for the application of the reasonableness test. The matters to which regard is to be had are any of the following which appear to be relevant:

(a) The strength of the bargaining positions of the parties relative to each other.

(b) Whether the customer received an inducement to agree to the term or, in accepting it, had an opportunity of entering into a similar contract with other persons but without having to accept a similar term.

(c) Whether the customer knew or ought reasonably to have known of the existence and extent of the term having regard amongst other things to any custom of the trade and any previous course of dealing between the parties.

(d) Where the term excludes or restricts any relevant liability or some condition is not complied with, whether is was reasonable at the time of the contract to expect that compliance with that condition would be practicable.

(e) Whether the goods were manufactured, processed or adapted to the special order of the customer.

Given the novel character of much of the contract research work attracted to a university, there is obviously scope in the guidelines to protect the university. However, if the university represents to the customer that the carrying out of a piece of consultancy or testing is a routine matter then this reduces the "specialness" of the circumstances on which the university could rely for a defence.

It is important to note that Schedule 1 provides that ss.2-4 of the Act do not extend to certain classes of contract. From the point of view of universities this is particularly important as one exclusion is "any contract so far as it relates to the creation or transfer of a right or interest in any patent, trade mark, copyright, registered design, technical or commercial information or other intellectual property or relates to the termination of any such right or interest". Note that the exclusion refers only to a contract relating to the creation or transfer of a right. It is arguable, for example, that a software licence creates a right or interest in technical information, but even if that is correct, the exclusion clauses (excluding liability for breach of contract and negligence) do not relate to the creation of the right of the licensee to use the software but to the exclusion of liability for consequential losses if that material is defective in some way. It follows that the exclusion of intellectual property items in Schedule 1 is of very limited use to a university as licensor seeking to avoid the effects of the Act. Thus, it is argued that for all practical purposes the Act applies. A term in a software licence which attempts to exclude liability for loss and injury will be effective only if the university can rely upon the guidelines for the reasonableness test. Similar considerations will clearly apply to other intellectual property items such as patents, registered design, trademark, etc.

3.3.9 Insurance Cover

Given the problems introduced by the Unfair Contracts Terms Act 1977 in relation to exclusion and indemnity clauses, it is obviously wise, in view of the theoretically unlimited liability of chartered corporations, to consider the extent to which such risks can be reduced or eliminated by insurance cover and other means. Professional indemnity insurance is an important feature of University research and consultancy activities.

The essential cover provided by the policy extends to negligence on the part of the University and individual members of its academic staff whether in contract or tort. Cover should also extend to infringement or alleged infringement of third party intellectual property rights.

However, insurance cover is hardly likely to be fully comprehensive. A typical policy will contain a large number of exceptions which will relate to certain types of research and consultancy activities. For example, there is typically excluded any claim or costs arising from

a) advice, design or specification which to the knowledge of the insured will be incorporated in aircraft or aerial devices;

b) trials involving drugs;

c) the provision of computer services (see below);

d) claims arising from the manufacture or supply of any product (the supply of a prototype is not the supply of a product); and

e) claims under contract for penalties or liquidated damages.

Cover does not usually extend to other claims or liabilities which can arise in respect of the death or bodily injury of employees arising out of the course of their employment or other risks which would be covered by different types of insurance. Because of the very considerable damages awarded by Courts of the United States a typical professional indemnity insurance policy will exclude claims first brought in a Court in the United States.

The general professional indemnity insurance market has changed very markedly in recent years, principally because of the major claims made against professional partnerships. Insurance premiums have risen dramatically. Thus, in a university with a research grant and contract turnover of, say, £5,000,000 per year, means a premium of about £18,000. There are no signs that the insurance market is prepared to distinguish between types of organizations or activity. Accordingly, for the exploitation of some high risk technology the university may be better advised to use the device of a limited company to limit liability rather than expose itself to continual increases in insurance premiums.

4. INTELLECTUAL PROPERTY RIGHTS

4.1 Introduction

The report of the CVCP Working Party on Patents and the Commercial Exploitation of Research Results in 1978 indicated that a survey of universities showed wide divergencies in policy and practice. Some universities explicitly excluded themselves from involvement in patents; some had no formal procedures and had dealt ad hoc with any problems which had arisen; some had detailed regulations including the specification of various scales for the division of revenue between the inventor and the institution; and some, although not having formal regulations, had nevertheless evolved schemes which permitted modest financial support to be provided for a member of staff seeking to take out a patent which was usually reflected in the agreement with the employee governing any revenues accruing from the patent. It also emerged from the replies in 1978 that several universities were currently either formulating a patents policy or reviewing their existing one.

The CVCP Working Party was prompted by a report of the Comptroller and Auditor General who had made the observation to the UGC that there should be an examination of the issues and the aim of introducing greater uniformity into existing arrangements. The other impetus to the work of the Working Party was the enactment of the Patents Act 1977 which, as will be seen, made significant changes to the law relating to ownership of patent rights.

Recent evidence suggests that universities are taking a more structured approach to these questions in response to the significant increase in industrially sponsored research work and other technology transfer activities and that more attention by academic and administrative staff is being paid to legal aspects.

4.2 Vesting of rights

The mechanism by which intellectual property rights are vested will require an analysis of both contracts of employment, which will vary for academic, research and other staff, and various statutes. This may also involve an analysis of fiduciary obligations which employees owe to their employers. It is likely that contracts of many long-serving members of academic staff will be silent on the question of the ownership of intellectual property rights. Some may have incorporated into their contract of employment the Statutes, Ordinances and Regulations of the university as they prevail from time to time and these may contain references to property rights. Where a statute such as the Patents Act 1977 makes provision for the first vesting of patent rights in the employer there may be an express reversal of that provision in a contract of employment held by a member of academic staff. There may also be custom and practice prevailing in the institution which reverses the statutory provision. This may, for example, be on the basis of a declared policy by the university, that it does not intend to hold patent rights as an institution.

4.3 Statutory provision and changes

An extended treatment of the Law of intellectual property is outside the scope of this book. Suggestions for further reading are made at the end of this chapter. The brief descriptions which follow reflect the law as at 31 July 1988. However, in November 1988 Parliament enacted the Copyright Designs and Patents Act 1988[10] which reformed and restated the law of copyright, provided a new regime for the protection of original designs and made a number of changes to the administration of the patent law system. Within the reforms of copyright, provision was made for two significant changes which may have particular significance for universities. One is the possibility for ascribing authorship in cases of so-called "computer-generated" works, which is believed to be the first copyright legislation anywhere in the world attempting to deal with the advent of artificial intelligence. The other change relates to the introduction of the moral rights of copyright owners whereby an author has the right to claim authorship of his work (the "paternity right") and to object to derogatory treatment of the work which is prejudicial to his honour or reputation (the "integrity right").

Employed authors do not enjoy the "paternity right" and their "integrity right" is limited. Academic staff enjoying the benefit of a university Statute or Ordinance which reverses the statutory presumption that work produced in the course of employment vests in the employer will presumably be exceptions to the new rule that employed authors do not enjoy the "paternity" right.

4.4 The Patents Act 1977

A short description of the position under the Patents Act 1977 is contained in the CVCP Working Party Report of 1978. Briefly, to be patentable an invention has to satisfy three criteria:

it has to be novel, that is, there must be no prior art:

it must not be obvious, that is, there must be an inventive step which is not obvious to a person skilled in the art concerned:

it must be capable of industrial application.

Many inventions and discoveries are not capable of being patented by reason of policy decisions. Such exclusions cover a discovery, scientific theory or mathematical method, an aesthetic creation, a scheme, rule or method for performing a mental act or a program as such for a computer. Computer programs which drive equipment, however, may be included under patentability. In addition to these exclusions the old objections to patents for methods for human or animal treatment are continued. Apart from microbiological processes and products thereof patents cannot be secured for any variety of animal or plant or essentially biological processes or their production.

Prima facie, ownership of a patentable invention is vested in the inventor and it is he (or his assignee or other successor in title) who may be granted a patent. However, where the invention is made by an employee in the course of his employment, first ownership may instead be vested in the employer. Prior to the 1977 Act the legal position largely depended upon general principles of common law of master and servant. However, in relation to inventions made after 1 June 1978 the Act codifies the old law and introduces important qualifications. S.39 of the Act states:

i) Notwithstanding anything in any rule of law, an invention made by an employee shall, as between him and his employer, be taken to belong to his employer for the purposes of this Act and all other purposes if

(a) it was made in the course of the normal duties of the employee or in the course of duties falling outside his normal duties, but specifically assigned to him, and the circumstances in either case were such that an invention might reasonably be expected to result from the carrying out of his duties; or

(b) the invention was made in the course of the duties of the employee and, at the time of making the invention, because of the nature of his duties and the particular responsibilities arising from the nature of his duties he had a special obligation to further the interests of the employer's undertaking.

(ii) Any other invention made by an employee shall, as between him and his employer, be taken for those purposes to belong to the employee.

Obviously of importance is the construction of the terms "in the course of normal duties" of the employee and "in the course of duties falling outside his normal duties but specifically assigned to him". The CVCP Report in 1978 gave the example of a Professor of Classics who happens to be an amateur radio enthusiast and who makes an invention. He will in law be the owner of it, notwithstanding that he may have made use of the university's laboratories and other facilities. This is not to say, however, that if the Professor makes a profit from the exploitation of his invention he does not have a duty to account to the university for reimbursement of the cost of facilities provided by the university or even a share of the profits of exploitation. The CVCP Report also warned against the assumption that every invention made by a teacher in the fields of science and engineering will necessarily belong to the university. A Professor of Theoretical Physics who invents an electronic device might argue successfully that it was not made in the course of his normal duties and that no invention could reasonably have been expected to result from the carrying out of his duties. In other cases the university might plausibly argue that any Professor has particular responsibilities and a special obligation to further the interests of the university.

However, for a number of categories of university staff the position will be relatively straight forward. If a member of staff has a duty as a lecturer to carry out research then, notwithstanding that the university has not defined the areas of his research, the university can argue that inventions might reasonably be expected to result from the carrying out of the duties and hence the ownership of the invention vests in the university. Unfortunately, a number of organisations involved in technology transfer have raised doubts about the title of universities to patentable inventions. It is suggested here that in order to resolve the position and for avoidance of doubt the university should have a formal agreement with members of staff, either collectively or individually, so as to govern their relationship in the matter of ownership, rights to exploitation, income, etc. This subject is, of course, now considerably more important for many universities in view of the ending in 1985 of the NRDC monopoly on Research Council funded work.

4.5 The Copyright Act 1956

As mentioned above the Copyright, Designs and Patents Act 1988 has reformed and restated the law to take account of technological changes in the last thirty years. However, it is likely that much case-law dealing with interpretation of the 1956 and earlier Acts will survive. Copyright is essentially different from other kinds of intellectual property in that it is a collection of separate legal rights protecting original literary, dramatic, musical and artistic works, published editions of such works, sound recordings, films (including video films) and broadcasts of all kinds. Computer programmes are now protected as literary works. There are no registration formalities and thus the owner bears the responsibility of proving the date of creation. This can be done in several simple ways, for example by registering a computer code listing with a responsible independent organisation. While not a complete monopoly in the manner of a patent, copyright gives legal rights for the control of the exploitation of work. Copyright is a property right which means it can be exploited, used, bought, sold, given away and assigned or bequeathed.

A major difference compared to a patent is in the term of copyright which can extend to the life of the author plus fifty years for literary, dramatic, musical and artistic works. The material need have no novelty or aesthetic or cultural value. It needs to be the result of independent intellectual effort.

Copyright is of great value in protecting industrial articles if they are recognisably derived from a drawing - an artistic work. Articles with distinct "eye-appeal" independent of function can attract under protection by registration under the Registered Designs Act 1949.[24] The 1988 Act has created a new design right to apply to original, non-commonplace designs of the shape or configuration of articles other than of articles which are artistic works.

It is likely that existing case-law defining questions relating to ownership of copyright will survive and be applied to the new Act. As mentioned earlier work made in the course of employment will normally belong to the employer. This is taken to mean work made in the course of the author's employment by another person under a contract of service or apprenticeship. Under the Act the copyright vests immediately in the employer as soon as the work is made and it never belongs to the employee. The law distinguishes between a contract of service and a contract for services, between an employee and an independent contractor. The distinction can often be difficult to draw. The modern test is whether the person performing services is in business on his own account.[25] If the answer is yes, then the contract is for services. If no, the contract is a contract of service.

It is often the case that a team of academic and non-academic staff, students and outside independent contractors are all engaged in the production of a report, book or software. Sorting out the ownership of valuable property is a matter best dealt with at an early stage, especially if it flows from a research contract to the university.

The fact that an employee is under a contract of service does not automatically vest all copyright in his work in his employer since the Act requires the work to be produced in the course of employment.[9] Employees may carry out work beyond their contract. For example, a biochemist employed as a research officer may produce computer software to organise and analyse his work because he has acquired the requisite expertise but this need not be a requirement of the job or be mentioned in his contract or job description. Such work may therefore be produced as an incidental matter, a bonus to his employer in some senses but not necessarily be the property of the employer even if the employer's resources have been needed to create it. The authority for this observation is drawn from the case of Stephenson, Jordan and Harrison Ltd v Macdonald and Evans.[26]

As mentioned earlier,[27] the statutory presumption is often reversed by university Statute or Ordinance in order to protect the academic freedom of university staff. Thus, first ownership of work produced in the course of employment in that situation will vest in the member of staff. However, it may be argued that it is the legal title which is vested in the employee and that the beneficial ownership may lie with the employer or with the employer and employee jointly if significant resources and materials belonging to the employer have been used to create the work. Alternatively, it could be argued that the legal and the beneficial ownership vests in the employee but that the employer has an entitlement to recover a fair share of the proceeds of exploitation which could be enforced by the Courts under an order to account.

5. UNIVERSITY COMPANIES AND JOINT VENTURES

5.1 Introduction

Since the 1970s there has been a large increase in the number of new high technology companies being formed in the United Kingdom. This phenomenon is well described as a specialised aspect of the literature in business policy. High tech companies associated with universities are attracting increasing attention such as in the report by Julian Lowe for the CVCP on University Companies and Science Parks.[28] There is increasing encouragement from

Government and from the financial community to scientists and engineers to form their own businesses. Specialist knowledge, technical skills, even pure intellect, can all provide a highly priced commodity for which there may be a strong commercial market. Starting a business from the shelter of a university research department can be very attractive and, in the formative stages of a company, can save a great deal of risk capital. Setting up any new business takes a great deal of time to evaluate the options, draw up a business plan and discuss it with co-founders, advisers and financiers. University departments may provide an environment in which this preparatory work can take place easily. In the Lowe report, a distinction was drawn between the type of university company primarily concerned with industrial liaison, and the "soft" or "hard" companies established to exploit a particular set of skills or products emerging from University departments.

5.2 The options

The choices for routes to exploit technology and promote technology transfer are many. They can include the following:

(a) University in-house research and development contracts for sponsorship and licensing

(b) Technology management agreements with, for example the British Technology Group or Research Corporation Limited, etc

(c) Direct outward licensing of technology

(d) Joint ventures

(e) University-owned companies

(f) Promotion through research/science/technology/business parks

(g) Creation of spin-off companies by academic staff, in which the university may have limited interest.

5.3 Reasons for Formation of "University Companies"

A survey by University Finance Officers in 1985 revealed nine main reasons for forming the university company. These were:

1. The need for limited liability to protect the university's assets.

2. Better and faster commercial decision-making.

3. Better images for dealing with outside bodies.

4. Proper payment for university facilities.

5. Ability to attract venture capital.

6. Facilitation of extra payments to academic staff.

7. Eligibility for Government (and EC) grants and contracts.

8. Better overheads on Government and EC contracts.

9. Less conflict with the university's charitable status.

To which might be added:

10. Long-term benefits of capitalising on investment by selling shares in the company.

11. Avoidance of product/design liability actions against the university by third party licensees or assignees.

12. Introduction of industrial and commercial partners into academic environments with opportunities for further university/industry interaction.

5.4 Formation of a limited liability company

This is very straightforward and can be accomplished on a "do it yourself" basis for about £100. There are a large number of company formation firms from which a company can be bought "off the shelf" and its Memorandum and Articles of Association amended for the purposes of any particular business or venture at a cost of about £300. The formation or acquisition of a company can be initiated either by the university through its Council, or by individual members of the university acting with the consent and approval of the university.

There are many excellent short summaries of company law to which reference should be made. The essentials of a limited company formed for trading purposes are:

(a) That it is a legal personality separate from those who have formed it.

(b) That its liability in law is limited to a sum of money which is stated either in the Memorandum and Articles of Association or in a contract between the company and its members.

(c) The company will have an existence independent of its founders and can survive them.

5.5 Liability Limited by Guarantee or by Shares

The principal alternatives are a company limited by guarantee or a company limited by shares.

A company limited by guarantee is the traditional form for research institutes, learned societies and the general type of industrial liaison company formed by universities during the 1970s. The liability of the members of the company, whether the university and/or individual members, is limited to a sum of money often described as a subscription, which they bind themselves to pay in the event of the company going into receivership or otherwise finding itself unable to meet its financial obligations. The subscription may be collected on an annual basis and deployed on servicing the membership with information about the company. Otherwise, it is not collected unless the company in liquidation or in receivership makes a call upon the members to pay the agreed sum. It will be readily appreciated that whilst this limitation of liability has advantages, its major disadvantage is that the company may have no capital base which might be used to expand its activities.

A company limited by shares is the more usual form for a company engaged in trading. The capital of the company is authorised in its Memorandum and the way in which the shares are allotted is described in the Articles of Association. The share capital of a company can be increased and varied as to classes, rights between classes, etc, by a special resolution of the members of the company in general meeting. Traditionally, a start-up company will have either a hundred or a thousand shares with a nominal value of 10p. (The capital duty payable on the formation of a company was abolished in the Finance Act 1988.[29]) When trading operations commence and it is necessary to raise finance, the share capital may be increased significantly. Shareholders may either pay up all of their shares by cash injection into the company, or can agree, within the resolution authorised in the share capital, to do so in stages. To the extent that the shares of each shareholder are not fully paid up, the directors of the company usually have a general power to make calls on sums outstanding. In the final analysis, a company in receivership or in liquidation will call upon the shareholders to pay up the outstanding sums to the limit of the nominal value of their shares. Thus, a shareholder with, say, 1,000 shares at £1 each has his liability limited to £1,000, even if the company crashes owing millions of pounds.

5.6 The doctrine of notice

The principle of limited liability is supported by the doctrine of notice. The Memorandum and Articles of a company, together with details of its accounts and legal charges made on the company, are open to public inspection at the office of the Registrar of Companies by those lending further monies to the company or trading with such company or extending credit to it. To the extent that a company has a large share capital with a significant amount not paid up, there is provided, in theory, for a creditor a reserve of cash upon which to draw in the event of the company getting into financial difficulties. A problem for the potential trader or creditor is knowing the state of a company's accounts at any point in time. Accordingly, in small start-up companies the founder members or shareholders often are required to give separate guarantees as collateral for loans or the performance of specific obligations by the company. This may be the case if even the university is the main or sole shareholder.

As noted above, one of the reasons for company formation in universities lies in the attraction of limited liability. Since a chartered corporation has unlimited liability, it exposes itself to considerable financial risk if it engages in trading operations which result in financial loss to itself or third parties, who then sue the university for damages. Whilst the university may be able to insure against certain risks, such as in the field of professional negligence, there are limitations to such cover and in the final analysis the assets of the university are put at risk.

5.7 "Lifting the veil" of incorporation

However, it should not be assumed that separate legal personality and limited liability provide total protection for a university which has formed a company. The Courts have developed a doctrine known as "lifting the veil of incorporation". An authoritative statement of this doctrine is contained in L.C.B. Gower's "Company Law".[30] This describes the circumstances in which the form of a company can be cast aside to reveal the substance, behind the veil of incorporation, of directors or shareholders manipulating the company in order to avoid responsibilities to third parties. Even where a university has given additional guarantees to third parties, if these are insufficient to meet the losses suffered, then the university might find itself being sued jointly with the company under this doctrine. If the share capital of the company is not mainly owned by the university but is shared amongst a number of investors, then it may prove extremely difficult to lift the veil of incorporation unless there is evidence of conspiracy. Theoretically, therefore, there are no particular reasons why a company formed by a university and other parties should enjoy any less privileges than a company formed by other organisations.

5.8 Liabilities of directors and "shadow" directors

Recent years have seen increasingly complex legislation in the field of company law following upon fiscal requirements of the Government and Directives of the European Economic Community on the harmonisation of company law in preparation for the EC's "single market" policy. Whilst major responsibilities fall on directors of companies, similar responsibilities and obligations can fall on those in accordance with whose wishes the company is required to act. This may mean, for example, that if a university has formed a company and is its main shareholder, then its Council may be held responsible as a "shadow director" for actions following from advice or direction given by it to the directors. There may be circumstances in which individual officers or members of the university Council may become personally liable in respect of the affairs of the company, even if they are not themselves appointed as directors.

There are many excellent studies in company law which set out the responsibilities, obligations and liabilities of company directors. In short, company directors are responsible, under the Articles of Association of the company, for the general management and administration of the company between general meetings.

The potential liabilities of directors have always been considerable as they occupy personal offices of trust. They have to take into account their responsibilities to the company itself, its shareholders, its employees, the general public, its clients and its creditors. Recent years have witnessed increasing legislative controls on directors in an effort to protect shareholders and creditors from malpractices. Some provisions also affect the director acting innocently if incompetently. Exposure to personal liability can arise in many ways - negligent advice or mis-statement, unauthorised payments or borrowing, failure to disclose conflicts of interest in contracts with the company or with clients of the company, trading after the company is technically insolvent, false or negligent accounting, imprudent investments in other companies, insufficient care in the appointment or supervision of delegates and agents, vicarious liability for tortious or illegal acts of the company carried out by subordinates and failure to supervise the general affairs of the company by not insisting on proper procedures.

Under the Insolvency Act 1986[31] directors may be held personally liable for the company's debts if it goes into insolvent liquidation and the court hold that they knew, or ought reasonably to have known, that there was no reasonable prospect of avoiding that situation. Before 1986 there had to be proof of fraud by the directors. Note that now there is an objective test of a reasonable belief which will be assessed by a Court in possession of the subsequent facts which the directors did not possess about, for example, the state of the market. If the directors decide to take a risk by accepting an order, for example, at a low price to keep the company afloat in the hope of keeping up cash flow to finance more profitable later transactions, then they will be judged by reference to what a reasonable board would have done at that time. Directors may well be tempted to put the company into liquidation at an earlier stage rather than go on and incur personal liability which will affect them financially, expose them to criminal sanctions and destroy their capacity to act as directors of other companies. The Company Directors Disqualification Act 1986[32] provides for the disqualification of a director where it can be demonstrated that conduct as a director of an insolvent company shows him to be unfit to occupy such an office. This scrutiny can be extended to any director holding in the three years before insolvency by means of a report by the liquidator of the company to the Secretary of State for Trade and Industry.

5.9 Indemnity and insurance

Limited protection is available to directors. The Articles of Association of the company may contain an obligation for the company to indemnify the directors for loss provided that they have attracted no civil or criminal liability as a result of their actions as directors. However, this assumes that the company has assets available to honour the indemnity. Even if the court holds a director to be at fault and thus debarred from the company's indemnity, the court may grant relief under section 727 of the Companies Act 1985[33] and make the company liable for the director's legal expenses.

To reduce the uncertainty of such situations for both directors and the company, it is possible for the company to take out insurance cover which will indemnify directors against damages awarded by the court or against out-of-court settlements and against the legal expenses of directors in defending civil and criminal actions and in representation at official enquiries. Cover can also protect the company if it has to honour its promise to give an indemnity under the Articles of Association. Usually, insurance cover operates for the whole of a board of directors and for senior offices such as the company secretary. This will be especially valuable to non-executive directors who will not normally be in touch with the day-to-day detail of the work of the full-time directors. Cover will not, of course, benefit the director who has acted dishonestly fraudulently or maliciously and neither is it usually available where directors initiate court proceeding against each other.

There is some uncertainty as to the effect of s.310 of the Companies Act 1985 on indemnity policies where the company pays the full premium. Accordingly, it should be agreed with the insurers that they will not invoke s.310 to avoid their obligations under the policy. No guidance can be offered in this work on the cost of such policies as circumstances of companies will vary enormously and insurance market conditions can change rapidly.

It is unlikely in the absence of an express term in a contract of employment that a university could oblige a member of its staff to become a director or officer or employee of a company established by the university. This would have to be based in a separate contract between the university or the company and the member of staff concerned.

5.10 Relationship between the Company and the University

As indicated above, both the university and a company formed by it alone or in association with others have separate legal personalities. In the case of the early university companies, there was usually no formal contractual relationship between them beyond a covenant to pay profits to the university. Usually, there is a deed of covenant subsisting under which the net trading profits of the company are covenanted to the university, enabling the university to recover any tax paid by the company. In practice, an agency and principal relationship may have emerged for the purposes of the promotion of the university's expertise to the commercial and industrial worlds. A typical reason for incorporating such a company would be the exploitation of the spare intellectual and physical facilities of the university by way of consultancy, research and development and training activities commissioned by outside organisations. Either the university company would act as agent with power to make a contract on behalf of its principal with a third party, or it would introduce the third party to the university which would then make a separate contract with the third party. On another analysis, the university company would contract directly with the third party for the provision of certain services and would then enter into a sub-contract with the university to meet those obligations. There may or may not be a standard sub-contracting arrangement established between the university company and the university in these matters.

There is always a danger that the identities of the university and of its creature company might appear to be almost merged. Certainly, in a number of difficult situations which have been faced at some universities, the untangling of these issues has been extremely difficult and complex. It is outside the scope of this work to analyse the reasons for the failure of university companies, but it is suggested that a major source of confusion has been the lack of a clear statement of principles at the initial stages of the company's operations. It is further suggested that the formation of university companies in which non-university organisations have a major interest will invariably see a much greater attempt at clarification of the relationship between the company and the university, in order to protect the investment of other parties. Whether or not third party investors are involved, it is surely wise to have clear statements or codes of practice for managing the relationship between a university company, which may be housed within a university department, and the university itself. Where academic members of staff are also directors of companies, they have a duty to the university to ensure that their managerial responsibilities for managing university resources are not compromised because of their activities as directors of the company. In this regard, it is particularly important that any contract for sub-contracting or for access to accommodation and equipment should be fully documented and costed at arm's length, so that there is full disclosure between the company and the university of their respective rights and obligations. At the root of many high tech companies' problems will lie questions on the ownership of intellectual property.

6. VALUE ADDED TAX

6.1 Introduction

Detailed guidelines on the interpretation of the law concerning VAT in the university context are set out in a CVCP circular[34]: the guidance was agreed jointly with HM Customs and Excise.

6.2 Trading activities in universities

The main features of VAT, however, should be known and understood by those responsible for any form of trading activity taking place in the university. VAT is a broadly based tax on general consumer expenditure and is charged upon most supplies made in the course of business by taxable persons, unless specific exemptions have been agreed by HM Customs and Excise. The basic feature of the tax is that a taxable person must charge tax at the standard rate of 15% on his supplies unless they are the subject of specific reliefs contained in the law. The law is mainly set out in the Value Added Tax Act 1983.[35] This provides for two main forms of relief - zero rating under Schedule 5 and exemption under Schedule 6. The difference is that zero rating allows tax to be recovered on purchases whereas exemption does not. The major exemption affecting universities relates to supplies of education and research. It should be noted that grants and donations which are freely given without conditions and which do not confer any unique benefit on the recipient are not the consideration for a supply and are therefore not taxable.

Supplies of education and research provided by universities are exempted under item 1 of Group 6 of Schedule 6. The CVCP guidelines reproduce this in full. The exemption applies only to a university, college, institution, school or hall of a university in the United Kingdom. It does not cover supplies of university staff acting independently, even though the accounting arrangements may be handled by the university, nor of companies or consortia set up by universities. These may, however, qualify for exemption if the provision of education or research is of the kind provided by a school or university or training or retraining for any trade, profession or employment otherwise than for profit.

The exemption for supplies of education by universities applies not only to full-time students but to all supplies of education such as extramural courses and individual courses. Tax should be charged on any "English as a foreign language" course provided for a profit, that is, for which fees are designed to cover more than the full overhead inclusive costs. These should be identified at the budgeting stage when fee levels are determined. In some cases, courses are budgeted to break even or to make a loss, but because of a successful take up or a reduction in costs they eventually make a profit. Such courses remain exempt because the crucial test is one of intention which can only be decided by when the courses begin. Where an educational charity budgets for and achieves a surplus of income over expenditure for the purpose of applying all of the surplus for educational charitable purposes, the charity is not registerable for VAT.[36]

6.3 Holiday courses and conferences

Holiday courses for sporting and recreational activities are taxable. In the case of conferences organised solely by universities, supplies of lectures, talks, etc. are exempt as supplies of education and so are supplies of accommodation, catering and other facilities to those attending the conference as supplies incidental to the supply of education. A conference organised jointly between a university and another body will similarly be exempt from VAT, provided its subject matter falls into the general pattern of university teaching and research or the administration of education and it is both managed and administered financially within the university. If, however, the educational content supplied by members of the university is small in proportion to the whole of the event, the university will be deemed to be making a mixed supply of exempt and standard rated items and the charge must be apportioned accordingly. It may be easier in practice to standard rate the whole supply.

6.4 Research

University supplies of research are exempted under Group 6 item 1 of Schedule 6. Supplies by other bodies, such as companies set up by universities are also exempt, but only if they are of a kind provided by a university and they are made otherwise than for profit. That is, the fees or charges are designed to cover only the full inclusive costs. For exemption, research must have the same meaning as that used in a letter from the Chairman of the UGC to the CVCP in May 1985, and now accepted by HM Customs and Excise, namely:

> "Research for the purposes of this exercise is to be understood as original investigation undertaken in order to gain knowledge and understanding. It includes the use of existing knowledge in experiemental development to produce new or substantially improved materials, devices, products and processes including design and construction. It excludes routine testing and analysis of materials, components and processes, e.g. for the maintenance of national standards - as distinct from the development of new analytical techniques. In the humanities it includes scholarship which leads to a new or substantially improved understanding."

Where the supply of research does not meet the above definition it is chargeable to VAT.

This exemption from VAT means that tax suffered on purchases of supplies or materials which are necessary to enable a university itself to supply research or education cannot be recovered. Accordingly, it is of vital importance that quotations and estimates given to third parties for supplies of education and research should indicate that they are made exclusive of VAT if applicable. Thus, in cases of doubt which are resolved against the university and where VAT is imposed by an officer of HM Customs and Excise or by a VAT tribunal, the university will be able to add the VAT to the invoice to the customer or recover it later. If this caveat is not entered before the contract for supply is made then, in the event that VAT is chargeable, the university will have to make over the tax out of the receipts, thereby suffering a loss of some 15%.

Where recipients of university supplies of education or research are themselves taxable persons then this caveat, if brought into effect, will not be detrimental to that taxable recipient because output tax will be set off against input tax.

Conversely where a university is trading in supplies which are not exempt under legislation or under guidelines jointly agreed between the CVCP and HM Customs and Excise then it will need to make sure that its VAT records are kept as accurately and comprehensively as those of a commercial trader.

Although in general, universities will not be able to recover VAT on goods purchased for the purposes of research there is a limited relief for goods used for certain medical research which is fully explained in the VAT leaflet "Donated Medical and Scientific Equipment". As universities are charities, their own funding is regarded as charitable and they can purchase eligible equipment at the zero rate of VAT when it is used solely for the purposes of medical research or medical treatment. This area of law is subject to piecemeal amendment and revision from year to year and thus enquiries should be made to the VAT office on any occasion where doubt is likely to arise.

6.5 Other University supplies

The CVCP guidance also deals with other university supplies such as the provision of catering to those to whom it provides exempt education, supplies of accommodation to non-university members during vacations and supplies of accommodation to staff, visiting students and other visitors. The guidance also deals with the letting of halls with or without bedded accommodation, car parking, letting of sporting facilities to outside organisations and individuals, catering, the sales of confectionery, vending machines, supplies by bookshops and libraries, photocopying services, self-supply of stationery, language tapes, pay-phones, consultancy, computer services and granting of rights (all of which are taxable unless the supply is made to a person outside the jurisdiction), part-exchange transactions, supplies to students' unions, university clubs, veterinary, architectural and other supplies (which are now chargeable to VAT). If, however, a university asks for donations for veterinary services those donations would not be subject to tax. Further guidance is awaited from HM Customs and Excise and CVCP in relation to inter-university supplies, supplies consortia and joint ventures of universities.

7. INCOME AND CORPORATION TAXES

7.1 Exemption of tax for charities

S.505 Income and Corporation Taxes Act 1988[37] provides that there may be exemption of tax under Schedule D in respect of the profits of any trade carried on by a charity, if the profits are applied solely to the purposes of the charity and either (i) the trade is exercised in the course of the actual carrying out of a mainly primary purpose of the charity or (ii) the work in connection with the trade is carried out by beneficiaries of the charity. This continues the exemption formerly provided in s.360 of the Income and Corporation Taxes Act 1970.[38] It will be seen that the trade must relate to a primary purpose of the charity. Therefore, the provision of education and research as primary objects of the university will fall within this category provided the profits are ploughed back into the purposes of the charity. Given the traditional difficulty of achieving a full economic recovery of all the costs associated with research projects and given the availability of significant allowances which could potentially be set against tax liability in respect of capital purchases, it is not likely that profits arising from a research and development contract would lead to a significant tax liability even if it fell outside the exemption provided by s.505 of the 1988 Act. However, should trading activities of a university fall to be taxed because they do not qualify under the exempting provision then consideration might usefully be given to transferring the activities to a separate company. Provided that this was so arranged that no losses would fall on the university from trading operations then the company could covenant to pay its net profit each year to the university. The university would be exempt from tax under other provisions with s.505.

7.2 Scientific Research Organisation (SRO) status

There is a special provision in s.508 Income and Corporation Taxes Act 1988 which provides for essentially the same benefits in fiscal privileges for certain companies as are enjoyed by charities. The organisation must be established to undertake scientific research which may lead to or facilitate an extension of any class or classes of trade and must be approved by the Secretary of State. The Memorandum of Association or other similar instrument regulating the functions of the body must preclude the direct or indirect payment or transfer to any of its members of any of its income or property by way of dividend, gift, division, bonus or otherwise howsoever by way of profit. The Board of Inland Revenue may allow in the case of the association such exemption from tax as falls to be allowed under s.505 in the case of a charity, the whole income of which is applied to charitable purposes.

A company established by a university to carry out trading operations by way of research consultancy, etc. may often be limited by guarantee rather than by share issue and may sometimes seek charitable status. The scheme provided by s.508 is a valuable alternative which does not involve prolonged negotiation as has been known to occur in the case of applications to the Charity Commissioners. Scientific research under s.508 means any activities in the field of natural or applied science for the extension of knowledge. The SRO status can be given up at any time on report to the Secretary of State.

The condition in s.508(1)(b) concerning payments to the members shall under s.508(2) not be deemed to be complied with in the case of any association by reason only that the memorandum or similar instrument regulating its functions does not prevent the payment to its members of reasonable remuneration for goods, labour or power supplied or services rendered, of reasonable interest for money lent or of reasonable rent for any premises. Therefore, such a company set up by a university can make reasonable payments for the services of staff or for the provision of premises by the university for the purposes of the company. Unlike a company limited by guarantee which has charitable status or a charitable trust whereby remuneration to members of the Council of Management is not compatible with charitable status, such considerations do not appear to apply to the payment of reasonable sums for services rendered by staff of the university who happen to be directors or officers of the company with SRO status.

Footnotes to Chapter 6

1. Charter of the University of Bath, Article (X)
2. Charter of the University of Bath, Statutes, Section 30
3. 1948 (11 & 12 Geo 6 c.38) to 1985 (c.6)
4. 1972 c.68
5. Memorandum from the CVCP, N/79/40, April 1979
6. For example,see the Charter of the University of Bath, Ordinance 5.3 on the duties of Heads of Groups
7. cf n.3 supra
8. Charter of the University of Bath, Article (5)
9. 4 & 5 Eliz 2 c.74, s.4(4)
10. Copyright, Designs and Patents Act 1988 c.46 ss.77-89 (The Act came into force fully on 1 August 1989)
11. 1982 c.29
12. 1967 c.7
13. 1977 c.37
14. 1979 c.54 s.62(2)
15. Atiyah The Sale of Goods 7th edn, London, Pitman 1985

16. 1977 c.50
17. [1932] AC 562
18. 1987 c.43
19. 9 & 10 Eliz 2 c.40
20. 1978 c.38
21. 1986 c.29
22. 1974 c.37
23. 5 & 6 Eliz 2 c.31
24. 12, 13 & 14 Geo 6 c.88
25. Market Investigations Ltd v Minister of Social Security [1969] 2 QB 173
26. Stephenson, Jordan and Harrison Ltd. v MacDonald and Evans [1952] 69 RPC 10
27. $3.1.3 supra
28. Lowe J, University of Bath 1985
29. 1988 c.39
30. Gower L C B et al Gower's Principles of Modern Company Law 4th edn London, Stevens 1981
31. 1986 c.45
32. 1986 c.46
33. 1985 c.6
34. Circular N/87/14 of February 1987
35. 1983 c.55
36. Bel Concord Educational Trust Ltd v Customs & Excise Commissioners "Times" 9 February 1989 (CA)
37. 1988 c.1

CHAPTER 7

THE UNIVERSITY ESTATE

1. INTRODUCTION

1.1 Coverage of this section

The law relating to land, its ownership and usage in all three jurisdictions in the United Kingdom is extremely complex. There are substantial differences between English and Scots law in this area, although it is argued[1] that Viscount Dunedin's statement in 1935 that

> "there is no more identity between the two systems than there is between chalk and cheese"[2]

may in the 1990s be in need of revision. We will not attempt to cover the general subject in any depth, but concentrate on those areas in which the university administrator is most likely to need practical advice. The detailed discussion will be centred on English law, although we have attempted to draw attention to the major differences between the English and Scots systems. While the statutory basis is different and procedures vary, the practical differences between English and Northern Ireland law are relatively minor.

1.2 The position of universities in the law of land

A chartered institution, as explained earlier, can generally speaking do anything that an ordinary individual can do. Thus in relation to land a chartered university may be landowner, lessor, landlord, lessee or tenant just as a natural person may be and will incur all the rights, liabilities, privileges and duties which apply to a natural person within the applicable jurisdiction.

Universities created by statute can of course do only those acts as are authorised directly or indirectly by the creating statute, but such statutes invariably permit the institution to act in relation to land in the same way as a chartered university. Either type of institution may own land and the buildings erected on it, take leases on buildings, rent buildings to third parties or to members of the university, e.g. students, student unions, shops, banks, etc., or have or be subject to rights of others over the land which they own or lease, for example rights of way, easements and wayleaves for the passage of electricity cables over, or drains under, the ground, and so on.

1.3 Areas of interest to university administrators

Perhaps in the days of expansion it would have been necessary to deal in depth with issues relating to the purchase of land, planning new buildings, roadworks and so on. In the 1990s issues of disposal of property, converting and adapting buildings - subject to statutory planning and building controls - and ensuring that buildings comply with the mass of statutory regulation of use, health and safety and fire precautions are perhaps most significant. These subjects are covered in considerable detail later in this section: again the English system is described in full and major differences in the Scots system are drawn out in $18. No attempt will be made to deal with questions of conveyancing, which the university administrator is most unlikely to have to tackle. This includes such matters as the creation of a legally-binding contract to purchase property, which as the general reader will be aware is different in England and Scotland. The general reader should however have some basic knowledge and the next three paragraphs will provide an introduction.

1.4 The ownership of land in English law[3]

1.4.1 Introduction

The applicable law in England (and Wales, which is treated as England for this purpose) is the law of real property (or realty), based on common law and a number of statutes, principally six Acts of 1925 and one of 1922 which all came into force on 1 January 1926 and which are referred to collectively as the "1925 property legislation". The division of property into real (realty) and personal (personalty) is based on early law. The courts would restore real property (the "res" or thing itself) to a dispossessed owner, but give the dispossessor the choice of either returning personal property or paying the value thereof. Land was realty and could be specifically recovered; swords, gloves (typically) were personalty and were not thus recoverable. Leaseholds (or "terms of years"), which are strictly personalty rather than realty, are nevertheless classified as "chattels real" and the law relating to them is customarily treated along with the law of real property.

1.4.2 Tenure and Estates

The basis of the law of land in England is that all land is owned by the Crown; the majority of it is occupied by tenants holding either directly or indirectly from the Crown. In the modern law, there is only one feudal tenure, that of socage, or freehold, and one non-feudal tenure, leasehold. Discussion here will be confined to the "estate in fee simple absolute in possession", which is what you would understand from the term "freehold residence" used by an estate agent, and the "term of years absolute", commonly called leaseholds. These two estates are the only ones capable of existing at law. Parallel with the legal ownership or tenancy of land there may run a beneficial ownership or tenancy based in equity and the law of trusts, relating to the rights of individuals and not attached to the land. Discussion of these issues is beyond the scope of this work but the reader should appreciate that equitable interests can and do exist, for example restrictive covenants dealt with in the next paragraph.

1.4.3 Charges, Easements, etc.

In addition the law allows interests or charges in or over land to be created, including easements, rights, privileges and charges by way of legal mortgage, equivalent to one of the two permitted estates. An easement is defined as "a right to use, or restrict the use of, the land of another person in some way",[4] for example rights of way, rights of light and rights of water. In each case there is a "dominant" and a "servient" tenement (i.e. parcel of land), the former having the relevant right over the latter. There are also quasi-easements, such as the right to support in certain circumstances, licences, which can only exist in equity, and restrictive covenants, the law of which is an equitable extension of the law of easements. Restrictive covenants are often attached to property on transfer, although the burden of them runs only in equity: no inspection of the land will reveal the existence of a restrictive covenant against burning lime or keeping swine, both common restrictive covenants imposed in the Victorian era. Attention should also be drawn to "profits a prendre", the right to take something from another person's land, e.g. profit of pasture, allowing the grazing of animals; profit of turbary, allowing removal of turf or peat as fuel; profit of estovers, allowing removal of wood for building or fuel; profit of piscary, the right to catch and take away fish. Subject to all these restrictions and the rights of others, if any, over the land, the owner who is seised - from "seisin" - the symbolic transfer of a twig or clot of earth - of an estate in fee simple absolute in possession can do whatever s/he likes with the land which is otherwise consistent with the general law. The most significant right of the normal householder is to mortgage the land and its buildings in order to raise funds to acquire it.

1.4.4 Leases

The usual type of lease is the occupational lease, where the tenant holds at a rent and either occupies it or sub-lets it. A lease is a document creating a legal interest in land for a fixed period of certain duration: it should be distinguished from a licence to occupy premises, which is an equitable arrangement. The grantor of the lease is the lessor (or landlord) and the person to whom it is granted is the lessee (or tenant). There may be considerable formality about the creation of a legal lease for other than a short period; the complexities of conveyancing are beyond the scope of this work. Rent Acts provide for security of tenure of tenants, and the control or regulation of rents, but educational tenancies are excepted from protection, in common with holiday homes, public houses, etc. by an amendment to the Rent Act 1971[5] in 1974.[6] The position is now governed by Schedule 1 Part I of the Housing Act 1988[7]: if the landlord (the university) wishes to terminate the tenancy for breach of conditions, and can establish its right to possession at common law, the Court has no discretion but to grant possession.[8]

1.4.5 Registration

The 1925 property legislation introduced a system of registration of title which has gradually been introduced into England and Wales. The Land Register is not open to inspection by the public although certain indexes are. There is a separate system of registration of incumbrances, the two types of register being the central Land Charges Register and the various Local Land Charges Registries maintained by local authorities. The central Register is essentially a register of private rights whereas the local Registers deal with public rights such as planning, making-up of private roads, etc. The central Land Charges Register is of decreasing importance as more land is the subject of registration of title, but the local Registers often contain critically important information and it is essentially that these should be "searched" before any binding contract to purchase a property is entered into.

1.5 The ownership of land in Scots law[9]

1.5.1 Introduction

Scots law shares with English law the basic theory of the universal derivative tenure of all land from the Crown (except in the udal landholding of Orkney and Shetland): land with its pertinents is the typical instance of heritable (or immovable) property. Buildings are counted as part of the ground and rights connected with land, such as leases and servitudes, are heritable. The feudal relationships of superior and vassal still exist although major changes in conveyancing law since 1971 have meant that increasingly the relationships are of practical significance only where conditions of a feu charter control the use and future development of land.[10] Sasine, like seisin in English law, was the symbolic transfer of heritage by delivery, e.g. handing over earth as the symbol for transfer of land. The owner of land can use his land for any purpose which is not inconsistent with the common law, statute law, conditions of his title or rights which may have been created in favour of third parties.

1.5.2 Registration

The system of registration of title to heritage by registration of writs in the Register of Sasines, a register open to public inspection, is a long-standing feature of Scots conveyancing. The person who appears in the Register as the owner of the land is said to be infeft, infeftment depending on the registration of the deed transferring the land. A person owning security over land acquires his charge over the land by registering the appropriate deed: the current form of security over land is the standard security which has replaced earlier, more complex arrangements. Land Registration in the English sense is a relatively recent appearance in Scotland and so far confined largely to the Glasgow area, although there are plans to computerise the system.

1.5.3 Servitudes

In Scots law the land may be subject to the burden of servitudes, such as rights of way, rights of support, stillicide (the right to discharge rainfall), and light or prospect. The average university administrator is unlikely to come across the servitude of fuel, feal and divot which corresponds to turbary in English law. However it is possible that in an urban situation a projected development may disturb the rights of other owners to, for example, support or light and in some scientific subjects the right of aquaehaustus, to take water from a well or stream, may be of significance. The general rule that burdens on heritage do not affect singular successors unless they appear in the Register of Sasines does not apply and there is considerable case law relating to the creation of servitudes which is beyond the scope of this work.

1.5.4 Leases

Leases in Scots law are created by contract whereby "certain uses, or the entire possession and control of lands, houses or other heritable subjects are given to the tenant for a return, known as rent or lordship, in money or goods".[11] Certain long leases may be recorded in the Register of Sasines, and there is a statutory limitation upon the residential use of property let under long leases. The position in relation to the Rent Acts is the same as in England and Wales.[12]

1.6 Recovery of possession

1.6.1 England and Wales

The one area of the law of land and procedural matters relating to its ownership and possession in which most university adminstrators, certainly in the decade from 1968 onwards, were likely to come into contact was recovery of possession following a student sit-in or similar disruption. In England and Wales a number of universities have from time to time taken steps in the courts to restrain students from disruptive activity or to regain possession of buildings unlawfully occupied.[13] Where repossession of premises unlawfully occupied is sought, the university may proceed under RSC Order 113 by application to a judge of the High Court. This is again a highly technical matter, the law being arguably unsuited to such cases, which now almost invariably result in substantial costs being levied on student unions. Procedure requires the service of summonses which delay recovery of the property and this can have a serious effect on the operation of a university. Any administrator facing such a situation must immediately consult a solicitor who is familiar with High Court procedures and take steps to ensure that careful accounts are kept of any time and other resources spent or irrecoverably lost through the action so that those responsible can be properly held to account.

1.6.2 Scotland

In Scotland the procedure is different. An interdict may be granted against named persons where there is actual or explicit threat of trespass, but otherwise procedure should be under the criminal law of trespass.[14] According to CVCP advice of 1974[15] the category of trespassers would include persons who lawfully obtain entry to premises, e.g. to an examination hall or to a hall of residence, but who refuse to leave when the period for which they had express or implied permission to remain expires. The civil action of summary ejection is unsuited to most disruptive activity since

> "the defender's possession..[must be].. violent, fraudulent or forcible, or precarious i.e. at the will of the pursuer, and he can claim no title to the occupation challenged."

and there are inbuilt procedural delays.

2. TOWN AND COUNTRY PLANNING

2.1 Introduction

In England and Wales at common law, a landowner could, prior to 1909, develop his property as he chose, but since that time, local authorities have been given increasing powers to control the use and development of land, beginning with the Housing, Town Planning, etc., Act 1909.[16] The modern system of control was introduced by the Town and Country Planning Act 1947,[17] as amended by the Acts of 1954[18] and 1959,[19] and the Caravan Sites and Control of Development Act 1960.[20] Control is now exercised by means of the Town and Country Planning Act 1971,[21] as amended in 1972, 1977 and 1985, and a number of regulations embracing such subjects as advertisements, fees for applications, listed buildings, local plans, tree preservation orders and conservation areas.

The system of planning control enshrined in the Act has two main elements, both of which fall to the local authority to administer. Firstly, authorities were required to take a strategic look at those areas under their control and draw up structure plans, formulating their development policy, for approval by the Secretary of State. This process also involves the establishing of local plans for specific areas and purposes and enables local authorities to determine, for example, which areas are to be zoned for housing and which for commercial or industrial development. Secondly, the Act requires local authorities to control development on a day-to-day basis, a function which is normally undertaken by a council committee with permanent officials providing advice on whether or not applications are in line with structure and local plans and so on. It is this day-to-day aspect of planning control with which most of those managing the universities' estates will be familiar.

2.2 What constitutes development

The Act defines "development" as

> "the carrying out of building, engineering, mining or other operations in, on, over or under land, or the making of any material change in the use of any buildings or other land".

Maintenance works, improvements or alterations are not classified as development provided that they do not materially affect the external appearance of the building. There are also exemptions for certain work undertaken by local authorities and for land and buildings used for agricultural purposes. Further exemptions for minor development are specified in the Town and

Country Planning General Development Order 1977 as amended, which lists no less than 23 separate classes of this "permitted development".

Before development proceeds, therefore, an application for planning permission is required, and should be submitted, together with the appropriate fee, to the local planning authority. Notices of applications to be considered are normally published in the local newspaper and sent to interested parties, e.g. neighbours, and representations received as a result are taken into account by the authority when determining the application. An authority may grant permission, with or without condition, or refuse the application and give reasons. In the case of the latter, the applicant may appeal within six months to the Secretary of State, who appoints an Inspector to adjudicate. Depending on the particular circumstances, the appeal may be by written representations or public enquiry. The Secretary of State's decision is final.

2.3 Applications for planning permission

Applications may be made for full planning permission or for permission in outline only. In cases where the complete extent of the proposed development is known, the application may be made in detail. However, if the development potential of a piece of land needs to be explored, the application may be made in outline, with all matters of detail being "reserved", i.e. for consideration at a later date. Often land is sold "with the benefit of outline planning permission", a process by which prospective purchasers are aware of the type of development which will be acceptable. In addition, the vendor can be satisfied that the sale price reflects accurately the value of the land and its development potential.

2.4 Developments without planning permission

Where development is undertaken without or contrary to planning permission, the local planning authority may serve an enforcement notice detailing the steps which it deems need to be taken and the timescale in which to take those steps. The notice is quite likely to require that the property or land be returned to its original state (i.e. that which existed prior to the development in question) regardless of the cost and inconvenience involved. The developer may appeal to the Secretary of State against the terms of the notice, and until the appeal is determined the notice is not deemed to take effect. Again, the Secretary of State's decision is final. Non-compliance with an enforcement notice may result in the local authority instigating criminal proceedings against the developer.

2.5 Listing of buildings and conservation areas

The Act also establishes powers for the listing of buildings of special architectural or historic interest. Listed building consent should be sought from the local planning authority before any such building is demolished, altered or extended in any way, and the penalties for ignoring the requirement can be heavy. Listing applies to the whole building, and not just part, but approval to alter a less important aspect will be easier to obtain. Listed building consent (applications for which are free) must also be sought for the demolition of any building, whether listed or not, in a conservation area.

With the approval of the Secretary of State, local planning authorities have the power to determine which parts of their areas, if any, are areas of special architectural or historic interest and designate them as conservation areas. Effectively, the planning authority exercises a higher degree of control over applications for development within conservation areas than outside them. Whereas the existence of a conservation area does not rule out development, consent tends to be more difficult to obtain, and sketch designs are often required in connection with applications for outline planning permission which would not be needed for applications relating to proposed development outside a conservation area.

2.6 Simplification of the planning system

The declared intention of the Secretary of State when issuing and bringing into effect the Town & Country Planning (Use Classes) Order 1987 was to simplify control by making it unnecessary to apply for planning permission for a change of use within the same class. For example, development is not deemed to be taking place when a travel agency is replaced by a hairdresser or a shop selling cold food for consumption off the premises by a post office (all class A1). However, a change from any type of shop to one selling hot food for consumption on or off the premises is development and planning permission is required (change from class A1 to A3). Again, change of use is not involved when a residential school becomes a nursing home (class C2) or a single person or family dwelling is used by up to six persons living as a single household rather than as a family (class C3). However, development is still deemed to be taking place when a single dwelling is converted into two flats and planning permission is required.

3. BUILDING CONTROL

3.1 The Building Act 1984[22]

The four main sections of the Building Act 1984 deal with the Building Regulations, the procedure for supervising building work other than by a local authority, the power of local authorities to require certain improvements to existing buildings and, finally, the duties of local authorities, procedures to be used etc.

Part I empowers the Secretary of State to make Building Regulations, to exempt certain classes of buildings from the regulations, and, in certain cases, to relax the regulations. It further identifies the scope of the regulations, the system for implementing them, the powers and duties of the local authority and the penalties for contravening them.

Part II identifies the procedures for the supervision of building work by an approved inspector rather than by the local authority.

For Part III refer to $5.2 infra.

Part IV details the duties of local authorities, the procedures to be followed, the notices and documents to be used, the methods of serving the notices etc. Local authorities are also given powers to enter a building in order to ascertain whether there is any contravention of the Act or the Building Regulations. Work required by local authorities can be done by them, with the owner's consent, and a charge raised for it. Finally, the procedure is identified whereby building owners may appeal against the terms of a notice served by a local authority.

3.2 Building Regulations

The latest Building Regulations came into force in 1985. They apply to the construction of a new building, an extension or alteration to an existing building, or the change of use of an existing building, and the local authority in whose area the work is to be undertaken should be notified of the proposals. The purpose of the Regulations as laid down in the Act is primarily "to ensure the health and safety of people in or about the building", but they also include provisions for energy conservation and access to buildings for the disabled. (See also $4.1 infra).

In theory, good practice dictates that all work should comply with the Regulations. In effect, however, it is only generally considered necessary for new buildings, extensions and material alterations to do so. Where alterations become "material" can be a matter of interpretation and best resolved by seeking the advice of the local authority.

Once it is established that the Regulations do apply to the proposed work, there are now three procedures which may be followed, with supervision being provided either by the local authority or by an approved inspector. The institution commissioning work will expect the architect or designer, whether a retained professional or employee, to ensure that the project conforms with the Regulations and to arrange appropriate supervision. In the context of the Regulations, supervision relates merely to ensuring that the work complies with them. Further, more detailed on-site supervision will almost certainly be arranged on the client's behalf.

Arguably, the method offering most protection, albeit limited, is to deposit full plans with the local authority together with the prescribed fee. The authority must pass or reject the plans, normally within five weeks, and will then inspect the work at various stages. A second method, also involving local authority supervision, is to issue a Building Notice to the authority, together with the prescribed fee and certain particulars of the work proposed. The authority may request further information or plans, but they are not required to pass or reject them. (This method cannot, however, be used if the Building Regulations relating to means of escape in case of fire apply (B1). In the latter case, plans must be deposited so that the local authority can consult the fire authority.) In both methods work may start on site provided 48 hours notice is given to the local authority, whose inspectors, if they consider that any part of the work contravenes the Regulations, may serve a notice requiring that it be taken down or altered.

The third method involves supervision by an Approved Inspector. The Regulations specify that the Inspector and institution commissioning the work should jointly send the local authority an Initial Notice together with certain plans and evidence of insurance. The Notice must be accepted or rejected within ten working days. Once the Notice has been accepted, the authority's powers to enforce the Regulations are suspended and work may start on site. The fee payable to the Inspector is subject to negotiation, and he/she may require similar notice to that specified by the local authority regarding the commencement of particular stages of the work. The Inspector is also empowered to serve a notice requiring remedial action if the work is considered to contravene the Regulations. When the project is complete, the Inspector will issue a final certificate to the Institution and the local authority.

Schedule 1 of the Regulations contains eleven parts and gives a broad outline of the requirements on such matters as the structure, fire, sound transmission, ventilation, drainage, stairways and fuel conservation. Each of these parts is supported by further more detailed documentation giving practical guidance on ways in which the requirements of the Regulations may be met.

4. FIRE PRECAUTIONS

4.1 Building Regulations

Such is the awareness of the dangers to life from the outbreak of fire that the Regulations contain mandatory rules for means of escape in case of fire, which apply, in broad terms, to a dwellinghouse of three or more storeys, a building of three or more storeys containing a flat or flats, and a building which contains an office or a shop (Schedule 1, paragraph B1). If the building in which the proposed work is to be undertaken falls within the definitions contained in paragraph B1 as well as requiring a certificate under the terms of the Fire Precautions Act 1971,[23] compliance with the Building Regulations is normally sufficient, and the fire authority is unlikely to require further structural or other alterations as a condition to issuing that certificate. (The fire authority can, of course, require the provision of alarms and fire fighting equipment under the terms of the 1971 Act in addition to the means of escape before granting the certificate.)

4.2 Fire Precautions Act 1971

The Act specifies that certain types of building use may require a fire certificate and empowers the Secretary of State to issue Orders in respect of those uses. The scope of the Act is extremely wide and covers sleeping accommodation, institutions providing treatment or care, places of entertainment, recreation or instruction, places used for teaching, training or research and buildings to which the public have access whether by payment or not. However, it also specifically excludes single dwellings and certain houses in multiple occupation, for example. The Act goes on to lay down the procedure for appeals, the method of application for and issue of fire certificates, the duty of the Fire Authority to survey a building and the contents of the fire certificate itself.

If a building is within a category for which a fire certificate is necessary, it is a criminal offence not to have one, punishable by fine or imprisonment. However, recognising the fact that issuing certificates for all buildings which required one would take some time, the Act regards the building owner's application for a certificate as being sufficient to discharge his or her responsibility. The onus then rests with the Fire Authority to detail the steps required to achieve certification.

Building owners are required to notify the Fire Authority if they wish to make material alterations to, extend, or undertake alterations to the internal arrangements of a building for which a certificate has been issued or requested. Failure to do so is a criminal offence. In response to such a notification, the Fire Authority is required to review the current arrangements with regard to fire safety and specify further work if they are no longer considered adequate.

Whereas the local authority is responsible for enforcing the Building Act 1984[22] and Housing Act 1985[24] in respect of means of escape from fire, it is the Fire Authority which alone enforces the Fire Precautions Act. However, the Fire Authority is required by the Act to consult with the local authority when considering applications for fire certificates. (See also $ 4.1 supra.)

Finally, the Act empowers the Secretary of State to make regulations specifying the fire precautions required in premises which it covers.

4.3 Orders under the Fire Precautions Act 1971

Since the Act came into force, two Orders have been issued covering specific building uses for which fire certificates are required. The Fire Precautions (Hotels and Boarding Houses) Order 1972 embraces the term "sleeping accommodation" contained in the Act, and the Fire Precautions (Factories, Offices, Shops and Railway Premises) Order 1989 brings into the scope of the Act building uses previously covered by the Offices, Shops and Railway Premises Act 1963.[25] The existence of a certificate issued under the terms of the latter is considered as being sufficient to satisfy the 1971 Act at least until such time as re-inspection is deemed necessary.

Although many Fire Authorities do not consider that university halls of residence come within the scope of the Act, specifically when occupied by students, several universities have applied for fire certificates to the standard required for hotels and boarding houses in order to use their halls for all types of conferences and for casual lettings, eg holidays.

Academic buildings, whether new or existing, only come within the scope of the Act if they contain offices as defined in the Offices, Shops and Railway Premises Act 1963. Office work is broadly deemed to be administrative or clerical (eg filing) or to involve handling money, and the enabling Order of

1976 restricted the application of the Act to buildings in which office employees exceeded twenty at any one time and in which there were more than ten such employees elsewhere than on the ground floor.

In practice, applications for fire certificates are made on the appropriate form which is available from the Fire Authority. At some point thereafter, the Fire Authority will inspect the building and prepare plans and a scheme for meeting its requirements. It will then issue a notice specifying the action required of the building owner and the timescale for compliance. At the end of that period, or later if an extension has been requested and agreed, the Fire Authority will re-inspect and, if all requirements of the notice have been met, issue a fire certificate.

The purpose of the Act is to protect life, and although some of the measures stipulated in the notice will have the effect of reducing the risk of fire damage to a building, this is incidental. Insurance companies very often require additional measures to protect expensive equipment, such as computer installations for example. Among the aspects covered in the notice will be the protected routes for escape purposes, the parts of the building which need to be of fire resisting construction, the location of fire resisting doors, the detection and alarm system, fire fighting equipment, exit notices, and areas where emergency lighting is needed.

4.4 The Fire Certificate

The fire certificate will take the form of a comprehensive booklet recording the facts that, at the time of inspection, the means of escape specified in the plans attached to the certificate had been provided; that the means specified in the plans existed for securing the use of the means of escape at all times; that the means specified in the plans for fighting fire and the means for giving warning in case of fire had both been provided; and, if applicable, that the location and quantities of explosive or highly flammable material stored or used in the building were as specified in the appendix.

The plans attached to, and forming part of, the certificate will show self closing doors and areas of fire resisting construction and record the provision of exit notices, fire fighting equipment, alarm points and sounders and emergency lighting. The certificate will also include schedules detailing the standards of protection which have been achieved and are to be maintained, the requirements for fire instruction, drills and inspections, the maximum number of persons allowed to use the building at any one time and the responsibilities of the building occupants and owner(s). The Act requires that the certificate be kept on the premises to which it relates, so that it is available for inspection at all times.

Fire Prevention Officers are normally able to offer informal advice on the requirements of the Act, its application and interpretation, and the Home Office and Scottish Home and Health Department have jointly published three guides to the Act, covering in outline the requirements for Hotels and Boarding Houses, Factories, and Offices, Shops and Railway Premises. (HMSO, Guides to the Fire Precautions Act 1971, 1 : Hotels & Boarding Houses; 2 : Factories; 3 : Offices, Shops and Railway Premises.)

5. PUBLIC HEALTH

5.1 The Public Health Act 1936[26]

The Public Health Act 1936 contained many sections of relevance to those managing a university's estate, but the most significant have now been superseded by the Building Act 1984 (regulations for building and means of escape from fire in certain buildings) and the Control of Pollution Act 1974[27] (waste disposal).

However, s.25 still forbids the construction of a building or extension over a public sewer of the type required to be recorded on a map kept by the local authority. S.27 prohibits the discharge into a public sewer, or a drain connected to a public sewer, of any material likely to damage the sewer or interfere with the flow through it, of any chemical refuse, of steam or liquid hotter than 110° F or of petroleum spirit. The penalty for infringement is a fine. S.34 lays down the right of building owners to drain their property into a public sewer. Finally, s.262 enables local authorities to require the culverting of water courses and ditches when building operations are in prospect.

5.2 The Building Act 1984[22]

Part III broadly restates many of the powers given to local authorities by the Public Health Act 1936, the relevant section of which it now replaces. Whereas Parts I & II deal with new buildings and extensions, Part III relates to existing buildings, and gives local authorities wide powers to ensure the safety of building occupants and users. Where local authorities consider that building drainage, sanitary provision or water supply are unsatisfactory, they are empowered to serve a notice requiring the facilities to be improved to an acceptable standard. They are also enabled to instruct that dangerous or defective buildings are repaired, and, if the work is not done, to carry out the repairs, recovering the cost by means of court proceedings if necessary from the building owner. In addition, local authorities may take immediate action in emergency situations.

As in the Public Health Act 1936, local authorities are empowered to serve a notice on a building owner after consultation with the fire authority requiring the provision of satisfactory access and egress which they consider suitable for the purpose for which the building is used and for the number of people likely to resort to it at any one time. They must also be satisfied with the means of escape from fire from each storey of a building whose floor is more than 20 feet above street or ground level (a measurement amended by certain local authority Acts). This applies to buildings exceeding two storeys, the floor of any of which is more than 20 feet above street or ground level (see above), which are (a) let in flats or tenement dwellings, (b) used as an inn, hotel, boarding house, hospital, nursing home, boarding school, children's home or similar institution or (c) used as a restaurant, shop, store or warehouse and have an upper floor/sleeping accommodation for persons employed on the premises.

6. LEGISLATION RELATING TO SPECIFIC USE OF BUILDINGS

6.1 The Offices, Shops and Railway Premises Act 1963[25]

6.1.1 Introduction

A substantial proportion of the Act has now been superseded by subsequent legislation such as the Health & Safety at Work etc Act 1974[28] and the Fire Precautions Act 1971.[23] However, the Act continues to have force in respect of many of the working conditions enjoyed by employees.

6.1.2 Definitions

An office is described as a place where persons are employed under a contract of employment for an aggregate of at least 21 hours per week, and office work as administration, clerical work, handling money and operating telephone or telegraph equipment. Clerical work includes writing, bookkeeping, sorting and filing papers, typing, duplicating and drawing. A shop is a building, or part of a building, where retail or wholesale trading takes place or where goods are brought by the public for repair or treatment, and also solid fuel depots. (Thus the Act would cover shops within university owned buildings or on university owned land whether they were run by a private company, the students' union or the university itself.) A canteen or restaurant which serves office workers is regarded as office accommodation for the purposes of the Act, although other legislation or regulations will also apply, in the areas of hygiene and food preparation for example.

6.1.3 Cleanliness and overcrowding

The Act requires that all premises within its scope should be kept in a clean state, as should all furniture, furnishings and fittings. Accommodation should not be overcrowded, with a minimum of $3.7m^2$ floor space and $11m^2$ breathing space allowed for each person. For calculation purposes, furniture is ignored, and the numerical standards do not apply to a shop because members of the public are admitted. Furniture is, however, taken into account when assessing whether or not accommodation is overcrowded.

6.1.4 Heating, ventilation and lighting

An effective system of heating must be maintained which can deliver a temperature not below 16° Celsius after the first hour of working in areas where the work undertaken does not involve physical effort. The requirement does not apply to rooms to which the public has access nor to shop areas in which it is not reasonably practicable to maintain such a temperature or in which that temperature would cause the deterioration of goods. A thermometer should be displayed on each floor of a building to which the Act applies, and although no maximum temperature is specified, that too should be reasonable. Ventilation of premises should be effective, as should its lighting, whether natural or artificial. Windows should be kept clean and free from obstruction, unless they are shaded for the purposes of reducing heat gain or glare.

6.1.5 Sanitary arrangements

Premises should be provided with sufficient and suitable sanitary conveniences which are conveniently accessible, clean, properly maintained and effectively ventilated and lit. Conveniences do not have to be solely for employees but may be shared so long as they are easily accessible. The Sanitary Conveniences Regulations 1964 lay down certain minimum standards for the number of water closets and urinals to be provided related to the number of employees. They also contain provisions for siting, ventilation, weather protection, privacy, marking for separate sexes and disposal of sanitary dressings. There should also be suitable and sufficient washing facilities, including a supply of clean, running hot and cold or warm water, soap and towels or other methods of cleaning and drying. Such facilities should be kept clean and properly maintained. The Washing Facilities Regulations 1964 lay down certain minimum standards, again related to the number of employees. An adequate supply of wholesome drinking water should be provided and maintained at suitable places conveniently accessible to the persons employed in the premises.

6.1.6 Cloakrooms, seating arrangements, etc.

Suitable places should be provided for persons employed to hang clothing which is not worn during working hours, and there should also be reasonably practicable arrangements to enable clothing to be dried. Similar arrangements should also be made for special work clothes which are not taken home. The security of employees' clothing will be a factor in deciding whether or not accommodation is suitable. Sitting facilities which are conveniently accessible should be provided for persons who, in the course of their work, have reasonable opportunity to sit down without detriment to their work. If work is or can be done sitting down, seats should be provided of suitable design, construction and dimension, including footrests if employees cannot readily and comfortably support their feet. If employees in a shop eat in their place of employment, suitable facilities should be provided.

6.1.7 Floors, stairways etc.

Floors, passages and stairs should be of sound construction, properly maintained, kept free of obstruction and of substances likely to cause persons to slip, so far as is reasonably practicable. Staircases should be provided with at least one handrail, located on the open side if there is one. Staircases with two open sides should have two handrails. All handrails on open sides should be suitably guarded to prevent persons falling through the openings beneath. Openings in floors should be fenced unless the nature of the work renders this impracticable.

6.1.8 Machinery and lifts

Any dangerous parts of machinery used as or forming part of the premises' equipment should be fenced unless its location or construction renders it as safe as if it had been fenced. If a fixed guard cannot be provided, it is permissible to fit a device automatically preventing the operator from coming into contact with any dangerous part. This requirement excludes persons who are examining, lubricating or adjusting parts which can only be examined, lubricated or adjusted while they are in motion. All guards and fencing should be substantial and properly maintained. No person under the age of 18 should be allowed to clean machinery forming part of the premises if they are at risk from any moving parts. Any person working on prescribed machinery should be fully instructed on its dangers and properly trained and supervised. The Offices, Shops and Railway Premises (Hoists and Lifts) Regulations 1968 give a building owner the responsibility for ensuring that all such equipment is of good mechanical construction, sound, of adequate strength and properly maintained. Hoists and lifts should be examined every six months by a competent person who should send a report to the building owner. Lifts should be effectively enclosed with gates fitted with an interlocking device which prevent their being opened other than at a landing and the lift from moving if they are not closed. The maximum load which the equipment can carry should be conspicuously marked, and, if it also carries persons, it should be fitted with automatic devices to prevent over-running.

6.1.9 Enforcement, penalties and standards

Failure to comply with the requirements of the Act is a criminal offence for which the building owner can be fined. Depending upon the nature of the activity carried out in the premises, the responsibility for enforcement will lie either with the local authority or with the Health and Safety Executive. In practice, the majority of offences tend to be dealt with by the Health and Safety Executive under the terms of the Health and Safety at Work etc Act 1974. When enforcing legislation or regulations in which there is no absolute definition of requirements, for example where the words 'reasonable' or 'reasonably practicable' are used, the Inspectors rely upon standards contained in other legislation (eg the Factories Act 1961[29]), regulations, British Standards or recommendations of professional bodies (eg the Institute of Electrical Engineers).

6.2 Housing Act 1985[24]

6.2.1 Repair Notices (Part VI)

If a local authority decides that a house is unfit for human habitation or, whilst still being fit, is in a state of disrepair, it may serve a notice on the person controlling the building requiring repairs to be undertaken. The notice will specify the work to be done and the time limit by which it should be completed. Even though the local authority is the instigator, the person controlling the building has to bear the expense. However, there is provision for that person to appeal to the courts to have the notice modified or quashed. If a building cannot be repaired or made habitable at reasonable expense, the local authority may apply for a compulsory purchase order, but, once having bought the property, it must carry out all of the specified works and bear the cost. Except in cases involving compulsory purchase, local authorities are also empowered to undertake the specified repair works and recover the cost from the controller of the building. However, it must first give notice of its intention so to do.

6.2.2 Improvement notices (Part VII)

A local authority may serve an improvement notice on the person controlling a house if it is without one or more of the standard amenities. The notice will specify the work to be done, give an estimate of the cost and set a time limit for the completion of the improvements. As with repair notices, there is provision of appeal to the county court and for the local authority to undertake the work if it is not done within the specified period, recovering the cost from the controller of the building. Special provisions are made for notices relating to properties in a housing action area or general improvement area, which the Act also empowers local authorities to establish.

6.2.3 Overcrowding (Part X)

A house is deemed to be overcrowded if either the space standard or room standard is contravened. Contravention of the room standard occurs when the number of persons sleeping in the dwelling and the number of rooms available as sleeping accommodation is such that two persons of opposite sexes who are not living together as husband and wife must sleep in the same room. For these purposes, children under the age of 10 are discounted.

The space standard is contravened when the number of persons sleeping in a dwelling is in excess of the permitted number having regard to the number and floor area of the rooms available for use as sleeping accommodation. For the purposes of calculating space standards, children below the age of 1 are discounted and those between the ages of 1 and 10 counted as half a person. The Act contains two Tables relating numbers of people to numbers of rooms (e.g. two rooms provide sleeping accommodation for three people, two in one room and one in the second) and floor area to numbers of people (e.g. a room of 70-90 sq.ft. can accommodate one person and one of 110 sq.ft. or more two persons). Both occupiers and landlords are guilty of an offence if they allow overcrowding.

6.2.4 Houses in multiple occupation (Part XI)

The Act defines a house in multiple occupation as being a house occupied by persons who do not form a single household.

Local authorities are empowered to introduce registration schemes for houses in multiple occupation in their area, but only after they have been confirmed by the Secretary of State. The Act also contains a number of control provisions, enabling, for example, a local authority to prevent a house being used as a house in multiple occupation unless it is registered.

By means of a notice, a local authority can require work to be done in a house in order to render it fit for the number of occupants in respect of lighting (natural and artificial), ventilation, water supply, personal washing facilities, sanitary arrangements, facilities for storage and preparation of food and space heating. Provision is contained within the Act for appeals against such notices to be made to the county court.

A local authority may also apply a limit to the number of occupants of a house in multiple occupation, again by means of a notice. An occupier or manager of a house who allows overcrowding is liable to a fine. Unlike Part X, this part of the Act contains no space or room standards, and the local authority may therefore specify the number of occupants it considers suitable for the premises concerned. Interestingly, in this part of the Act, children under the age of 12 are discounted, whereas in Part X the age limit is 10. Appeals against notices specifying the number of occupants may be made to the county court.

If it appears to a local authority that a house in multiple occupation is not provided with means of escape from fire which it considers necessary, it may by means of a notice require work to be done or, if appropriate, to forbid occupation of part of the house in question. Before serving such a notice, the local authority is obliged to consult the fire authority although it does have the discretion to ignore, amend or accept the latter's recommendations. The notice will specify the work to be done and the period of time within which it has to be completed, although there is provision for this limit to be extended, and it will be served on the person having control of the house who may appeal to the county court. The local authority is empowered to undertake the required work and to recover the cost. Anyone failing to comply with the requirements of the notice is liable to a fine.

Of particular interest in the matter of means of escape from fire is Kingston upon Hull District Council v The University of Hull.[24] The Council considered that houses owned by the University and occupied by students who paid rent individually to the University were houses in multiple occupation. Similar powers to those in the 1985 Act were available to local authorities under the terms of section 16 of the Housing Act 1961, and the Council served notices on the University of Hull in 1976. Four houses were cited in the first instance, although the university owned many more which were also used for student accommodation. The main requirements of the notices were the installation of a detection/alarm system, the provision of fire resisting, self-closing doors and the making of the understairs cupboard into a protected cupboard. The university appealed to the County Court where only the fire resisting/self-closing doors of the main requirements were found to be necessary. This judgment was upheld in the Court of Appeal.

In order to achieve a degree of uniformity throughout the country, environmental health officers have agreed on a series of standards, which are available in booklet form from local authorities. The areas covered include room size, washing facilities, sanitary arrangements and means of escape. Some degree of interpretation is still needed, however, and in certain cases it may prove impossible to meet the minimum standards contained in the booklet, a situation which would have to be resolved by discussion with the local authority.

6.2.5 Grants

Part XV of the Act enables local authorities to make grants available towards the cost of improvements and repairs to dwelling houses and improvements (including means of escape) to houses in multiple occupation.

6.3 The Health and Safety At Work, Etc. Act 1974[28]

6.3.1 Introduction

Certain implications for universities in relation to staff and their trades unions are dealt with in Chapter 5 supra. However, there are aspects of the Act which relate directly or indirectly to the management of the university's estate.

6.3.2 Employer's duties to employees

S.2 of the Act details the duties of employers, the primary one of which is to ensure, so far as is reasonably practicable, the health, safety and welfare at work of all employees. S.2(2) lists the employer's duties as follows:

(i) the provision and maintenance of plant and systems at work that are, so far as is reasonably practicable, safe and without risks to health;

(ii) the making of arrangements for ensuring, so far as is reasonably practicable, safety and absence of risks to health in connection with the use, handling, storage and transport of articles and substances;

(iii) the provision of such information, instruction, training and supervision as is necessary to ensure, so far as is reasonably practicable, the health and safety at work of his employees;

(iv) the maintenance, so far as is reasonably practicable, of any place of work under the employer's control in a condition that is safe and without risks to health, and the provision and means of access to and egress from it that are safe and without risks;

(v) the provision and maintenance of a working environment for his employees that is, so far as is reasonably practicable, safe, without risks to health, and adequate as regards facilities and arrangements for their welfare at work.

The failure of an employer to implement these requirements may result in criminal liability under s.33, and, if there is an accident, to a claim for damages at common law or in an action for breach of statutory duty.

6.3.3 Employer's duties to others

S.3 of the Act extends the employer's duties to include others who use the premises concerned, and, in the university context, this would be interpreted as meaning students, members of the public or contractors working in a university building. The fact that an accident may occur during an act of trespass does not diminish the employer's responsibility to maintain a safe environment at all times. (See also $$ 13 and 16 infra on Trespass and Occupier's Liability.)

6.3.4 Emission to atmosphere

S.5 identifies a further duty of the employer to prevent by the best practical means any emission into the atmosphere of noxious or offensive substances and to render harmless and inoffensive such substances as may be so emitted. In this context, both the way in which plant is used and the supervision of the operation involved should be designed to take due heed of the requirement.

6.3.5 Articles supplied or imported

S.6 of the Act states that it is the duty of any person who designs, manufactures, supplies or imports articles to ensure that they are safe and without risks when properly used.

6.3.6 Duties of employees

S.7 states that it shall be the duty of every employee while at work:

(i) to take reasonable care for the health and safety of himself and of other persons who may be affected by his acts or omissions at work;

and

(ii) as regards any duty or requirement imposed on his employer or any other person by or under any of the relevant statutory provisons, to co-operate with him so far as is necessary to enable that duty or requirement to be performed or complied with. In addition, employees have a duty not to interfere with or misuse anything which is provided by the employer in the interests of health, safety and welfare in the work place.

6.3.7 Responsibilities of those managing the estate

It is clear, therefore, that those in charge of managing the universities' estates have considerable responsibilities for the health and safety of anyone making use of university facilities or entering its buildings, residences or grounds whether employees, students, contractors or the general public. Not only is there a duty to maintain the premises, equipment and plant so that they are safe and present no hazards to health, but the maintenance itself must be undertaken in a safe manner, as must any new construction work. Both direct labour personnel and contractors' employees should use safe systems of work, and it is the responsibility of those supervising the operations to see that they do. Whilst the onus in relation to the university's own employees is clear and unambiguous, many still believe that the responsibility for ensuring that contractors' employees adopt safe working practices is the contractors'. However, unless the operations concerned are being carried out within a defined site area for which the contractor has taken responsibility, those initiating the work do still have a duty in this respect. Many universities now produce a handbook for the guidance of non-university personnel working within or around its buildings. However, issuing copies to the employer is not enough - those supervising work must be satisfied that the individuals involved are aware of safety procedures, eg evacuation and assembly points in case of fire, and that they are employing safe methods of work.[30]

6.3.8 Training

Training is a key area, for in the event of a notifiable accident, the Inspector is certain to ask whether or not the employee had received instruction on the safe method of work, use of equipment etc. required in that particular operation. It is also a double-edged requirement for just as failure to train can result in an employer being prosecuted under section 33, so can failure to implement job safety lead to an injured employee losing the right to compensation. In ICI Ltd v Shatwell,[31] the employees, who were two trained and experienced shotfirers, voluntarily took on a risk in the course of their work, even after careful instruction given to them by the employers. They lost their claim because it was held that the employers had not breached any statutory duty, were not vicariously liable and had shown no negligence, and that the employees were trained men who were fully aware of the risks involved. This type of case will be rare, since the duty of employers in the area of safety and training is extremely rigorous, and was decided purely upon its own unusual facts.

6.3.9 Access and egress

The means of access to and egress from the place of work must be maintained in a safe condition at all times, and those managing the estate need to ensure that the same standards of maintenance specified in subsection 2.2 are applied. In addition, however, egress also includes the means of escape in case of fire, a topic which is dealt with in $4 supra. Let it at this stage suffice to note that the Act has the effect of amending the Fire Precautions Act 1971[23] so that general fire precautions in the majority of places of work can be dealt with by the fire authorities under the 1971 Act.

6.3.10 Responsibilities for design

Whilst the duty of a person who designs, manufactures, supplies or imports articles is to ensure that they are safe and without risks when properly used, many alterations to university buildings and maintenance works thereof are designed "in house", and it follows, therefore, that the person responsible for that process has a duty to ensure that the modified or maintained building can be used in safety and without risk.

6.3.11 Responsibilities for emissions to atmosphere

The duty to prevent the emission into the atmosphere of noxious or offensive substances and to render harmless and inoffensive any such substances as may be so emitted is particularly relevant in the context of laboratory fume cupboards and biological safety cabinets. Whilst the operations undertaken in such facilities are primarily the responsibility of the department concerned, those managing the estate will, in most cases, have a duty to ensure that the equipment is functioning satisfactorily. For example, an extract fan which is no longer operating to its specification could lead to poor containment within the fume cupboard, with fumes escaping into the laboratory as a result, or a low dilution factor leading to higher than acceptable concentration of the substance concerned being emitted into the atmosphere. In order to prevent such problems, periodic testing and monitoring will be necessary, but the precise division of responsibility between department and estate manager will vary depending on the equipment and the practices adopted in each university.

6.3.12 Civil and criminal proceeedings: compensation

The failure of an employee to take care for himself and others and to co-operate with the employer in matters of safety may lead to criminal proceedings under s.33, as would the misuse or abuse of anything provided by the employer in the interests of safety. Where injuries arise as a result of the employee's conduct, there may well be civil proceedings in addition to any at criminal law brought by the Health & Safety Executive's Inspector. Any compensation payable to an injured employee will be assessed on the basis of the amount of contributory negligence on the part of employer and employee.[32]

Whilst the Health & Safety Executive may bring criminal proceedings against an employer or an employee for breaches of the Act or any statutory regulation issued under its aegis, s.47(1) specifically precludes either employee or employer from bringing an action for damages under the Act itself. If any employee wishes to claim damages in respect of an accident at work, he must do so at common law or in an action for breach of statutory duty. In cases of injury where there has been no specific breach of statutory regulations, an employee can claim damages by alleging negligence - a common law action in tort - and if there has been a criminal action brought by the Health & Safety Executive, he may cite that in support of his claim. Where injury arises as a result of a breach of statutory regulations, this can be used directly to found a a claim for damages (section 47(2)).

7. RATES

7.1 Definition

A rate is not a tax upon land. It is a personal charge on the occupier of the land, and payable according to the annual value of the occupation to the occupier. The basis of the charge is the rateable value of the property which, in circumstances where this is practicable, is calculated by reference to the hypothetical tenancy of the property, that is, the rent at which the property might reasonably be expected to be let. The rateable value is the net annual value after deducting certain hypothetical expenditure.

Until the passing of the Local Government Finance Act 1988, which received the Royal Assent on the same day as the Education Reform Act 1988, the principal legislation regulating rates was the General Rate Act 1967, now repealed.

7.2 Position of Universities as Charities

Under the General Rate Act registered charities, and bodies wholly or mainly devoted to charitable purposes were entitled to a certain measure of rating relief and eligible for 100% relief. However by s.40(2) no mandatory relief was to be given in the case of a hereditament occupied by a charity and wholly or mainly used for charitable purposes for any period during which it is occupied by any of the universities in England and Wales.

This withdrawal of mandatory relief was not unreasonable when first enacted because it was the practice of the U.G.C. to meet the cost of rates on all property occupied by a university, by an earmarked grant, that is, a grant which has to be accounted for for a specific purpose.

7.3 The Local Government Finance Act 1988

However, the passing of the Local Government Finance Act 1988 alters the situation fundamentally in relation to rates. As far as universities are concerned there are two main consequences of the Act. First, it replaces domestic rates with a flat-rate personal community charge, and secondly, it retains rates for business premises, but in the form of a uniform national business rate. The personal community charge has implications for students and staff in service tenancies but no implications for the university estate.

As far as non-domestic rates are concerned two lists are to be drawn up (a) a local non-domestic rating list which will list all relevant non-domestic hereditaments situated in the authority's area and their rateable values and (b) a central rating list with a view to secure central rating en bloc of certain hereditaments. The local rating list will show whether the hereditament consists entirely of property which is non-domestic, or is a composite hereditament one of which "part" is domestic for which there is no rate liability: the personal and standard community charge being the source of local authority income, and the other part is non-domestic. For the non-domestic "part" it must show the rateable value of such part of the hereditament as is neither domestic property nor exempt from local non-domestic rating. S.64(9) reads "A hereditament is composite if part only of it consists of domestic property."

At the time of writing it is uncertain as to whether university residential accommodation will be classified as domestic or composite, that is, divided between its status as residential accommodation for full-time students, and its occasional use for short courses and conferences. The only judicial interpretation of the meaning of the word "part" is that it is a physical part[33] and not a division by time. Wynn v Skegness UDC[34] is support for the view that in a dispute before the Rating and Valuation Tribunal over whether or not a hall of residence (or a student house) was or was not a composite hereditament. In that case a dispute arose over a holiday centre for miners and their families, in which the same accommodation was sometimes used by members of the general public. The facts were that the centre could be used by the general public when there was surplus accommodation, and such admission was necessary to meet overheads and to keep the charges for qualified persons to an amount which would enable them to attend. It was held that the hereditament was wholly used for charitable purposes and not in part for other purposes because

(1) The charity was registered under the Charities Act 1960 which was a conclusive presumption that its purposes were exclusively charitable.

(2) The power to admit members of the general public to the centre was ancillary to the purposes of the charity.

(3) In admitting and charging members of the general public the trustees had been seeking to meet overheads and to act economically so as to serve the purposes of the charity.

(4) [not a relevant consideration for universities] The use of the hereditament was a charitable use by virtue of the Recreational Charities Act 1958.

7.4 Rating relief for Charities - The Present Position

S.43(5) and (6) provide that in respect of an occupied hereditament a charity will have its non-domestic rate bill automatically rebated by 80% and s.47 permits the rate rebate for charities to be increased to 100%. For universities which are not registered charities s.47(2)(b) would apply. A university is not established or conducted for profit and each of its main objects are charitable.

A zoo was held to be an educational charity because it was not conducted for profit despite the fact that it, as might a university, occassionally made a financial surplus on its operations.[35] S.49 empowers a charging authority to reduce or remit any amount that a person[36] is liable to pay provided that it is satisfied that the rate payer would suffer hardship in paying, and provided that it is reasonable, having regard to the liability to pay community charges.

7.5 The Calculation of Rateable Value[37]

As is pointed out above a rateable value is calculated by reference to the "rent" that might be paid. In circumstances where neither actual rents nor the profits of trading afford adequate evidence of an annual rental value, as in the case of university buildings, a valuation is made by reference to the cost of construction or the structural value. This is known as the effective capital value, that is, the value leaving out "frills" and allowing for age and obsolescence. Once the effective capital value has been calculated or assessed a percentage rate is applied to that value to give the annual value. This is known as the Contractors Test and it is based on the thesis that the hypothetical tenant will be unwilling to pay more as an annual rent than it would cost him in annual interest on the capital sum necessary to build a similar building.

The capital value can be assessed by reference to the original cost, the current capital value, or the estimated value of a substitute building. The percentage rate needs to be related to the rate at which the occupier could borrow money: the more "blue chip" the borrower the lower the percentage rate that the valuer can apply.

8. LIABILITY OF CONTRACTORS AND CONSULTANTS

8.1 Building Contracts

8.1.1 Introduction

Essentially, a contract is a straightforward affair in which, for example, two parties agree that one shall undertake a particular task for the other and receive consideration upon fulfilment. However, building contracts are arguably the most prolific source of litigation that exists, and most universities will have at least some experience in the field.

The precise nature and extent of the contract will depend upon the task to be undertaken, the service performed or the article supplied, and the university, as a consumer, can expect exactly the same in law when buying goods and services as the general public or, indeed, its own customers in the area of any trading activities (see Chapter 6). In short, goods should be fit for their usual use, of proper quality and as described by the vendor whether orally or in writing. Services should be performed to a reasonable standard, materials used should be of good quality and reasonably fit for use, goods being repaired or serviced should be taken reasonable care of by the repairer and the work done should be as agreed.

8.1.2 Supply of Goods and Services Act 1982

Building contracts, whether small or large, whether involving new construction or repair, are basically services and fall within the realm of common law and of the Supply of Goods and Services Act 1982.[38] Part I of the Act applies to the materials used in the execution of a contract and Part II to the service element or the actual work itself. Contracts covered by the Act include maintenance contracts (for example the servicing of refrigeration equipment with the firm involved supplying both parts and labour), building and construction contracts (in this case the builder will supply labour and materials to undertake, for example, the conversion of a building from one use to another) and installation and improvement contracts (for example, the installation of a heating system or the redecoration of a laboratory). The implied terms are similar to those contained in the Sale of Goods Act 1979[39] and cover title or ownership, description, merchantable quality, fitness for purpose and sample. Assuming that the implied terms are a condition of the contract, any breach discharges the customer from his obligation to pay the agreed price, and he may in addition recover damages. Part I of the Act also covers contracts for the hire of goods, for example telephone and construction plant and equipment, which must also be of adequate quality and fit for its purpose.

Part II of the Act covers the service element involved in a contract and is concerned to deal with such matters as slowness to complete work, quality of workmanship and overcharging. Not only does Part II apply to those undertaking the type of building, installation or maintenance contract listed in the previous paragraph, it also covers the professional services offered by architects, surveyors, engineers and other consultants. Such persons are expected to perform their services with reasonable care and skill, and the customer is entitled to expect a standard of service akin to that which would be offered by a reasonably competent member of that person's profession or trade. Thus an incompetent consultant may well be liable for poor advice even though he has acted to the best of his ability.

8.1.3 Redress

The remedy at law available to the customer who regards, for example, the installation of a new air conditioning system to be unsatisfactory is an action for damages. However, apart from the redress offered by the 1982 Act, there may well be circumstances in which an action based on the common law tort of negligence may be appropriate.

8.1.4 Elements of a building contract

Even though the basic elements of a contract are straightforward enough, the wealth of published material and the number of cases heard by the courts indicate that many are much more complex affairs. This is partially true of the building industry.

Perhaps the main reason for problems in this field is the failure of either or both parties to understand fully what has been agreed. Where a contract involves a client, a main contractor and many sub-contractors, there is plenty of scope for misunderstandings, for there will often be offers or promises followed by counter offers and so on until agreement is reached between the parties. But unless each has taken care to understand and record what has happened at each stage and understood that it is the last shot which counts, there will inevitably be problems. A contract may contain many documents - the enquiry, a specification, drawings, a programme, the quotation and the contract document itself, for example - and it is as well for every party involved to establish precisely which are relevant and which not.

Acceptance of a contract may be oral or written or by action, ie making a start. Once this stage has been reached, the contractor is obliged to continue and the client obliged to allow him to do so and to pay at the end.

Although the popular assumption relating to the broken contract is that of the contractor failing to complete on time or to ensure a satisfactory standard of workmanship, equally important are the obligations of the other parties, the client for example. If he makes it impossible for the contractor to fulfil his side of the agreement, eg by denying access, then the latter has a right to compensation if he has incurred any loss as a result.

8.1.5 Forms of building contract

Mention has already been made of the fact that the nature of a contract will vary depending on the type of work or service which it covers. As far as building or maintenance works are concerned, there is at the one end of the scale the verbal instruction to repair a leaking gutter, for example, followed no doubt by an official order confirming the request, and at the other an extremely lengthy and complicated standard form of contract dealing with the construction of a new building. Both are contracts at common law and in the terms of the Supply of Goods and Services Act 1982.[38] Between the two extremes will be other standard forms relating to minor works or contractor's design, for example, and the official order together with its implied and/or explicit terms.

Custom and practice will vary from institution to institution, reflecting local conditions and needs and the nature of the work to be undertaken or service supplied. Some contracts will include a requirement to perform work to a standard specification while others will comprise a drawing and schedule of work. Some will involve competitive tendering, with some or all of the tender documents being part of the contract, while others will be on a time and materials or negotiated rate basis. The possibilities are almost endless, and each problem has to be dealt with strictly on the issues involved.

8.1.6 The Standard Form of Building Contract

The Standard Form of Building Contract[40] issued by the Joint Contracts Tribunal comprises many sections and has continually been the subject of seminars and training courses since its introduction. Such is the complexity of the document, that contracts managers scrutinise each one they receive looking for loopholes, ambiguities and straightforward - or complex - "fiddles". Although the subject of much criticism and arguably the originator of more litigation than satisfactory construction, the Contract is widely used in connection with both new and refurbishment works, if only, some may argue, in the absence of anything better. In view of the complexity of the Standard Form and the fact that no two contracts will be identical, it is not proposed to study it in great detail.

The Standard Form begins with the Articles of Agreement, which names the parties, the architect, the quantity surveyor, the contract sum and the provisions governing arbitration of dispute. Part 1 continues with definitions, contractor's obligation, provisions for payments, variations, supervision, insurance, practical completion and defects liability. Part 2 deals with nominated sub-contractors and suppliers and Part 3 with fluctuations.

Although the architect, or supervising officer if that person is not entitled to use the name 'architect', is named in the Articles of Agreement, he is not one of the parties to the contract, these being the Employer (or client) and the Contractor. The architect, who will almost certainly have been responsible for the design of the building or refurbishment scheme, is the employer's agent, whose powers are conferred on him by the contract, and he is both entitled and obliged to protect the interests of the employer.[41] However, he is also expected by the RIBA Code of Professional Conduct to act impartially in all matters of dispute between contractor and building owner.

The basic purpose of the Standard Form is to provide a means whereby construction or refurbishment can take place under a series of terms and conditions which are familiar to the parties concerned and which identify their obligations, responsibilities and expectations.

8.2 The position of the architect and other consultants

Reference has been made briefly to the role of the architect in the context of the standard Form of Building Contract, but the relationship between Employer (or client) and architect deserves further examination. Again, this relationship is essentially a contractual one, although it is likely to be based on the booklet 'Architect's appointment' published by the RIBA, and, since a service is being supplied, it is also subject to the Supply of Goods and Services Act 1982,[38] as well as having its roots in common law. The booklet deals with the services which an architect is likely to be expected to provide (preliminary, basic and augmented), the conditions of appointment and the recommended fee scales. Architects wishing to use the standard conditions of engagement will produce a Memorandum of Agreement, again in standard form, which is signed by both client and architect and which includes a schedule of the services to be provided and the fees to be charged.

Although it is likely that the engagement of an architect will be based on the standard conditions, it is possible that the extent of the service does not warrant this approach or that the fees charged will be settled by tender or negotiation rather than being based on standard scales. Indeed, many architects in private practice will accept an agreement based on the client's own standard conditions rather than those of the RIBA, a system which is fairly commonly used by local authorities. Similar standard forms of engagement exist in respect of Quantity Surveyors and Consulting Engineers, and it is not uncommon for, say, a firm of Structural Engineers when asked for advice on a specific problem to agree to act on the basis of their own standard terms and conditions. Although it is common for the architect to be engaged directly by the client, the services of other consultants may be arranged on a similar basis or via the architect. Some architectural practices also employ Quantity Surveyors and are thus able to provide this service as part of the "package". Alternatively, such consultants may be engaged directly by the client or by the architect who then assumes a contractual responsibility for those thus appointed.

All of the standard terms of engagement seek to establish for the benefit of both parties the scope of the services to be provided and the level of fee to be charged. In addition to the safeguards offered by the Supply of Goods and Services Act 1982,[38] clients are also afforded protection by the Unfair Contract Terms Act 1977[42] which largely invalidates any attempt to exclude 'business liability' for negligence. Therefore, terms in a form of engagement which sought to exclude the firm from any liability for professional negligence would be completely invalid in cases where personal injury or death were the result of a poor design, for example. Where other cases of loss are concerned, such clauses or terms are only valid if the person relying on them can convince the court that they are 'fair and reasonable'.

8.3 Limitation of actions

The Limitation Act 1980[43] stipulates that certain types of action - which includes claims for negligence against builders, architects and consultants - cannot be brought

> "after the expiration of six years from the date on which the cause of action accrued".

The crucial matter, of course, is determining when a cause of action accrues, which in simple terms is the time when facts first exist upon which the plaintiff has the right to sue. In turn this is dependent upon whether the action is to be based on a breach of contract or on tort. Since an action in breach of contract can only be brought by one of the parties to that contract, the only recourse for third parties is a negligence action in tort. Originally the courts would not entertain such suits, but this situation has been dramatically altered in recent years.[44] Now persons who have subsequently established an interest may have the right to sue for negligence - for example, a houseowner, who is not the original purchaser, may be able to claim damages against the builder in respect of faults in the structure. In addition, a building owner may also be able to sue for negligence someone who was not a party to the original contract - a subcontractor for defective workmanship or the local authority's building control officer for inadequate supervision, for example.

An action based on breach of contract can be brought at any time from the point at which the breach occurs until six years thereafter, whereas a negligence action in tort can only be brought once loss is suffered or damage incurred, (the "Pirelli" case),[45] and the six year limitation period is deemed to run from that date. This judgement can be helpful to the client in building projects but not, of course, to the architect, consultant or builder since it extends almost indefinitely their responsibilities for taking reasonable care. However, determining the date on which the damage occurred could be well nigh impossible since buildings do not suddenly fail but rather gradually deteriorate, although, of course, the burden of proof is laid upon the defendant to show that the limitation period has expired and not vice versa. A strange feature of the Pirelli case is that it enables the defendant to plead that the building was 'doomed from the start' and that, if the claim arises more than six years after completion, it is statute barred, though this could hardly be good for business.

Since Pirelli, there have been several cases in which 'doomed from the start' was a factor, and, whereas there is guidance on when a building is not so doomed[46] there is none on when it is. The fact that an otherwise successful action cannot be brought in breach of contract because six years have elapsed since the breach does not guarantee the success or validity of an alternative action in tort. In another case,[47] the plaintiff sued for damages in respect of decorative cladding fixed by the defendant which had begun to fall from the building. The action failed because the Court of Appeal held that the builder had only been negligent to the extent that he had disregarded a requirement of the contract and used a different means of fixing the cladding from the one specified. Since negligence could only be demonstrated by reference to the contract, the plaintiff was bound by the contractual period of limitation, six years, which had expired.

For the position in Scotland see $18.1 infra.

8.4 Latent Damage Act

Further considerations now have to be taken into account in the area of actions for negligence as a result of the Latent Damage Act 1986[48] which has still to be extensively tested in the courts. This Act has the effect of amending the

Limitation Act 1980[43] in respect of actions for negligence where personal injury or death is not involved, but it does not apply to breach of contract or statutory duty. It effectively creates two new periods of time in which actions may be brought. Firstly, the plaintiff has up to three years to bring a claim from the date on which he knew he had a right of action. Secondly, there is a cut-off point of fifteen years from the date of the last negligent act, after which no claims may be made. However, rather than clarifying the situation, the Act is considered by many architects and consultants to be unsatisfactory and likely to add to the already complex arguments surrounding the date of accrual.

An action for negligence must, therefore, be brought either within six years of the accrual of the cause of the action or within three years from the starting date if that is later. The starting date is the point at which the plaintiff first knew

a) such facts about the damages as would lead a reasonable person who had suffered such damage to consider it sufficiently serious to justify instituting proceedings for damages against a defendant who did not dispute liability and was able to satisfy a judgement;

b) that the damage was attributable to the act or omission alleged to constitute the negligence; and

c) the identity of the defendant.

The plaintiff's knowledge includes everything which he could reasonably be expected to observe or ascertain with expert advice. Thus the plaintiff has to be in possession of a considerable amount of information before the date of knowledge can be said to have arrived. Indeed the date of knowledge may not arrive until the expert adviser actually informs the plaintiff that he has a right of action.

The fifteen year cut-off period is likely to run in most contracts from the date of practical completion, or in the case of a design/advice only service from the last occasion on which the consultant was involved. However, the period does not apply where a consultant has deliberately withheld information from the client concerning, for example, incorrect calculations which might lead to the failure of a staircase. The period does not also seem to apply to third party claims, with consequences for all involved in a major project. It is conceivable that a building owner could bring a successful action for negligence against a builder who in turn cites the architect as being partly to blame, with the result that the latter could face a court action over twenty years after practical completion.

9. NEIGHBOURS

9.1 Introduction

In managing the estate contact will inevitably be made with persons or organisations owning adjacent property, and questions will arise regarding the rights and obligations of the parties.

9.2 Fencing and Boundaries

Generally there is no legal requirement for a building owner to fence his land or to maintain that fence. However, there may be a covenant in the deeds stipulating the type of boundary fencing (or wall) and the responsibility for its future maintenance. Disputes over the precise line of a boundary are commonplace, and it has been known for neighbours to argue about, effectively, the thickness of a piece of string - even as far as the courts. In seeking to settle such disputes, the courts will consider the title deeds and documents to see whether there is any precise information contained in them, but they are often vague and any plans insufficiently detailed. Even the generally accepted practice of hedging on the far side of a ditch (with the boundary running on the near side) can be overruled by, for example, the landowner traditionally maintaining the hedge. In addition, if the title deeds define the boundary by reference to an Ordnance Survey map, the hedge and ditch rule may not be relevant, since the OS delineates boundaries along the middle of hedges rather than along the edges of ditches. Damage caused by animals straying across an unfenced boundary or through a poorly maintained fence, wall or hedge, can be held to be the responsibility of the owner of the animals in question - normally, however, only if he has been negligent. Exceptions to this rule are livestock (even if kept as pets), dangerous animals, animals which are normally harmless but which, for some reason, are dangerous and guard dogs.

9.3 Right to light

Although a landowner owns the airspace above his property, he does not enjoy an automatic right to have light enter his airspace or land. Thus if a property owner chooses to erect a high building or fence on his land, there may be no redress at all for neighbours affected by these activities except opposing the application for planning permission if such is in fact necessary. However, a right to light can be acquired by agreement or by prescription (ie continuous use over a period of twenty years or more), but it only applies to buildings and not to gardens or other open spaces, and the courts will assess the level of light as being sufficient for normal use of the room concerned - living rooms need more light than bedrooms for example. For these purposes, greenhouses are classified as buildings and demand sufficient light to enable plants to grow. Shading caused by a fence or a building can, therefore, be an infringement of this right.[49] Prescription applies to a new building provided it has been constructed largely on the same site and is not drastically different in size or character from one which has previously existed and acquired the rights in question.

9.4 Subsidence

Interestingly, soil enjoys a right to support, but buildings do not necessarily. Thus excavations affecting a neighbour's garden and causing the soil to subside can be stopped, but such protection only exists for buildings if they have acquired a right to support either by written deed or by a restrictive covenant or by prescription (see $9.3 supra).

9.5 Noise

Anything which interferes with a landowner's or householder's enjoyment of his property can be held to be a nuisance. Noisy operations, such as pile-driving at night, can be stopped by seeking and being granted an injunction, and the courts will decide what is reasonable, taking into account all the circumstances. For example, a health authority was given a specified period of time in which to cure noise caused by heating plant which was interfering with a neighbour's ability to sleep and had to pay damages for the nuisance before and during the intervening period.[50] Since applying to the courts for injunctions can be an expensive proposition, the originator of a nuisance may find himself being served with a noise abatement notice by the local authority, to whom an aggrieved party may have complained. In this context, the environmental health officer is empowered to take action by the Control of Pollution Act 1974[27] forbidding the noise completely or restricting it to certain times. Non-compliance with such a notice can lead to prosecution by the local authority in the magistrates' court, and a fine can result. If a local authority refuses to issue a notice or to prosecute for any breach, the aggrieved party can apply direct to the magistrates' court for action. Finally, there may be within local bye-laws means of stopping or controlling noise by prosecuting the offender, and in this case too the most likely originator of proceedings will be the local authority.

9.6 Trees

Overhanging branches can be regarded as a nuisance, and this is one of the few instances where self-help is permissible in law, because, if the owner of the tree refuses to prune the offending branches, the aggrieved neighbour may do so but he should return the branches to their owner. However, it is important to note that restrictions exist in respect of trees which are in a conservation area or the subject of a Tree Preservation Order, and these may only be lopped, pruned or felled after consultation with the local authority. Ignorance of the existence of such restrictions is no excuse, and offenders are liable to a fine. Roots may also be pruned, and if this operation necessitates digging through an ornamental lawn, for example, the tree owner can be liable for the cost of re-instatement as well as for the pruning itself. A tree owner can also be held responsible for damage caused by roots to neighbouring buildings, but not every piece of damage so caused will necessarily be his fault[51] and claiming poor construction is not a reliable defence if roots are responsible for damage.[52] In this context, local authorities can be held liable for damage caused by the roots of trees on pavements. Damage caused by falling trees or branches can be held to be the responsibility of the tree owner if he is found to have been negligent. For example, if a tree falls during a gale, the owner will probably not have been negligent, but if a tree falls because of disease or age, the owner may be held to be negligent for not having inspected it regularly - once or perhaps twice a year.

9.7 Smells

As with noise, the courts are likely to assess what is reasonable in all the circumstances, and what is deemed to be acceptable in one area may not be so in another. Since it is difficult to assess damages in such cases, awards have varied enormously, the judge having to put a monetary value on the enjoyment of fresh air for example. Again, as with noise, complaints may be made to the local authority resulting in the environmental health officer issuing a notice which requires the offenders to cease or restrict creating the offensive smell.

10. ASBESTOS

Growing awareness of the dangers of asbestos and asbestos-containing products has resulted in the introduction in recent years of three sets of regulations enforced by the Health & Safety Executive. Although some regulations existed in the past, it is really during the last six years that modern thinking has been translated into effective legislation.

The Asbestos (Licensing) Regulations 1983 established procedures for the licensing by the Health & Safety Executive of companies which worked with asbestos or asbestos-containing products. Undertaking such work without a licence is a criminal offence under s.33(1)(c) of the Health & Safety at Work etc Act 1974.[28] However, no licence is needed if the employer or self-employed person undertakes the work in premises of which he is the occupier and if he had notified the enforcing authority of the proposed work 28 days in advance. (The enforcing authority is likely to be the local authority in most cases, but it may in certain circumstances be the Health & Safety Executive, and there is provision for the responsibility to be passed from one to the other.) The regulations also specify that work with asbestos insulation or coating which does not exceed one hour in seven consecutive days for one person or two hours in total for all persons may be undertaken without a licence as can work involving only air monitoring or the collection of samples for identification purposes.

The Asbestos (Prohibition) Regulations 1985 forbid the importation, supply and use of crocidolite and amosite (blue and brown asbestos respectively) and products containing them - except for evaluation purposes. In addition, the Regulations also ban the spraying of asbestos, the installation of asbestos insulation and, by amendment in 1988, the use of certain paint or varnish containing asbestos. However, the term 'asbestos insulation' does not include asbestos cement or asbestos insulating boards and certain other compounds containing asbestos which are used for insulation purposes.

The Control of Asbestos at Work Regulations 1987 are designed to provide improved statutory protection for all those working with asbestos both within and outside the industry itself. Although the new regulations replace earlier ones dating from 1969 (simply named The Asbestos Regulations), the latter are still deemed to be relevant for certain purposes. The new regulations impose duties on employers for the protection of employees who may be exposed to asbestos at work and of others who are likely to be affected by such work. The employer must identify the type of asbestos, assess the nature and degree of employees' exposure to it and take steps to reduce that exposure. Work with asbestos must be notified to the enforcing authority and adequate information, instruction and training given to employees and others on the premises. Employers are required to prevent the exposure of employees and others to asbestos or to reduce it to the lowest reasonably practicable level, and if this is still not below specified control limits, to issue respiratory and protective equipment, which itself must be properly used and maintained. Protective clothing must be kept clean, the spread of asbestos contained and premises and plant associated with work involving asbestos also kept clean.

Areas in which exposure to asbestos exceeds or is likely to exceed the specified limit or level should be designated and marked accordingly with entry limited.

Provision is made for the monitoring of exposure, and employees who are likely to experience significant exposure are to be under regular medical surveillance. The Regulations require the provision of washing and changing facilities and specify rules for the storage, distribution and labelling of raw asbestos and asbestos waste. Finally, the labelling of products for use at work which contain asbestos is specified and detailed.

In addition to the 1987 Regulations, two codes of practice have also been issued giving practical guidance on how to comply with them - Approved Code of Practice on Control of Asbestos at Work (Control of Asbestos at Work Regulations 1987) and Approved Code of Practice on Work with Asbestos Insulation, Asbestos Coating and Asbestos Insulating Board.

11. SAFETY SIGNS REGULATIONS 1980

Essentially, the Regulations require that safety signs shall comply with BS5378 and shall not, except in certain respects, be used at places of work except to provide the safety information or instructions specified in Appendix A to the Standard. The regulations, which apply to all signs both new and existing, specify four main types each with its own characteristic shape and colour:

Prohibition - circular with a red border and crossbar over a black symbol on a white background (used for such signs as 'No Smoking', 'Not Drinking Water' etc).

Warning - triangular with a black border and symbol on a yellow background (used to denote potential hazards such as risk of fire, live cables etc).

Mandatory - circular on blue background with symbols in white (used when there is an obligation, for example, to keep a door closed or locked or to wear such equipment as eye or ear protection or a safety helmet).

Safe Condition - square or oblong on green background with symbols in white (used to denote emergency exits and routes, first-aid posts, emergency telephones etc).

Provision is also made for the use of supplementary signs where there is a need to give additional information, for example assembly points or the precise nature of the hazardous material which is present.

12. THE CONTROL OF POLLUTION ACT 1974[27]

12.1 Waste and Refuse

Part I deals with waste (household, commercial, industrial and other categories), the duties of local authorities regarding its collection and disposal and the licensing by local authorities of private disposal.

Generally local authorities are obliged to collect household waste and to collect, or arrange for the collection of, commercial and industrial waste if requested to do so. The Act specifies that a reasonable charge may be levied for the collection of waste other than household waste, with the latter being removed free. Although the definition of household waste specifically includes that emanating from any premises forming part of a university (s.30(3)), the enabling regulations (The Collection and Disposal of Waste Regulations 1988) allows local authorities to raise a charge for collecting certain types of household waste, and into this latter category falls waste 'from premises forming part of a university' (Schedule 2 of the Regulations). Thus local authorities are able to exercise discretion and may charge for the removal of waste from any or all university buildings. Policy will undoubtedly vary from local authority to local authority, probably reflecting the attitude of the district auditor towards the permissible recovery of expenditure.

In deciding whether or not to charge for the collection of refuse from halls of residence, local authorities may refer to Mattison v Beverley Borough Council.[53] The Council had advised the University of Hull that a charge for the service would be raised, since the refuse was 'other waste', for the removal of which the authority was entitled to charge (s.74, Public Health Act 1936).[26] Although the character of the waste was such that it could be regarded as 'house refuse', the Court of Appeal ruled that halls of residence were not dwelling houses, that waste from them was not, therefore, 'house refuse', and that the local authority was entitled to charge for its removal.

In determining whether a university should be charged for the removal of refuse from academic buildings (ie those other than residences), a local authority may well take into account both the nature of the waste and the activities undertaken rather than simply relying on the terms of Schedule 2. As a result, charges could be introduced for the collection of waste from a catering building or bookshop since both are liable to be viewed as commercial activities. Schedule 3 which defines industrial waste includes references to clinical waste and that from a laboratory, for the removal of which a local authority is entitled to charge.

12.2 Rivers and Coastal Waters

Part II deals with the control of pollution of rivers and coastal waters and with the discharging of trade sewage and effluent into them. Under its terms it is an offence to allow poisonous, noxious or polluting matter to enter a stream or controlled waters, or to impede their proper flow in a manner as to aggravate pollution, or to allow solid waste matter to enter a stream or restricted waters. It also enables water authorities to control the discharge of trade effluent into public sewers. For the purposes of the Act, 'trade premises' are any which are used or intended to be used for carrying on any trade or industry and 'trade effluent' as any liquid - with or without particles in suspension therein - wholly or partly produced in the course of trade or industry carried out in trade premises.

Although universities themselves are unlikely to be regarded as trade premises, certain activities may well fall within the scope of trade, eg catering facilities used for commercial purposes during vacations and university companies undertaking research work or testing for reward. In addition there are now several 'science parks' associated with universities, and, depending on the terms on which the development has taken place, the host institution may well have responsibilities if it is the 'landlord'.

12.3 Noise

Part III is concerned with noise and the provisions by which it may be controlled, for example by declaring a noise abatement zone, and enables the Secretary of State to set noise levels for plant and machinery by means of regulations. Local authorities are empowered to specify the hours during which noisy operations may be undertaken, to lay down noise levels and to control the type of machinery to be used when constructing a new building. The method of control in each case is a notice served by the Environmental Health Officer. The Act also requires that persons submitting applications for approval under the Building Regulations shall at the same time apply for prior consent for work to be undertaken on a construction site in order that the local authority may issue an appropriate notice to control noisy operations and equipment.

12.4 Discharges to atmosphere

Part IV deals with atmospheric pollution and empowers local authorities to investigate any emissions into the atmosphere. They are also enabled to serve a notice requiring the occupier of any premises to provide information on emissions of pollutants or other substances into the atmosphere and may as a result issue a further notice specifying steps to be taken to control or curtail such emissions. In this context, a member of the public, for example, may complain to the local authority about smells allegedly emanating from a university science building. The local authority may then require information on the nature of work being undertaken in laboratory fume cupboards and on the substance involved.

12.5 Legal Proceedings

Part V is concerned with legal proceedings. In the event of notices served by the Environmental Health Officer not being complied with or ignored, the local authority may initiate proceedings against the owner of the building, premises or construction site in the magistrates' court. Similar provisions are made in respect of any contravention of regulations issued under the Act's aegis. Persons convicted are liable to a fine.

13. TRESPASS TO PROPERTY

13.1 General

The act of trespass is a tort, or wrong, actionable at civil law. Whereas "Private Property - Keep Out" is an accurate statement of the law, the popular "Trespassers Will Be Prosecuted" has no legal basis in itself.

An owner of a piece of land, a house or building has the right to decide who can come onto or into his property, subject to the statutory right of access afforded to the police or to certain statutory bodies, eg the water authority for the purposes of laying a pipeline. However, the property owner must also have possession in order to sue for trespass. If property is leased, it is the lessee who is entitled to sue, although the lessor may also bring an action if the damage caused by the trespasser is such that it would affect his reversion at the expiry of the lease. When a person signs a contract for the purchase of a piece of land or a house, he becomes entitled to possession, and if an act of trespass occurs before he actually does take possession, he may sue in respect of that trespass when he goes into possession, his right to do so dating back to the point when the contract was signed.

Trespass is the interference with the possession of land and may take various forms. Entering onto land without invitation or authorisation is an act of trespass, as is leaving an article on another person's land, for example parking one's car in a neighbour's drive without permission. If a person is invited into a house and later asked to leave, he is trespassing if he does not do so. In addition, the abusing of the purpose for which a person is allowed to be on land is an act of trespass. In Hickman v Maisey,[54] the highway was used for making notes on the form of racehorses being exercised on adjacent land, and this was held to be trespass since the purpose of the highway is for passing and re-passing. A person crossing another's land by a right of way would be trespassing if he abused or exceeded the right to pass and re-pass.[55]

There are two main remedies available to the landowner. Firstly, he may ask the trespasser to leave, and, if the latter refuses, he may use reasonable force to eject him. However, the trespasser might consider that the degree of force used was unnecessary and prosecute the landowner for assault. Secondly, the landowner could sue for damages and obtain compensation for any loss or damage caused during the trespass. However, unless the trespasser actually causes damage, there is unlikely to be any quantifiable loss for which the court would be prepared to award compensation. Indeed, if the loss were only slight, the court might only assess damages at a few pence and not award the landowner his legal costs.

There is, therefore, little that can be done in practical terms about the casual trespass, someone taking a short cut across a university's campus or playing field for example, who does not cause any damage or disruption. However, if there is a persistent trespass, the landowner can ask the court for an injunction against the trespasser which requires him not to trespass in the future. Ignoring such an order is contempt of court and could render that person liable to a fine or imprisonment.

Although trespass itself is a matter of civil law, any criminal acts, such as assault or theft, committed during trespass give rise to criminal liability. Thus a member of the public who is trespassing and who is apprehended by a university's security patrol whilst stealing a bicycle from the campus for example can be handed over to the police who may instigate a criminal prosecution for that offence.

The occupier of land, who may or may not be the owner (see above), has a duty to ensure that all reasonable and practicable steps are taken to warn potential trespassers of any danger which may be present, or to exclude them from the property.[56] Where trespassers are or are likely to be children, the occupier must by means of effective warning or protection keep them from injuring themselves, for example by deterring them from playing with enticing and dangerous equipment.

13.2 Rights of Way

Whereas in general terms a person entering another's land is trespassing, this does not apply to rights of way which allow the restricted use of private land for a bona fide journey.

An individual may achieve the right to use a footpath across private land either by being given a written deed or by using it for a period of twenty years, ie prescription. However, for prescription to apply, the person must have used the path without asking for permission or offering payment, and the landowner must have implicitly accepted his right to do so, for example by not telling him to stop or challenging the right.

The general public may also acquire a right of way by the same means as an individual establishes his private foot path. Again, the route must be defined and permission must not have been sought or given. After twenty years' use, it is assumed that the landowner has accepted the existence of a public right of way and dedicated the land as such (Highways Act 1980). In order to avoid this, a landowner must demonstrate publicly that he does not want a public right of way to be created, either by displaying a sign stating that the land is not being dedicated as a public highway, or by depositing a formal notice with the local authority to this effect, or by blocking the road or path for one day every year thus asserting ownership and demonstrating that the path exists only by courtesy.

Local authorities maintain a definitive map showing the location and classification of all public rights of way in their area, ie footpaths, bridleways and by-ways open to all traffic. If the map shows a footpath in a particular location, this is conclusive evidence that the right of way exists. However, public paths can continue to be created, and the omission of a path from the map does not necessarily mean that it is not open to the public. A footpath cannot be lost because its use declines or even ceases - once it exists, it remains until closed or redirected by an order made under the terms of a statute. A person deviating from a path or not using it for its proper purpose becomes a trespasser, and, interestingly, local authorities are obliged to maintain the surface of paths which existed before 1949. The local authority has to agree to maintain any created since that date. The maintenance of gates and stiles along public rights of way, however, is the responsibility of the landowner.

13.3 Squatters

Since trespass is the interference with the possession of land, it follows that squatters are in fact trespassers. Anyone occupying premises without permission is a trespasser and has no rights over the land on which he is trespassing. However, it is possible for a trespasser or squatter to gain adverse possession (see below) and, as a result, derive certain rights.

As has already been noted, the act of trespass is not a criminal offence, but squatters who damage the property while entering (eg forcing a door or breaking a window) or in possession can be prosecuted for causing criminal damage.

Previously, squatters could be evicted by physical means and using reasonable force, but the Criminal Law Act 1977[57] created specific offences with squatters in mind and restricted the use of threats of violence in order to achieve repossession. Now only a displaced residential occupier is able to ask squatters to leave without first applying for a court order, and by refusing to do so a squatter is committing an offence, punishable by a fine or imprisonment. Displaced residential occupiers are tenants and owner occupiers who were using the property as their home prior to the squatter entering, and intending occupiers who are either owners or leaseholders (for a period of twenty one years or more). Squatters do not commit an offence if they refuse to leave when asked to do so by anyone who does not have, or is not intending to have, his home in the premises. Trespassing with an offensive weapon is also an offence punishable by a fine or imprisonment, and one can be committed quite easily, for the term 'offensive weapon' includes items such as crowbars and bolt croppers which although not offensive when used for their proper purposes could be used as weapons in a physical confrontation. Finally, the Act renders it an offence for a squatter to resist or intentionally obstruct an Officer of the Court who is attempting to put into effect a possession order granted by a court.

Since squatters can only be asked to leave by a displaced residential occupier, the only means of repossession available to a landlord, such as a university, is to apply for a court order. Procedures now exist which enable the High Court or county court to make a possession order within five days of the proceedings being started, and this applies even if the identity of the squatter(s) is unknown. Orders must be granted when the applicant has shown that he is entitled to the property and that those occupying it are in fact trespassing. Squatters can be ordered to pay the legal costs, but damages for nuisance, damage etc can only be sought by bringing a default action in the county court. Once a possession order has been made, arrangements will be put in motion for a bailiff to be sent to evict the squatters.

13.4 Adverse possession

Reference has already been made to 'adverse possession', which is a means whereby someone who is not the true owner may acquire a title. This may happen as a result of a person occupying and using land or premises for a period of twelve years or more without the actual owner's permission or any interference from him.[58] However, such adverse possession must be in the form of overt acts which are not consistent with the title of the owner, and the courts will take a strict view of possession and use.[59] Apparently contrasting views have been taken as to whether or not adverse possession necessarily involves inconvenience being caused to the true owner,[60] but tenants may only acquire title by adverse possession if they communicate to the landlord some form of disclaimer of the latter's title.[61]

14. LICENSING

14.1 Introduction

University premises require licensing for a great variety of operational functions, and failure to hold the appropriate licences may render both the university and individual members of staff liable to legal proceedings.[62] The following list of licences is believed to represent the complete requirements for university operations.

14.2 Anatomy

Licensing provisions relating to anatomy concern potentially all universities and not only those with medical schools. This is because medical research, within the meaning of the Anatomy Acts 1832 to 1984[63] and the Human Tissue Act 1961,[64] can be undertaken in any appropriate laboratories such as, for example, biochemistry, physiology, chemistry, physics, zoology. Under the Anatomy Acts the licensing is of persons,[65] and dissection may be undertaken by a licensed person on premises of which notice is given to the Secretary of State for Health by the licensed person, or the owner or occupier of the premises.[66] It is the intention that the premises themselves shall be licensed,[67] but the relevant legislation had not been brought into force by 1st August 1989.

By virtue of the Human Tissue Act 1961 parts of a body may be removed for medical purposes,[68] and research undertaken thereon, provided that the specimen remains in the possession of a licensed person. In this context "possession" can only be construed in a popular and not a narrow sense: in other words it covers more than actual physical possession. Thus human cornea can, for example, be entrusted to research workers in a physics laboratory provided that a consultant ophthalmologist is at all times in possession.[69]

14.3 Cultivation etc. of Cannabis Plants

It is an offence to cultivate cannabis without a licence from the Secretary of State for Health.[70] It is also an offence to allow smoking to take place as the owner or manager of premises unless authorised by the Secretary of State.[71] There is an express statutory defence in relation to cultivation where there is lack of knowledge,[72] and consumption must have been "knowingly".[73]

Where any offence under the Misuse of Drugs Act 1971 committed by a body corporate is proved to have been committed with the consent or connivance of, or to have been attributable to any neglect on the part of any director, manager, secretary or other similar officer of the body corporate, he as well as the body corporate is guilty of that offence.[74]

14.4 Distillers' etc. Licences

A distillers' licence is required for the manufacture of spirits (except methyl alcohol) and for the rectifying and compounding of spirits and keeping a still therefor.[75] A licence is also required for the keeping or using of a still and for the storage of methylated spirits and more than three gallons of petroleum substances.[76]

14.5 Late Night Refreshment House

A house, room or building kept open for public refreshment at any time between 10.00 p.m. and 5.00 a.m., and which is not licensed for the sale and consumption on the premises of alcoholic drinks requires (in Scotland may require) a licence.[77] The licensing is undertaken by the local authority. Although student union premises are commonly licensed for the consumption of alcoholic drinks it may be that some part of the accommodation allocated to a student union which is not licensed may be used in this manner.

14.6 Theatre Licence (Intoxicating Liquor)

In England and Wales intoxicating liquor may be sold without a Justices' licence at licensed theatres, if the licensee has given notice to the licensing magistrates. An application for a Theatre Licence may, however, be refused on the grounds that the applicant will not give an undertaking not to sell intoxicating liquor[78] but such a condition ought not to be imposed unless it is necessary in order to ensure order and decency in the theatre.[79]

14.7 Gaming etc. Licences

A licence is required for premises to be used for certain specified games: baccarat, punto banco, big six, blackjack, boule, chemin de fer, chuck-a-luck, craps, crown and anchor, faro, faro bank, hazard, poker dice, pontoon, French roulette, American Roulette, vente-et-quarante, ving-et-un and a wheel of fortune.[80] A licence is also required for premises to have gaming machines.[81] To obtain a licence local authority approval is required.

14.8 Tree Felling Licence

A licence is required for the felling of growing trees not included in a tree preservation order. There are however a large number of exemptions, the most relevant of which are those with a trunk diameter of less than three inches (six inches in a coppice), fruit or garden trees, to prevent danger or abate nuisance, to improve the growth of other trees (four inch diameter limit), where planning permission has been granted, or where the aggregate cubic content does not exceed 825 cubic feet, and not more than 150 cubic feet is sold.[82]

14.9 Cinematographic Exhibitions

Unless specifically exempted, all premises used for cinematographic exhibitions must (in Scotland, may) be licensed for that purpose by the local authority.[83] The relevant exemptions are where the premises are not used for exhibitions on more than six days in the calendar year, provided that written notice is given to the local authority, the chief officer of police, and the fire authority not less than seven days before the exhibition and all conditions imposed by the local authority complied with.[84] The second ground for exemption is that the public is not admitted. The third ground for exemption is that the exhibition is free or such charge as is levied is not for private gain,[85] and the fourth ground for exemption is that the exhibitor holds a certificate as an exempted organisation.[86]

14.10 Billiards

Any house room or place kept for public billiard playing requires a licence issued by the licensing justices unless the house room or place is included within the ambit of a justices' on-licence for the sale of intoxicating liquor.[87] Thus a student union building which admits "the public" may require such a licence if an unlicensed part of the premises contains snooker tables.

14.11 Gaming

Gaming is prohibited where any of the following conditions obtain: playing or staking against a bank: the chances are not equally favourable to all players: the chances are not so favourable to the players as they are to some other person. On the other hand these restrictions do not apply to a hostel or hall of residence where the players consist, at least mainly, of residents or inmates of such establishments.[88] No charges may be made for gaming on unlicensed (i.e. not licensed for the purposes of gaming) premises except in the case of clubs where limited permission applies.[89] The charges that may be imposed are very low, but where the gaming at any one time consists exclusively of bridge and/or whist higher charges may be authorised.[90]

14.12 Boxing, Wrestling, Judo and Karate

An entertainment licence[91] is required (in Scotland, may be required) for any public contest, exhibition or display of the above-mentioned sports. The test of "public" is not that members of the public are present but rather that members of the public could be present.[92] The licensing authority is the district council.

14.13 Hypnotism

Premises must (in Scotland, may) be licensed for public entertainment before any exhibition, demonstration or performance of hypnotism takes place thereat, whether on payment or otherwise, unless the licensing authority has given its authorisation, or the premises are a licensed theatre.[93] The licensing authority is the district council.

14.14 Scaffolding etc.

A licence is required in connection with the erection of scaffolding to alter, repair, maintain or clean any building which obstructs the highway.[94] The licence is issued by the highway authority. Likewise a builder's skip may not be deposited on the highway without the permission of the highway authority.[95] A close boarded hoarding may have to be erected to separate a building on the highway which is to undergo erection, alteration, repair or demolition.[96]

14.15 Public Entertainments etc.

Premises which provide public dancing, music or similar entertainment require (in Scotland, may require) an entertainments licence granted by the local authority. "Public" has the same meaning as in boxing etc.[97] The district council has wide-ranging powers to impose conditions in relation to safety, access, sanitary provision, and noise restriction, but no others.[98] The use of private places for entertainment may also require a licence if promoted for private gain, but private gain is defined as excluding circumstances in which any society is established wholly for purposes other than purposes of any commercial undertaking, or wholly or mainly for the purpose of participation in or support of athletic sports or athletic games. It similarly does not apply to the licensed premises occupied by a club[99]: a common position for the premises occupied by unions, but they may need a public entertainment licence.

14.16 Justices' Licences

It is impossible to summarise adequately the salient features of the law of England and Wales relative to licences for the sale for consumption on the premises of intoxicating liquor and reference should be to standard works on the subject.[100] For the position in Scotland see $18.3 infra.

There are three forms of licence controlling intoxicating liquor: excise licences, justices' licences, and club. Excise licences are required only for wholesale dealing in alcoholic drinks, but brewing of beer (but not other drinks) for authorised research is exempt.[101] There are certain exemptions from the requirement that premises be licensed. An occasional licence may be granted, authorising the holder of a justices' on licence to sell intoxicating liquor at such place other than the premises in respect of which the licence was granted for periods of up to three weeks at a time. Application must be determined according to the law and not according to some prescription of the licensing bench,[102] and there must be no system of "rationing" occasional licences: each application must be considered on its merits.[103] The position regarding theatres is discussed above.[104]

Justices have a discretion to grant a licence, and there is no limit on the kinds of objection that they may take into consideration. They may consider that there are already enough licensed houses in the particular district, or that the proposed house is too far removed from police supervision:[105] a factor for university campuses with buildings far removed from the public highway.

Prescribed conditions may be attached to the grant of licences. These are: a six day licence, early closing, midday only (for restaurant or residential licences), no off-sale, seasonal, a limited class of the public. Even without a seasonal licence a licensee is not required to keep the premises open throughout the year, unless there is a specific condition requiring him to do so.

A restaurant licence is granted for premises used, or intended to be used, for habitually providing the customary main meal at midday or in the evening, or both, and is subject to the condition that intoxicating liquor may not be sold or supplied on the premises except to persons taking meals seated at a table, counter or other structure serving the purpose of a table, and which is not used by persons taking refreshments. The consumption must be as an ancillary to a meal.[106]

A residential licence is a licence for premises providing for payment board and lodging (breakfast plus at least one other meal) but with consumption restricted to residents and their private friends. A residential and restaurant licence is for premises falling within both descriptions with the sale restricted to restaurant licence or residential licence.[107] The essential difference between a justices' on-licence and a restaurant and/or residential licence is that the latter may only be refused on certain specified ground: there is no discretion and any grounds for refusal must be communicated to the applicant in writing.[108]

Once a justices' on-licence has been granted there are restrictions on the operation of the licence that keep the premises under the continuing supervision of the licensing justices. The principal controls are in relation to the premises. No alteration which gives increased facilities for drinking, conceals from observation any part of the premises used for drinking, or affects communication between the public part of the premises and the remainder of the premises or the public highway may be made without the permission of the justices.[109] Alteration means that the identity of the premises must not be destroyed. It is for the justices to decide what is an alteration and what is an accessory improvement.[110] On renewal of a licence the justices also have the power to order such structural alterations as they think reasonably necessary to secure the proper conduct of business.[111] Once made no further order may be made for five years.

The hours during which intoxicating liquor may be sold are regulated in great detail and are known as the permitted hours. The permitted hours may be extended for persons taking table meals by one hour following the general licensing hours, provided that the magistrates are satisfied that the provision of substantial refreshment is bona fide and the supply of intoxicating liquor is ancillary.[112] Where entertainment is included the supply can be extended to 1.00 a.m. This is known as an extended hours order. Where licensed premises have a public entertainment licence, and are bona fide used for music and dancing and substantial refreshment to which the sale of intoxicating liquor is ancillary the justices must grant a special hours certificate.[113] The special hours extend to 2.00 a.m., but commence at a later hour than normal licensing hours. In such cases the "drinking up" time is extended from ten minutes to half an hour.[114]

There are two principal exemptions from the permitted hours for the supply of intoxicating liquor. The first relates to the bona fide guest of the licensee, manager, or employee. Private friends may be supplied at the expense of the licensee, manager or employee. The second is for consumption on the premises by persons employed there for the purposes of the business carried on by the licence holding, if the liquor is supplied at the expense of their employer.[115] Thus a "free bar" can be available to a Senate dinner taking place on licensed premises.

There is a wide range of offences under the licensing acts, and the following is no more than a brief summary of those that have been known to arise in a university setting. The principal possibility is the sale of intoxicating liquor without a licence, and the liability is not only of those undertaking the sale, but also of the occupier if he is proved to be privy to the sale.[116] "Occupier" is not defined, but it is felt that knowledge on the part of a cleaner or secretary would not make a university, as occupier, privy to the sale. If an unlicensed person sells on licensed premises an offence is committed and the licensee may be convicted of aiding and abetting the sale.[117] It is also unlawful to supply or consume intoxicating liquor at any party organised for gain and taking place on premises habitually used for parties. In assessing whether or not gain accrued, no account is to be taken of any expenditure incurred in connection with the party.[118] Intoxicating liquor may not be sold on a credit basis, i.e. it must be paid for before or at the time it is sold.[119] Drinks must all be sold according to a prescribed measure and a written statement as to the quantities must be displayed on the premises. There is an exception, however, when a drink is formed by mixing together three or more liquids. A licensee is not guilty of an offence where he does not know of consumption outside permitted hours, and it is not enough that an employee who had entrusted to him the control and management of the premises[120] was aware of what customers were doing. Children under 14 are not allowed in the bar except as a passage way to some other part of the premises which has no other convenient means of access or egress. Beer and cider can be sold to persons over 16 for consumption at a meal in a part of the premises which is not a bar.

A licensee has the power to refuse to admit, or expel from licensed premises, any person who is drunken, violent, quarrelsome or disorderly, and the right to demand assistance from the police[121]. The position in relation to those who "occupy" licensed premises without being quarrelsome or disorderly is not clear. In Dallimore v Tatton[122] the respondent used bad language on being ordered to leave (on account of previous disorderly conduct) but was not, on the second occasion, violent or disorderly. This was held not to be disorderly conduct.

To supply intoxicating liquor a club must be registered under the Licensing Act or hold a justices' licence for the premises.[123] Many of the rules regarding a club licence are the same as for a justices' on-licence, but not those regarding sale, as the members of the club are already owners of the liquor. If the club rules permit the admission of persons other than members or their guests and the sale to them of intoxicating liquor, as do the rules of many university unions, a separate licence is not required.[124] If, however, the rules do not so prescribe, and a steward sells liquor to non-members contrary to instructions, the club is not liable despite the fact that the proceeds were paid into the club account.[125]

14.17 Theatre Licences

Premises must be licensed for the public performance of plays. In this context "public" means the public or any section of the public, whether on payment or otherwise.[126] A theatre licence may be required even though the premises are not expressly used as a theatre and money is not taken at the door.[127] In granting a theatre licence the local authority is not permitted to prescribe conditions as to the nature of the plays or the manner of their performance, but it can impose restrictions in the interests of physical safety and health[128] and has a discretion similar in character to licensing justices. If a public performance of a play (any dramatic piece involving at least one person, and involving the playing of a role) is given in premises that are not licensed, offences have been committed by those concerned with organisation and management, and those who knew or had reasonable grounds to suspect that a performance would take place, nevertheless allowed the premises to be so used. A copy of the script of any new play performed must be delivered to the trustees of the British Museum free of charge within the period of one month of the beginning of the performance.[129]

14.18 Protection of Animals

The protection of animals used for experimental or other scientific procedures is governed by the Animals (Scientific Procedures) Act 1986. No scientific (i.e. other than veterinary, agricultural or animal husbandry) procedure may take place other than at the place specified in the licence granted to a person. A personal licence granted to an individual to undertake regulated procedures therefore specifies where the procedure should be performed. A project licence, authorising a programme of specified regulated procedures also specified the place or places where the procedures will be undertaken, and any place specified in a project licence must be designated by a certificate issued by the Secretary of State as a scientific procedure establishment.[130]

14.19 Radioactive Substances

The keeping of radioactive substances, beyond a certain threshold of radioactivity, on unregistered premises, is prohibited. Both the premises and the radioactive substances kept require registration.[131] Application for registration must be made to the Secretary of State for the Environment, and must state the premises, the undertaking, the materials, the quantities, and the manner in which it is proposed to use them. The Secretary of State has a discretion in relation to the application, but in considering the conditions he may wish to impose he must have regard to the amount and character of radioactive waste likely to arise from its keeping or use.[132]

Their use is now regulated by the Ionising Radiation Regulations 1985 made under the Health and Safety At Work, Etc. Act. They require notification of any new work involving radioactive substances 28 days prior to the commencement of work, and notification of any material change to the type of work being carried out. Persons registered under the Radioactive Substances Act 1960 are deemed to be registered under the Regulations. A university is also required to appoint a suitably qualified and experienced Radiation Protection Advisor.

Any releases, spillages or overdoses of radioactive substances must be notified to the Health and Safety Executive under the 1985 Regulations. Discharge into public sewers is also covered by the Regulations and specific consents may be required for such discharges.[133]

Substantial provision exists for safety and health in relation to the use of radioactive substances, and in relation to carriage. Carriage in a public service vehicle is prohibited. Other vehicles must be marked as carriers, and packages must also be marked. There are restrictions on travelling in vehicles carrying radioactive substances.

The disposal of radioactive waste is strictly regulated and there are restrictions on the amounts that may be discharged to the public sewer.

14.20 Biological Hazards

There are two principal sets of regulations to be considered: those relating to genetic manipulation and those relating to dangerous pathogens. S.16 of the Health and Safety At Work, Etc. Act 1974 has been employed to make regulations controlling genetic manipulation. Anyone intending to carry on such work must notify the Health and Safety Executive and the Advisory Committee on Genetic Manipulation. A principal requirement is the setting up of proper internal monitoring machinery under the supervision of which the work is carried out.

Work on dangerous pathogens is also controlled by the Health and Safety (Dangerous Pathogens) Regulations 1988 made under s.16 of the Health and Safety At Work, Etc. Act 1974. The movement of certain pathogens must be notified. The importation of animal pathogens is controlled by regulations made under the Animal Health Act 1981 and of plant pathogens and pests by regulations made under the Plant Health Act 1967. The holding of other pathogens may require licensing under the Pests Act 1954 or the Diseases of Fish Act 1937.

14.21 Broadcasting

In addition to the normal provision for the licensing of receivers there are three areas in which universities have particular concerns. They are:

(1) Private mobile radio licences for "walkie-talkies" used by security staff:

(2) Broadcasting licences for low level transmission for a student union radio service:

(3) Satellite receiving equipment licences.

14.22 Non-Statutory Licensing

The universities enter into a vast range of voluntary agreements without statutory obligations and it is impossible to do more than indicate two principal examples.

1. Performance

Agreements are entered into with Phonographic Performance Ltd., and the Performing Rights Society Ltd., with regard to the public use of sound recording and the public performance of music.

2. Copyright

Some universities have entered into a voluntary agreement with the Copyright Licensing Agency regarding the recording or the copying of material in copyright works.

15. A UNIVERSITY'S LIABILITY FOR GOODS ON THE PREMISES

15.1 Introduction

University staff, students and visitors bring a wide variety of chattels onto university premises and the question arises as to the nature and extent of that liability. Much of the ground is covered by the responsibilities of an occupier,[134] but there are additional considerations arising from the law of trespass. Trespass consists in committing, without lawful justification, any act of direct physical interference with goods in the possession of another person.[135]

> "The act of handling a man's goods without his permission is prima facie tortious".[136]

Even negligent damage, provided that it is direct, falls within the scope of trespass. Thus, if a porter, while applying a wheel clamp to a car improperly parked on a university campus scratches a door panel, there is a prima facie liability on the part of the university.[137] It is immaterial, however, that no damage has been done to the property:

> "The respondent ... has been guilty of a trespass. The wrong to the appellants in relation to that trespass is constituted whether or not actual damage has resulted therefrom either to the chattel or to themselves".[138]

It is not, however, a trespass to read documents.

> "Papers are the owner's goods and chattels: they are his dearest property: and are so far from enduring a seizure, that they will hardly bear an inspection; and although the eye cannot by the laws of England be guilty of a trespass, yet where private papers are removed and carried away, the secret nature of those goods will be an aggravation of the trespass, and demand considerably more damages in that respect".[139]

There is thus no right to privacy: the papers need to be handled before tort could, prima facie, be said to have arisen.

15.2 The Exclusion of Liability

The definition given above implies that the liability in relation to trespass to goods is strict, in other words, it is not necessary to prove intention or negligence in the defendant. However, the present rule appears to be that either intention or negligence must be proved.[140] In any case the university, as occupier, has liability as prescribed in the Occupiers Liability Act 1957 for the property of a visitor or person on the premises with his permission.

Liability to damage to property can be excluded if

(1) Warning has been given;

(2) The member of staff, student or visitor has accepted the risk - volenti non fit injuria;

(3) The extension, restriction, modification or exclusion of the duty of care has been undertaken;

(4) There is no fault on the part of the occupier.

15.3 The Giving of Warning

There has been a progressive tendency to restrict the right to exclude liability by the giving of a warning, but this applies particularly in the case of injury to the person. In the case of damage to property a less exacting standard obtains, but the notice must be sufficient to enable the person coming onto the premises to accomplish the purpose for which he had entered the premises.[141] An unlit hole on a campus road with a chalked warning on a blackboard would not suffice: the courts would expect the same standards as for a highway authority. The occupier has a liability which he cannot exclude by the giving of a warning, and the warning must be enough to enable the person on the premises to make his property reasonably safe.[142]

15.4 Acceptance of Risk

A person can accept risk to his property in circumstances which would otherwise be a trespass.[143] He can also consent to run the risk of accidental harm which would otherwise be the subject of an action for negligence.[144] The test is whether a real assent is given to the taking of the risk, and did that assent absolve the defendant from the duty to take care.[145] Knowledge of danger to property, such as parking a car in an unlit part of the campus or leaving a mink coat in an unattended cloakroom, does not automatically involve consent: the facts do not speak for themselves. This is now expressly regulated by the Unfair Contract Terms Act 1977 s.2(3):

> "Where a contract term or notice purports to exclude or restrict liability from negligence, a person's agreement to or awareness of it is not of itself to be taken as indicating his voluntary acceptance of any risk".

15.5 Extension, Restriction or Modification of the Duty of Care

The normal manner in which the duty of care is limited is by notice: "The university accepts no liability ..." This does not, as pointed out above, automatically exempt the university from liability. There may be some risks for which the university will still be liable, and the liability is less easily avoided for injury to person than property. For property, however, the rules are less strict, but a university might have certain difficulties in contemplating excluding liability in the event of its own negligence, quite apart from whether or not such exclusion would be held to be reasonable in the circumstances.

15.6 Lack of Fault

There are certain circumstances in which is is not necessary to prove fault on the part of the occupier. There is strict liability for the escape of dangerous things accumulated on the premises for some non-natural purpose, but this liability does not extend to a person who is not himself an occupier.[146] There may also be strict liability when an occupier is vicariously responsible for the act of another. Strict liability is not the same as absolute liability. The consequences were such as were not intended by the defendant and could not have been foreseen and avoided by the exercise of reasonable skill and care.[147] An accident is any expected damage resulting from any unlooked-for mishap or occurrence. An act of God may also exonerate.

An occupier may also be exempt from liability for a fire on the premises. If a fire is caused by the negligence of a servant or person lawfully on the premises, such as a student, there is liability, but not as the consequence of an act of God, or of a stranger whose activities cannot be controlled, but may well be foreseen.[148]

The Fires Prevention (Metropolis) Act 1774, which is not in its application limited to London, exempts occupiers from liability for any fire which begins accidentally, i.e. that is caused by chance, or from unknown cause.[149] Fires caused by negligence are still the subject of liability.[150] There is also liability in relation to the ignition of substances inherently volatile, such as petrol or, presumably, certain chemicals and solvents. In Musgrove v Pandelis the defendants' motor car caught fire, and damaged rooms above the garage in which it was kept.[151] The right of action would in such circumstances extend to anyone whose property was lawfully on the affected premises.

> "If I happen to be on somebody's land and my motor car or property is destroyed, I have just as much right against the person who allows the fire to escape from his land as the owner of the land on which I happen to be".[152]

15.7 Goods unlawfully on the Premises

Universities frequently experience a situation in which a trespasser brings property on to the campus: in the form, for example of a motor car, a bicycle, a skate board, or a football. The question will quite often arise (a) if there is any duty of care to the property of a trespasser (b) if the property of the trespasser can be seized so as to discourage the trespasser.

If a car is parked without authority it might happen that it is damaged by negligence whether or not it is in the physical posssession of the trespasser at the time of damage. The general position appears to be that the trespasser can expect the same standard of care to his property as a visitor who brings his car on to the property with lawful authority. On the other hand a car unlawfully on the premises can be immobilised, and a service fee charged to release the clamp or other form of immobilisation. It cannot however be seized, unless it has caused damage. This is because the self-help remedy of distress damage feasant can only be invoked where damage has been done.[153] The goods are seized as security for compensation. Thus, in principle, a football can be seized because its use will have occasioned some damage to blades of grass. Such would be unlikely to apply to skateboard or bicycle and the courts are, in general, not enthusiastic about self-help remedies and will tend to limit quite strictly their employment.[154] There are evident reasons of public policy why this should be so. An attempt to seize chattels could lead to a breach of the peace.

16 OCCUPIERS' LIABILITY

16.1 Definition

The rules governing occupiers' liability are those that govern the liability of that occupier for injuries to persons who come on to those premises, i.e. visitors to the premises. The first consideration is when is a university occupier of premises. The issue is not quite as straightforward as it might seem as there are many circumstances, and with varying degrees of formality, in which a university might be occupier, or have sufficiency of occupancy to render it liable to visitors. In the first place a university owns the premises and is in sole possession. Secondly, a university owns the premises but has leased them to a tenant. In the third place the university owns the premises but has licensed an occupant. Fourthly the university is itself the tenant of leased premises, such as a field station. Fifthly, the university is licensee of premises, or part thereof, for example, for mounting an exhibition. To be an occupier exclusive occupation is not required, and the test as to whether or not a university is the occupier is whether it has some degree of control which is both associated with and arising out of his presence in and use of or activity in the premises in question.[155]

For the purposes of defining the occupiers' liability some points are clear. The owner in possession of his land is an occupier. If the premises in their entirety are leased the tenant is the occupier. If, on the other hand, the university, as owner, leases only part of the premises, it remains liable as occupier for that part of the premises, e.g. a staircase, a lobby or a corridor, not leased to the tenant.[156] The manner by which the occupier is identified is to determine who has the right to admit or exclude people to or from the premises.[157] Control of access also gives an opportunity to warn those coming on to the premises of any defects in those premises.[158] For the purposes of occupiers' liability occupancy need not be exclusive, and the duty of care may be shared, either equally or in proportion to the responsibility for the premises. Thus a university, as landlord, would almost certainly be held solely liable for injury arising from structural failure in a tenanted property, but not in a case where the injury arose from a badly laid carpet, the laying of the carpet being the responsibility of the tenant.[159]

Such considerations also apply in the case of a contractor repairing or altering university premises, when the test of effective control indicates that the contractor rather than the university is in effective control of the premises.[160]

16.2 The visitor

The next question that needs to be answered in any issue of occupiers' liability is the nature of the visitor. Since the passing of the Occupiers' Liability Act 1957 there are only two classes of visitors: visitors as such and trespassers.[161] Liability for trespassers is not affected by the Occupiers' Liability Act: the tests are those of common law.[162] A visitor is someone who comes on to university premises or premises of which the university is deemed to be in occupancy. The statutory duty under the Occupiers' Liability Act 1957 applies to visitors only. A university, as occupier of premises, does have liabilities to those who are on the premises, whether as visitor or as trespasser.[163] The duty owed to a visitor is the common duty of care, and the common duty of care is defined as the duty to take such care as in all the circumstances of the case is reasonable, to see that the visitor will be reasonably safe in using the premises for the purposes for which he is invited or permitted by the university to be there, including the degree of care to be looked for in the visitor,[164] and as stated above, anyone who is neither invited nor permitted to be there (or has a statutory right to be there) is a trespasser, to whom no duty is owed by the Act. The only duty owed to a trespasser is not to injure him wilfully or to act with reckless disregard of his presence.[165] A relatively common problem relating to a visitor on premises is when he is injured while searching for a lavatory. A visitor can search in the immediate curtilage of a building to which he has been invited, or through doors off a passage, but not go into a plant room.[166]

16.3 The Standard of Care

The test of the standard of care towards visitors is one of fact and not of law. What needs to be taken into account is the nature of the danger, the length of time that danger was in existence, the steps necessary to remove that danger, and the likelihood or otherwise of an injury being caused. In Sawyer v H & G Simonds Ltd,[167] the plaintiff had been injured when he slipped in a hotel bar and cut his hand on some broken glass on the floor. Whilst occupiers do insure, it is no part of the legal liability of the occupiers to be insurers, and while broken glass is naturally dangerous it cannot very well be cleared up until the occupier knows that it is there: thus the liability is to keep a reasonable lookout for such a danger. In that case, and this is a situation which arises quite frequently, the danger was caused by the action of a third party. An occupier cannot disclaim liability merely because the danger was created by a third party. The test is whether he could have been expected to make allowance for his premises being made unsafe by a third party.

For university staff the situation of a union bar, and its contrast with a staff bar, will spring readily to mind. Vomit on the steps of licensed premises will not render the occupier liable, as the danger was not one which could reasonably be anticipated.[168] By contrast, an occupier was held to be liable for injuries caused by a drunken person on the premises. He had anticipated that very danger, as he employed "bouncers" for the purposes of ejecting the undesirable.[169] The occupier will be liable if negligence can be proved against him, or the doctrine of res ipsa loquitur (the fact speaks for itself), that is, where the only rational explanation of the facts is that the occupier has been negligent. Examples would be the collapse of a chimney, a tile falling off a roof, or the glass falling out of a window, each in the absence of storms.[170] However, a tree and its branches are upheld by natural means and no liability arises from their fall unless negligence is proved.[171]

The courts will determine whether an occupier of premises has discharged the common duty of care to a visitor, for instance where damage is caused to him by a danger due to the faulty execution of any work of construction, maintenance or repair by an independent contractor employed by the occupier. The principle to be followed is that the occupier is not to be treated without more as answerable for the danger, if in all the circumstances he had acted reasonably in entrusting the work to an independent contractor. This includes taking such steps as he reasonably ought to in order to satisfy himself that the contractor was competent and that the work had been properly done.[172] Thus, if a university is negligent through financial exigency in the maintenance of roofs and the private property of a lecturer is damaged thereby, the university will be liable. An occupier who has taken all reasonable care is not answerable to strangers to the contract, unless it expressly so provides for damages due to the faulty execution of any work of construction, maintenance or repair, or other like operation by persons other than himself, his servants or those acting under his direction or control.[173] The Unfair Contracts Terms Act 1977 restricts the power of the occupier to exclude himself from liability. A person to whom the Act applies cannot, by reference to any contract terms or to a notice given to persons generally or to particular persons, exclude or restrict his liability for damage or personal injury resulting from negligence.[174] For the use of a notice the requirement of reasonableness is that it should be fair and reasonable to allow reliance on it, having regard to all the circumstances obtaining when the liability arose.[175]

16.4 Liability to Persons not on the Premises

The liability of an occupier is not restricted to persons and property on the premises. There is a general duty to take reasonable care to prevent injury to persons or damage to property on adjoining premises and this includes the adjoining highway.[176] An occupier cannot even rely upon an act of God to escape liability. It is his duty to take steps to protect the public from injury. Thus, where a mass of snow had remained on a roof for several days, and had then fallen and injured a passer-by, the occupier was liable because he had had plenty of time to remove the snow, or warn the public of the danger.[177] In addition there is an absolute liability for the maintenance of any part of a building which projects over the highway.[178] "Absolute" means that a defence of reasonable care cannot be pleaded, but it is a defence that the offence was actually caused by some other person but the user had taken all reasonable precautions and exercised all due diligence to avoid the commission of an offence.[179] Thus, if a university owns and occupies a bridge building across a public highway, its liability for that bridge is absolute, but not, for example, if third parties throw materials off the bridge damaging cars parked underneath. Particular attention is devoted to the carrying out of building operations. If, in the course of carrying out building operations in or near a street, an accident occurs which gives rise to the risk of serious bodily injury to a passer by, the owner (not the occupier) of the land or building operation being carried out may be guilty of an offence.[180]

16.5 The duty to fence

To protect from dangers a duty is sometimes on the occupier to fence. This duty arises when there is anything on the land which is a cause of danger to persons using the street.[181] Fencing is also a means of discharging the duty of care under the Occupiers' Liability Act 1957, and even without a specific duty to fence, an owner or occupier may be liable for damages or injury through having no fence, or an inadequate or defective fence.[182] It is also particularly important to prevent children trespassing on land, especially where the land contains dangers, and the child might not appreciate the danger or be able to read notices warning of the danger.[183]

16.6 Trespassers

Liability to trespassers is now regulated by the Occupiers Liability Act 1984, in respect of injury suffered but not damage to property. It replaces the rules of common law[184] to determine "(a) Whether any duty is owed by a person as occupier of premises to persons other than his visitors in respect of any risk of their suffering injury on the premises by reason of any danger due to the state of the premises or to things done or omitted to be done on them.

(b) If so, what that duty is."

The Occupiers Liability (Scotland) Act 1960 by contrast provides that an occupier will automatically owe a duty to all who are not visitors who enter the land, and the content of that duty varies with the nature of that entry.

The duty exists in relation to the premises if

(1) the occupier must be aware of the danger or have reasonable grounds for believing that it exists;

(2) he knew or had reasonable grounds to know that the uninvited entrant either was or might come into the vicinity of the danger;

(3) the risk of entry to an uninvited entrant resulting from that danger was one against which in all the circumstances of the case the occupier might reasonably be expected to offer the uninvited entrant some protection;

(4) actual knowledge exists where the occupier ignores the obvious or fails to draw reasonable inferences from known facts.

There is no obligation to inspect the property, either for the existence of dangers or the presence of the duties.[185]

The standard of care varies with circumstances and character of the entry, the age of the entrant, the nature of the premises and the extent of risk. It might also vary according to the financial resources of the occupier.[186]

"Where an occupier of premises owes a duty to another in respect of such a risk, the duty is to take such care as is reasonable in all the circumstances of the case to see that [the uninvited entrant] does not suffer injury on the premises by reason of the danger concerned".

Thus an occupier would not be liable if he could not reasonably have known of either the danger or the presence of the trespasser, or it was unreasonable to expect him to take precautions against the risk.

The occupier may however discharge his duty by taking reasonable steps to give a warning of the danger concerned, or to discourage persons from taking a risk.[187] A notice can, however, be counter-productive particularly where an occupier, such as a university, faces a mixture of visitors and trespassers. "Danger. Guard Dogs patrolling" is not a sign to be recommended. It indicates that the occupier has created a danger upon his land, with all the consequences thereof. "Warning. Guard Dogs patrolling" is the preferable formulation. A particular problem with notices is that they are not much defence against child trespassers: a major potential problem of universities, given the use of their campuses as adventure playgrounds. If a child is not mature enough to take proper care for his own safety he is probably insufficiently mature to appreciate the nature of the risk to which he is exposing himself by entry on to the premises.[188]

In terms of hazards on a campus a university with an open campus has less of an obligation to warn than a university with an enclosed campus and a restricted number of entry points. In the latter case there is a clear duty to post the appropriate notices at all the (finite) number of entry points. In the former all that can be expected is the posting of a reasonable number of warnings. A warning sufficient to discourage a trespasser from taking a risk will discharge the (modest) duty of care to a trespasser. A warning for a visitor must, by contrast, be sufficient to enable the visitor to be reasonably safe.[189] Thus a knowledge of a risk plus entry makes a trespasser subject to the rule of law: volenti non fit injuria. He has willingly accepted the risk. To complicate matters further, however, that risk must arise from the static condition of the land, and not from activities carried out thereon.[190]

The duty to a trespasser to warn him of dangers is minimal but that duty certainly exists. It is a basic rule of law that an agreement to contract out of a statutory duty is void,[191] and the defence of volenti non fit injuria is not available for the breach of a statutory duty.[192] There is no provision in s.1 Occupiers' Liability Act 1984 of any right for an occupier to exclude liability to the person of a trespasser, but s.1(8) expressly excludes statutory liability for the property of a trespasser. Thus liability at common law for the goods of a trespasser continues to apply.

17. PUBLIC UTILITIES

17.1 Water

S.17 of the Water Act 1945[193] and s.70 of the Water (Scotland) Act 1980[194] enable the various district water authorities to introduce byelaws for the purposes of preventing waste, undue consumption, misuse or contamination of water. As a result each water authority drew up its own set of byelaws which did vary from area to area - for example most authorities allowed cisterns of 2 gallon capacity whereas at least one other stipulated only 1.5 gallons. Inevitably, such differences caused problems for manufacturers. Standardization has now virtually been achieved with authorities adopting the 1986 edition of the Model Water Byelaws for use in their area. The byelaws deal with all aspects of water installations, giving details of acceptable methods, designs and specifications. All new installations, modifications to existing installations and new fittings should comply with the byelaws currently in force in the area concerned, failure for which is punishable by a fine.

17.2 Gas

The Gas Act 1986[195] made provision for the appointment and function of a Director General of Gas Supply and the establishment and function of the Gas Consumers' Council. Perhaps most important of all, however, it enabled the privatization of the industry to take place with the then Corporation being replaced by a company, now quoted on the stock exchange as British Gas plc.

The Act also lays down the terms, conditions and duties relating to the supply of gas, methods of charging and the fixing of tariffs as well as enabling the Secretary of State to make regulations designed to ensure the safety of gas installations. Interestingly, there is provision too for other companies to apply for permission to use the existing distribution network for the purposes of supplying gas.

Prior to the Act coming into force, various regulations existed covering safety in the industry and many of these continue to have effect today. In general terms, these regulations are designed to ensure that all installations are safe and lay down requirements covering pipework, meters, governors, fittings, testing, gas escapes and equipment connected to the supply. Anyone contravening the regulations, and this includes those persons responsible for a building as well as those actually carrying out work on an installation, is liable upon conviction to a fine.

17.3 Electricity

The electricity industry was nationalised by the provisions of the Electricity Act 1947[196] which established the British Electricity Authority and Area Electricity Boards. The Act laid a duty on the Authority to generate or acquire supplies of electricity and to provide bulk supplies to the Area Boards and on the latter to provide supplies to "persons in their area who require them." The industry was subsequently reorganised by the Electricity Act

1957,[197] which had the effect of establishing an Electricity Council and replacing the British Electricity Authority by the Central Electricity Generating Board. Further changes in the industry were brought about by the Energy Act 1983[198] which, for example, enabled persons other than the area electricity boards to generate electricity (and sell it to the boards), and at least one university has availed itself of this facility. Other changes will doubtless take place when the industry is returned to the private sector in due course.

The 1947 and 1983 Acts enable the Secretary of State to issue regulations covering the various aspects of supplying electricity, carrying out electrical installations and ensuring that safety standards are met. In accordance with s.16 of the Energy Act 1983, s.64 of the Electricity Act 1947 and s.40(6) of the Electricity (Scotland) Act 1979,[199] the Secretaries of State for Energy and Scotland have jointly issued the Electricity Supply Regulations 1989, which contain provisions as to earthing and for electricity lines above and below ground. They also impose requirements on suppliers of electricity in such matters as maximum line voltage, safety signs and work on consumers' premises as well as enabling suppliers to refuse to supply electricity to consumers whose installations are not considered to be safe or are in such a condition as to cause interference to the system or the supply to others. Any person contravening the regulations is deemed to have committed an offence under s.16 of the Energy Act 1983, which is punishable by a fine.

17.4 Services-general

Not only must all gas, water and electricity installations comply with the relevant aspects of the particular byelaws or regulations in question, but Inspectors from the Health and Safety Executive will expect them also to meet standards recommended by professional bodies (e.g. the regulations issued by the Institution of Electrical Engineers) and to comply with the relevant code of practice or British Standard, if one exists, although none of these actually has any legal status in itself.

18. SCOTLAND

18.1 Town Planning, Building Control, etc.

The first statutory intervention in town planning in Scotland was in 1919: the basis for the current system is the Town and Country Planning (Scotland) Act 1947.[200] The Town and Country Planning (Scotland) Act 1972[201] provided for a new system of development planning which took effect in 1975 after local government reorganisation. There are a number of other relevant statutes and

Orders.[202] Since 1975 there has been a system of structure plans and local plans and the concept of "permitted development" under the 1972 Act. Otherwise, broadly speaking, the system is analogous to that operating in England and Wales.

The system of building control is governed by the Building (Scotland) Acts 1959[203] and 1970.[204] Almost all building operations in Scotland require a Building Warrant issued by the relevant local authority.

Scotland has separate but very comparable standard forms of building contract and of terms of engagement of architects (see $8.1 supra).

The law relating to prescription and limitation in Scotland is governed by the Prescription and Limitation (Scotland) Acts 1973[205] and 1984.[206] In general there is a prescriptive period of five years: an obligation is extinguished at the end of that period if there has been no relevant claim made nor any relevant acknowledgment of the obligation. The starting date for the prescriptive period, including cases of reparation for breach of contract, can be summarised as either the date on which the loss, injury or damage occurred or, where it was a continuing process, the date on which the act, neglect or default ceased or the date when the injured party could first, with reasonable diligence, have become aware of the loss, injury or damage.

18.2 Housing

The legislative framework is contained in the Housing (Scotland) Acts 1987[207] and 1988.[208] There are no significant differences between English and Scots law relevant to the discussion in this Chapter.

18.3 Licensing

So far as miscellaneous licensing functions of local authorities are concerned, arrangements in Scotland are broadly similar, though there are differences of detail. Perhaps the most interesting difference is that in a number of cases where in England a licence must be obtained, in Scotland a local authority has some discretion whether or not to require the issue of a licence.

The basis of the Scots law relating to the sale for consumption of intoxicating liquor is the Licensing (Scotland) Act 1976.[209] The equivalent of a justices' licence in Scotland is a licence granted by the Licensing Board which consists of district or islands council members. Such licences are:

(a) Public House licences, which authorise the sale of alcoholic liquor in a public house for consumption on or off the premises;

(b) Off-Sale licences, for consumption only off the premises;

(c) Hotel licences, on a similar basis to public houses;

(d) Restricted Hotel licences, restricting sale of liquor to hotel residents or persons taking meals in the hotel;

(e) Restaurant licences, for sale to persons taking table meals in the premises;

(f) Refreshment licences, which authorise the sale of liquor for consumption on the premises when food and non-alcoholic drink are also on sale;

(g) Entertainment licences, which authorise the sale of liquor for consumption in cinemas, theatres, dance halls and clubs.

Normally a licence is granted for three years at a time but the Licensing Board retains certain powers to suspend a licence or close licensed premises.

Club registration, also covered by the Act,[210] is separately carried out by the Sheriff Clerk but the form of application requires to be accompanied by a statement that the club is a bona fide club and not mainly for the supply of alcoholic liquor; this statement has to be signed by two members of the Licensing Board and also by the owner of the premises, if these are not owned by the club. Student Unions (and Athletic Clubs) are specifically exempted from the general requirements that a member be 18 or over[211] but it remains an offence to sell or supply liquor to any person under age 18.

For university and student union premises it is sometimes necessary to consider these various alternatives very carefully, particularly since more than one licence cannot be held or operated for the same premises.

While the Act lays down "permitted hours" (11 a.m. - 2.30 p.m., 5 p.m. - 11 p.m. on weekdays, 12.30 p.m. - 2.30 p.m., 6.30 p.m. - 11 p.m. on Sundays), Licensing Boards have powers to grant regular extensions as well as to deal with applications for occasional extensions. Student unions in Scotland commonly have substantial regular extensions of hours, usually granted for one year at a time.

The Boards meet quarterly to deal with applications for the grant of new licences, renewals where there are objections, transfers, extension of permitted hours, Sunday opening, etc. For full details reference should be made to a standard work on the subject.[212] Much of the discussion in $14.16 supra is relevant applying the statutory provisions mutatis mutandis. The liberalisation of licensing particularly in relation to permitted hours which the Act introduced to Scotland has now been echoed to a considerable degree in England and Wales by the Licensing Act 1988.[213]

18.4 Trespass to Property

In Scotland a proprietor of land is entitled to apply for interdict (approximating to the English injunction) to prohibit actual or explicit threat of trespass [214] unless permitted by statute[215] or public necessity.[216] While the criminal law of trespass is applied mostly in regard to poaching[217] the Trespass (Scotland) Act 1865[14] penalises occupation of private land or premises without the owner's permission.

For occupiers' liability to trespassers in Scotland see $ 16.6 supra

19. NORTHERN IRELAND

19.1 Land law, planning and housing

The "1925 property legislation" of England and Wales did not apply to Northern Ireland: the pre-1921 law of Ireland was adapted to Northern Ireland by subordinate legislation under the Government of Ireland Act 1920,[218] the provisions of which were expected to be temporary pending the re-unification of the two parts of the island of Ireland. From 1921 to 1972 Northern Ireland enjoyed a form of devolved government and these matters were within the province of the Northern Ireland Parliament, which enacted some relevant legislation.[219] Since 1972 however, except for brief periods Northern Ireland has been governed by "direct rule" from Westminster and most of the legislation enacted by Order in Council under the temporary provisions for its government has echoed developments in English law.[220] Some legislation has been statutory, for example the Fair Employment (Northern Ireland) Act 1976 and the Judicature (Northern Ireland) Act 1978.[221]

One major difference between Great Britain and Northern Ireland is the much greater concentration of power in the provincial or state government (although Northern Ireland is not constitutionally a state) as opposed to local authorities. Planning, for example, is controlled by the provincial Department of the Environment, with rights of appeal to an independent Planning Appeals Commission;[222] district councils have only a consultative role in the planning process. Public housing is controlled by a central Housing Executive.[223] The principles by which these and similar functions are exercised are so similar to those of England, Wales and Scotland as not to merit any special treatment here.

19.2 Licensing

Northern Ireland's liquor licensing laws are within its "domestic" legislation.[224] Although procedures vary, there is now no significant relevant difference for the purposes of this work between Northern Ireland and the rest of the United Kingdom.

Footnotes to Chapter 7

1. Kolbert, C.F. and Mackay, N.A.M. "History of Scots and English Land Law", Geographical Publications Ltd., 1977, p.342
2. Lord Dundein, "English and Scottish Law" Murray Lecture, 19
3. For further information on this subject see any leading textbook on the Law of Real Property, e.g. Megarry's Manual of the Law of Real Property. The "1925 property legislation" consists of the Law of Property Acts 1922 and 1925, and the Settled Land, Trustee, Administration of Estates and Land Registration Acts 1925.
4. Megarry, 5th edn, (1975) p.386
5. 1971 c.28 s.2(1)(bb)
6. 1974 c.51 s.2(1)
7. 1988 c.50
8. Part II of Schedule 3 to 1971 c.28 Case 11C added by 1974 c.51 s.3(2) and as consolidated in the Housing Act 1988 Schedule 1 Part I para 8. Business Tenancies are subject to the special regime of the Landlord and Tenant Act 1954 2 & 3 Eliz 2 c.56, Part II.
9. For further information on this subject see any leading textbook on the law of Scotland e.g. Gloag and Henderson.
10. Conveyancing and Feudal Reform (Scotland) Act 1970; Land Tenure Reform (Scotland) Act 1974; Land Registration (Scotland) Act 1979
11. Gloag and Henderson, 8th edn (1980) p.442 W Green & Son Ltd Edinburgh
12. See $.1.4.4. above
13. See in relation to student unions chapter 5 supra
14. Trespass Act 1865 28&29 Vict. c.56

15. Note by Professor D M Walker of the University of Glasgow appended to letter of 4 July 1974 from the Executive Secretary of CVCP to Principals of Scottish Universities.
16. 9 Edw 7 c.44
17. 10 & 11 Geo 6 c.51
18. 2 & 3 Eliz 2 c.54
19. 7 & 8 Eliz 2 c.53
20. 8 & 9 Eliz 2 c.33
21. 1971 c.78
22. 1984 c.55
23. 1971 c.40
24. Housing Act 1985 c.68 now consolidated in Housing Act 1988 c.50; Kingston-upon Hull District Council v The University of Hull [1979] LAG Bulletin 191 (CA)
25. 1963 c.41
26. 26 Geo 5 and 1 Edw 8 c.49
27. 1974 c.40
28. 1974 c.37
29. 9 & 10 Eliz 2 c.34
30. R v Swan Hunter Shipbuilders [1982] 1 All ER 264
31. ICI Ltd v Shatwell [1965] 2 All ER 999
32. Ross v Associated Portland Cement Manufacturers Ltd [1964] 2 All ER 452; Boyle v Kodak Ltd [1969] 2 All ER 439
33. St Thomas's Hospital (Governors) v Charing Cross Railway Company [1861] John and H 400 per Page Wood V-C at pp 404-406
34. [1966] 3 A11 ER 336
35. North of England Zoological Society v Chester RDC [1959] 3A11 E.R. 116
36. A person, unless the contrary is indicated, includes a body of persons corporate or unincorporate: Interpretation Act 1978 s.5, Sch 1
37. For a fuller account of how rateable value on non-domestic hereditaments is calculated refer to the latest edition of Shaw's Practical Guide to Valuation for Rating.
38. 1982 c.29
39. 1979 c.54
40. See "The Standard Form of Building Contract JCT80", John Parris, Granada
41. Sutcliffe v Thackrah [1924] AC 727
42. 1977 c.50
43. 1980 c.58
44 Dutton v Bognor Regis UDC [1972] 1 QB 373; Anns v London Borough of Merton [1978] AC 728; Junior Books Ltd v Veitchi Co. Ltd [1982] 3 WLR
45. Pirelli General Cable Works v Oscar Faber [1983] AC 1

46. Ketteman and Others v Hansell Properties Ltd [1988] 1 All ER 38 (HL)
47. William Hill Organisation v Bernard Sunley and Sons Ltd [1983] 22 BLR 1
48. 1986 c.37
49. Allen v Greenwood [1970] 2 WLR 188
50. Allison v Merton and Sutton and Wandsworth AHA [1975] CL 2450
51. Russell v Barnet LBC [1984] "The Times" 19 April
52. Bunclark v Hertfordshire CC [1977] CLYB 2148
53. Mattison v Beverley Borough Council "The Times" 6 February 1987
54. [1900] 1 QB 752
55. Harrison v Duke of Rutland [1893] 1 QB 142
56. British Railways Board v Herrington [1972] AC 877; the judgment has effectively been put into statutory form by the Occupiers' Liability Act 1984.
57. 1977 c.45
58. Hayward v Challoner [1967] All ER 122
59. Littledale v Liverpool College [1900] 1 Ch 19
60. Wallis's Caton Bay Holiday Camp v Shell-Mex and BP [1974] 3 All ER 575; Treloar v Nute [1976] 120 SJ 590
61. Smirk v Lyndale Developments Ltd [1974] 2 All ER 8
62. See Chapter 2 supra
63. 2 & 3 Will 4 c.75; 1984 c.14
64. 9 & 10 Eliz 2 c.54
65 Anatomy Act 1832 s.1
66. Ibid., s.12
67. Anatomy Act 1984 s.3
68. Human Tissue Act 1961 s.1
69. Ibid. s.1(8)
70. Misuse of Drugs Regulations 1973 S.I. 1973/797 reg. 12
71. Ibid. Reg.13
72. Misuse of Drugs Act 1971 c.38 s.7
73. Ibid. s.8
74. Ibid. s.21
75. Customs and Excise Act 1952 15 & 16 Geo 6 and 1 Eliz 2 c.44 ss.92, 99
76. Ibid. S.226(1); Alcoholic Liquor Duties Act 1979 c.4 s.90; Petroleum(Regulations) Acts 1928 and 1936 (Repeals and Modifications) Regulations 1974, S.I. 1974/1942 Reg.2
77. Late Night Refreshment Houses Act 1969 c.53 s.1; in Scotland a licence may be required: Civic Government (Scotland) Act 1982 c.45 s.9
78. Theatres Act 1968 c.54 s.12 and Licensing Act 1964 c.26 s.199(c)
79. R v Flint County Council County Licensing (Stage Plays) Committee ex.p. Barrett [1957] 1 QB 350
80. Betting & Gaming Duties Act 1972 c.25 ss.13, 15
81. Ibid. s.21

82. Forestry Act 1967 c.10 s.9
83. Cinemas Act 1985 c.13 s.1
84. Ibid. s.3
85. Ibid. s.5
86. Ibid. s.22
87. Gaming Act 1845 8 & 9 Vict c.109 s.10
88. Gaming Act 1968 c.65 s.2
89. Ibid. s.40
90. S.I.1969/1108
91. I.e. a licence granted under the Local Government (Miscellaneous Provisions) Act 1982 c.30 Sch 1: s.1
92. Beynon v Caerphilly Lower Licensing JJ [1970] 1 All ER 618, D.C.
93. Hypnotism Act 1952 15 & 16 Geo 6 and 1 Eliz 2 c.46 s.2; Theatres Act 1968 c.54 s.19, Sch 2
94. Highways Act 1980 c.66 s.169
95. Ibid. s.139
96. Ibid. s.172
97. See $ 14.12 supra
98. Local Government (Miscellaneous Provisions) Act 1982 c.30
99. Private Places of Entertainment (Licensing) Act 1967 c.54 s.2
100. See, for example, Paterson's Licensing Acts (London Butterworths 1979) Vol. 26 Intoxicating Liquor: note that the Licensing Act 1988 c.17 has made significant changes in licensing laws, both in relation to public houses and to clubs.
101. Customs and Excise Act 1952 15 & 16 Geo 6 and 1 Eliz 2 c.44 s.125
102. R v Rotherham Licensing JJ, ex.p. Chapman [1939] 2 All ER 710
103. Chandler v Emerton [1940] 2 KB 261
104. See $14.6 supra
105. Sharp v Wakefield [1891] AC 173, HL
106. Licensing Act 1964 c.26 ss.93-4
107. Ibid. s.94
108. Ibid. s.98
109. Ibid. s.20
110. R v Pownall [1890] 63 LT 418
111. Licensing Act 1964 c.26 s.19
112. R v Liverpool Licensing JJ ex parte Tynan [1961] 2 All ER 363
113. Licensing Act 1988 c.17 s.3
114. Licensing Act 1964 c.26 s.76
115. Ibid. s.63;
116. Ibid. s.160
117. Peckover v Defries [1906] 96 LT 883
118. Licensing Act 1964 c.26 s.84
119. Ibid. s.166
120. Ferguson v Wearing [1951] 1 KB 814

121. Ibid. s.174
122. 78 LT 469
123. Licensing Act 1964 c.26 ss.39 & 55
124. Ibid. s.49
125. Stevens v Wood [1890] 54 JP 742 DC
126. Theatres Act 1968 c.54 s.18(1)
127. Archer v Willingrice [1803] v Esp 186
128. Theatres Act 1968 c.54 s.1
129. Ibid. s.11
130. Animals (Scientific Procedures) Act 1986 c.14 s.6
131. Radioactive Substances Act 1960 8 & 9 Eliz 2 c.34 ss.1 & 19
132. Ibid. s.1
133. Ibid. s.9
134. Occupiers' Liability - see $ 16 infra
135. Heuston RVF and Buckley RA Salmond and Heuston on the Law of Torts (London, Sweet & Maxwell 1987) p. 104
136. R v IRC ex parte Rossminster [1980] A.C. 952 at p. 1011, per Lord Diplock
137. Learne v Bray [1803] 3 East 593; Faulds v Willoughby [1841] 8 M & W 540 at p. 549, per Alderson B
138. William Leitch & Co v Leydon [1931] AC 90 at p. 106 per Lord Blanesburgh. Quoted in Heuston & Buckley op.cit. p. 105
139. Entick v Carrington [1765] 19 St.Tr 1030 at p. 1066 per Lord Camden CJ
140. Heuston & Buckley op.cit. p. 106
141. Heuston & Buckley op. cit. p. 306
142. Occupiers Liability Act 1957 5 & 6 Eliz 2 c.31 s.2(4)
143. Leitch v Leydon [1931] A.C. 90
144. Heuston & Buckley op.cit. p. 557
145. Seymour's Case [1956] 2 OLR 369m cited in Heuston & Buckley, op.cit. p. 559
146. Weller v Foot and Mouth Disease Research Institute [1966] 1 QB 569
147. McBride v Stitt [1944] N.I.7, cited in Heuston & Buckley op.cit. p. 37
148. Hargrave v Goldman [1964] 110 C.L.R. 24 and Holderness v Goslin [1975] 2 NZLR 46 cited in Heuston & Buckley op.cit. p. 374
149. Collingwood v Home & Colonial Stores [1936] 3 All ER 200
150. Mason v Levy Auto Parts of England [1967] 2 QB 530
151. [1919] 2 KB 43, cited in Heuston & Buckley op.cit. p.377
152. R v Hawson [1966] SSD.LR (2d) 583, cited in Salmond, op. cit. p. 686
153. Lagan Navigation Co v Lambeg Bleaching, Dyeing and Finishing Co [1927] AC 226 at 244 cited in M Brazier Street on Torts (London Butterworth) 1988 p99.
154. Sochacki v Sas [1947] 1 All ER 344 at p. 345 per Lord Goddard CJ cited in Heuston & Buckley op.cit. P. 378. On liability for fires generally see Heuston & Buckley op.cit. pp. 374-8

155. Occupiers' Liability Act 1957 5 & 6 Eliz 2 c.31 sl
156. Wheat v E Lacon & Co Ltd [1966] AC 552; Fisher v CHT Ltd (No2) [1966] 2 QB 475; Miller v Hancock [1893] 2 QB 177; Videan v British Transport Commission [1963] 2 QB 650
157. Cavalier v Pope [1906] AC 428
158. North, PM, Occupiers Liability (London, Butterworths 1971) P 24 discussing Wheat v Lacon, n.156 supra
159. Savoy v Holland and Hannen & Cubitts (Southern) [1964] 1 WLR 1158 per Lord Denning at 1163
160. Occupiers' Liability Act 1957 5 & 6 Eliz 2 c.31, Preamble
161. R. Addie and Sons (Collieries) Ltd v Dumbreck [1929] AC 358 at 365
162. Occupiers Liability Act, 1957 s.1. For trespassers, British Railways Board v Herrington loc.cit. n.56 supra; see also Bolton v Store [1951] AC 850
163. Occupiers' Liability Act 1957 s.2(3)
164. R. Addie and Sons (Collieries) Ltd v Dumbreck [1929] AC 358, 365 Fierce guard dogs are permitted: Sarch v Blackburn [1830] 4 C & P 297, 300, Animals Act 1971 c.22 s.5(3)(b), but they must be under control, and not able to escape from the premises in 'hot pursuit'. Barbed wire is also permitted, The Carlgarth [1927] 136 LT 518
165. Walker v Midland Rail Co [1886] LT 489
166. Clerk JF & Lindsell WHB (edited by Armitage AL & others) S 1021
167. [1966] 197 Estates Gazette 877
168. Simons v Winslade [1938] 3 All ER 774
169. Lehnert v Nelson [1947] 4 DLR 473
170. Tarry v Ashton [1876] 1 QBD 314
171. Noble v Harrison [1926] 2 KBD 332
172. Occupiers' Liability Act 1957 s.2(4)(b)
173. s.3(2)
174. Unfair Contract Terms Act, 1977 c.50 s.2(1)
175. s.11(1)
176. Castle v Augustine Links [1922] 38 TLR 614 in relation to a highway. Fay v Prentice [1845] 1 CB 828 in relation to adjacent premises
177. Slater v Worthington's Cash Stores (1930) Ltd [1941] 1 KB 488
178. Tarry v Ashton n.170 supra
179. Highways Act 1971 c.41 s.36(1)(b)
180. Ibid. s.36(3)
181. Highways Act 1959 7 & 8 Eliz 2 c.25 s.295(1)
182. Indermar v Dames [1866] LR1 CP 274
183. Edwards v Railway Executive [1952] HC 737; Cooke v Midland Great Western Rail Co of Ireland [1909] AC 229
184. Occupiers' Liability Act 1957 s.2(b); the rules of common law prior to the passing of the Act are comprehensively stated in British Railways Board v Herrington [1972] AC 877.
185. Harris v Birkenhead Corporation [1976] 1 WLR 279.

186. Occupiers Liability Act 1984 s.1(4)
187. Ibid. s.1(5)
188. Bragg and Brajier "Occupiers and Exclusion of Liability" (1986) 130 Sol. Jo. 251 & 274.
189. Occupiers Liability Act 1957 s.2(4)(a)
190. Titchener v British Railways Board [1983] 3 All ER 710.
191. See 15.7 supra.
192. ICI Ltd v Shatwell [1965] AC 656
193. 8 & 9 Geo 6 c.42
194. 1980 c.45
195. 1986 c.44
196. 10 & 11 Geo 6 c.54
197. 5 & 6 Eliz 2 c.48
198. 1983 c.25
199. 1979 c.11
200. 10 & 11 Geo 6 c.53
201. c.52
202. Local Government (Scotland) Act 1973 c.65; Town and Country Amenities Act 1974 c.32; Town and Country Planning (Scotland) Act 1977 c.10; Local Government, Planning and Land Act 1980 c.65; Local Government and Planning (Scotland) Act 1982 c.43; Housing and Planning Act 1986 c.63; General Development and Use Classes Orders 1981 and 1973.
203. 7 & 8 Eliz 2 c.24
204. c.38
205. 1973 c.52
206. 1984 c.45
207. 1987 c.26
208. 1988 c.43
209. 1976 c.66
210. Ibid. ss.102-118
211. Ibid. s.107(4)
212. e.g. J Allan & C D Chapman The Licensing (Scotland) Act 1976 Edinburgh, W Green & Son 1977
213. 1988 c.17
214. See $1.6.2 supra in relation to recovery of possession from student trespassers in unlawful occupation of buildings
215. e.g. Health and Safety at Work,Etc. Act 1974 s.20
216. e.g. Shepherd v Menzies [1900] 2 F 443
217. Night Poaching Acts 1828 and 1844; Day Trespass Act [Game (Scotland) Act] 1832; Poaching Prevention Act 1862

218. Government of Ireland Act 1920 10 & 11 Geo 5 c.67 ss.69 & 70; Government of Ireland (Adaptation of Enactments) (No.3) Order 1922/183. Also see Northern Ireland (Land Registry) Adaptation of Enactments Order 1948/485; Northern Ireland (Registration of Deeds) Adaptation of Enactments Order 1948/487
219. e.g. Registration of Deeds Act (Northern Ireland) 1970 c.25 (NI)
220. See currently Northern Ireland Act 1974 c.28 and Orders made under Schedule 1 paragraph 1 thereof
221. 1976 c.25; 1978 c.23
222. Planning (Northern Ireland) Order 1972/1634 and Regulations/Orders made thereunder
223. Housing Act (Northern Ireland) 1971 c.16 (NI); see also the Housing (Northern Ireland) Orders 1981/156, 1986/1301, 1988/1990
224. Licensing Act (Northern Ireland) 1971 c.13(NI); Licensing (Northern Ireland) Order 1987/1277

SUGGESTIONS FOR FURTHER READING

CHAPTER 1 UNIVERSITIES AND THE LAW

Committee on Higher Education, Higher Education Appendix 4 - Administrative, Financial & Economic Aspects of Higher Education (London, HMSO 1963) (The Robbins Report)

D.G. Cracknell Law Relating to Charities (London; Oyez Publishing 1973)

The University & The Law (H. Janish ed. 1975)

House of Commons, Education, Science & Arts Committee Session 1982-83, Higher Education Funding - Minutes of Evidence Monday 28 March 1983 (London HMSO 1983)

GW Keeton & LA Sheridan The Modern Law of Charities (Belfast, Northern Ireland Legal Quarterly Inc., 1971)

Chapter 1, GW Keeton The Modern Law of Charities (London, Pitman 1962)

DH McMullen, SG Maurice & DB Parker, Tudor on Charities (London, Sweet & Maxwsell 19167)

J.G. Riddell The Law of Trusts (London, Butterworths 1982)

G Taylor & JB Saunders The Law of Education (London, Butterworths 1976)

CHAPTER 2 UNIVERSITY GOVERNMENT AND MANAGEMENT

GHL Fridman, The Law of Agency (London Butterworths 1971)

S Kyd A Treatise on the Law of Corporations

BS Markesinis & RJC Monday An Outline of the Law of Agency (London Butterworths 1986)

V Powell-Smith Blackwell's Law of Meetings (London Butterworths 1967)

Sir Sebag Shaw & ED Smith The Law of Meetings - Their Conduct & Procedure

CHAPTER 3 THE LAW GOVERNING STUDENTS

UCCA Handbook

University Entrance: The Official Guide (CVCP)

British Universities Guide to Graduate Study (CVCP)

Higher Education in the United Kingdom (Longman, for ACU)

Calendars and Prospectuses published by individual universities

CVCP Codes of Practice

CHAPTER 4 UNIVERSITY STAFF AND EMPLOYMENT LAW

There are several good modern guides to Employment Law. Wedderburn's The Worker and the Law (3rd edition 1986, available in Penguin) is lengthy but very readable. Michawl Whincup: Modern Employment Law (6th edition 1988, Heinemann) is a briefer alternative.

An indispensable reference tool, which should be held by all university Personnel Offices, is Croner's Employment Law (available on subscription, in loose-leaf form, with frequent updates).

For Administrative Law there are several standard textbooks, including H W R Wade: Administrative Law (6th edition 1988, available as an Oxford paperback).

CHAPTER 6 UNIVERSITY TRADING AND ENTREPRENEURIAL ACTIVITIES

W R Cornish Intellectual Property (London, Sweet & Maxwell 1981)

CHAPTER 7 THE UNIVERSITY ESTATE

GC Cheshire (Revd. JD Davies) The Modern Law of Real Property (London, Butterworths 1967)

Megarry, Sir Robert & HWR Wade The Law of Real Property (London, Stevens 1975)

CHAPTER 7 (cont)

PM North Occupiers' Liability (London, Butterworths 1971)

M Dewis The Law on Health & Safety At Work MacDonald & Evans

Roderick Davies The Offices, Shops & Railway Premises Act 1963 Oyez Publications

Encyclopaedia of Health & Safety at Work Law and Practice, ed M J Goodman, Sweet & Maxwell

Encyclopaedia of Planning Law and Practice, ed Sir Desmond Heap, Sweet & Maxwell

Encyclopaedia of Environmental Health Law and Practice, ed Charles A Cross, Sweet & Maxwell

INDEX

Index

SPELLING

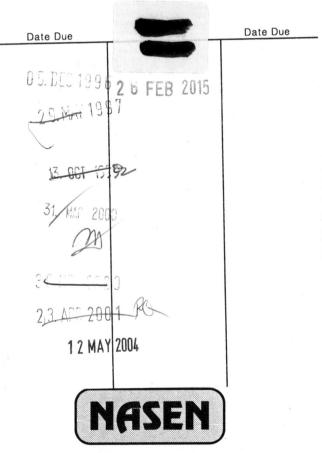

A NASEN PUBLICATION

Published in 1995

ISBN 0 906730 74 0

NASEN

Published by NASEN Enterprises Ltd.
NASEN Enterprises is a company limited by guarantee, registered in England and Wales. Company No. 2637438.

Further copies of this book and details of NASEN's many other publications may be obtained from the Publications Department at its registered office:
NASEN House, 4 and 5 Amber Business Village, Amber Close, Amington, Tamworth, Staffs., B77 4RP. Tel: 01827 311500; Fax: 01827 313005.

Copy editing by Nicola von Schreiber
Typeset in Times and printed in the United Kingdom by Impress Printers.